RICHARD HACK

DUCHESS OF DEATH
THE UNAUTHORIZED BIOGRAPHY OF
AGATHA CHISTIE

Drawing on over 5000
unpublished letters,
documents and notes

BOOKS

First published in Great Britain in 2010 by
JR Books, 10 Greenland Street, London NW1 0ND
www.jrbooks.com

A catalogue record for this book is available from the British Library.

ISBN 978-1-906779-83-2

1 3 5 7 9 10 8 6 4 2

Printed by Clays Ltd, St Ives plc

To Jared N. Stein,

who knows the reason why.

TABLE OF CONTENTS

PROLOGUE

Mystery At Newlands Corner

*"...you're so beautiful—so beautiful.
Promise me you'll always be beautiful."*

"You'd love me just the same if I weren't."

*"No. Not quite. It wouldn't be quite the same. Promise me.
Say you'll always be beautiful..."*

Agatha Christie
Unfinished Portrait

DECEMBER 3, 1926. AGATHA CHRISTIE DREW ASIDE THE thick velvet drapery and peered expectantly through the bedroom window. The fog, so typical of Sunningdale in December, had moved across the road and now threatened to block her view of the front drive completely. She hated fog; hated the way it leaned into familiar shapes, turning them sinister and threatening. As her body shivered, she protectively pulled closed the curtain, blocking the cold draft that found its way through the window at night, turning the room damp. It was a little after nine p.m., and she knew her husband wasn't ever coming home.

After twelve years of marriage, mystery writer Agatha Mary Clarissa Miller Christie was thirty-six years old, famous and alone. Not alone in the sense that there was no one else in the large, brooding brick house named Styles. Her seven-year-old daughter, Rosalind, was sleeping in the next room, and Lilly, a chambermaid, was downstairs doing whatever it was she did at night before getting ready to sleep herself. In less than an hour, Rosalind's nanny and Agatha's secretary, the always punctual Charlotte Fisher, would be returning home on the last train from London, just forty minutes away.

She would normally welcome Charlotte's arrival, for she regarded her as her closest friend. Only the previous evening, she and Charlotte (whom she nicknamed Carlo) had danced the Charleston, or tried to, as they were taking classes together in Ascot, one town over. Dear Carlo. Loyalty paid for by the hour.

She would need to leave Carlo a note to explain what she was about to do. *But how,* she thought, *does one explain that your life is over? How do you explain the overwhelming isolation of feeling alone?*

Moving to her writing desk, she found a correspondence card and her fountain pen, and then struggled to get beyond "Dear Carlo." A writer without words. Even at a time like this, the irony amused her. Despite having authored eight books, Agatha still found writing difficult. Imagining the *stories* was easy; that was fun. Writing them down, explaining them, that was the difficult part.

Her first book had taken years to be published, and even after it appeared in bookstores across the country when Agatha was thirty, she never thought of writing as a career. Her husband wouldn't have accepted that. To him, her mystery stories were little more than amusing diversions, like needlepoint or gardening. He thought of them as "silly"— almost as ridiculous as he now thought her to be.

It wasn't always that way, of course. When Agatha Miller eloped with Archibald Christie in December 1914, hers was the "happily ever after" love of fairy tales and dreams come true. He was tall, movie-star handsome and an aviator in Britain's Royal Flying Corps. In the two years he had courted her, she could think of none other. Back then, she had a flawless complexion, long wavy red hair, a tall, fashionably full figure and a plan to be his wife forever. Even then, he was hardly ever comfortable with her touch or talk of the future, but she steadfastly refused to admit that her husband believed the commitment of marriage was less about eternity and more about the companionship of an eternally attractive wife. "Promise me you'll always be beautiful," she later wrote in a novel, mimicking Archie's words.

Determined to be ever available to her husband, she never allowed him to see her writing, not that he had shown any interest. He was so structured, so utterly obsessed with his fledgling investment career, that any hope she had once held of rating a passing smile or compliment had been dimmed in the shadow of his neglect. As one year followed another, Archie showed less and less interest in her, often spending nights at his club in London and weekends on the golf course. She wanted his touch, needed his attention. Yet the more she tried to draw him close, the harder he pulled away. All the while, she quietly produced one book and then the next and the next, with her meager royalties bolstering the family's finances, which, at the time, were barely adequate.

Now it has come to this, she thought, looking back at the too quiet room. She felt movement at her feet and reached down to stroke her beloved wirehaired terrier, Peter, as he repositioned himself to lick the back of her hand. She barely felt his moist, warm tongue, her mind muted as if shrouded in layers of cotton wool, unable to command itself to think. Still, she needed to finish, quickly now, and leave before logic and reason shattered her plan.

After removing her wedding ring, Agatha placed it inside a small mahogany box on the desk, where she was certain it would be discovered. She stood and crept toward the door, lowering her head, as if embarrassed, and never slowing until she reached her daughter's room. Inside, she watched silently as Rosalind exhaled rhythmic breath in the cadence of peaceful sleep. She then kissed her child on the forehead, as she did every night, just as her own mother had done with her. It was only as she left the room that she allowed herself to remember the smell of her mother's violet cologne as her face drew near. Agatha wiped away the tears summoned by the memory.

Eight months earlier, everything had been so different. Then, Agatha's mother, Clara, was still alive, living in Ashfield, the family's estate in Torquay. Her mother would have known what to do. Clara had a way of always knowing what was right.

Yet the suddenness of her mother's death in April 1926, at the age of seventy-two, fueled a depression that left Agatha bereft of joy and spirit. A gray wash of numbness was her only comfort. "Sometimes one feels so eager to get out of this body," her mother had told her, during one of her frequent illnesses near the end. "One longs to be released from this prison."[i] Suddenly Agatha understood.

Archie was no help in times of sadness. He was awkward around grief, and had, in fact, "a violent dislike of illness, death and trouble of any kind."[ii] In place of compassion, Archie made jokes. At the time of Clara's death, he suggested traveling—a vacation in Spain. It would be "fun," he said. It would "distract."

Distract? Agatha didn't want distraction. "I wanted to be with my sorrow and get used to it,"[iii] she said. Leaving her husband in London, she drove herself to Torquay, three hours away, dreading the chore of closing a house that had been her childhood haven of fantasy and safety. Once there, Agatha was engulfed by her suffering, stalled like a storm front, shuffling silently through her task on slippered feet. She had only meant to be gone for weeks, not months, and certainly not half a year. But there it was.

Archie declared he found it inconvenient to travel to Ashfield on weekend visits, suggesting instead that the pair take an extended trip to Italy in August to visit an obscure health resort in Alassio, on the Gulf of Genoa. Agatha readily agreed, hoping that the vacation would rekindle love, clutching onto the plan with such anticipation that when her husband eventually arrived at Ashfield on August fourth, she was packed for two weeks of mineral baths and therapeutic scrubs. Her eagerness manifested itself in nervous whispered chatter, like the swarming of a thousand bees, when simple silence might have served her well.

Archie thought Agatha looked edgy and in extremely poor health. While her letters had made mention of her inability to sleep as well as her lack of appetite and mental despair, he was horrified at what he saw when she rushed to meet his car. His shock translated itself into superficial conversation, polite but without emotion.

It was that coldness that terrified her. "I think the nearest I can get to describing what I felt at that moment is to recall an old nightmare of mine," Agatha wrote in her autobiography. "The horror of sitting at a tea table, looking across at my best-loved friend, and suddenly realizing that the person sitting there *was a stranger*."[iv]

What she did not admit then, or later, was the complete absence of love in her husband's face. If her eyes were glazed with disappointment, his shifted with the uneasiness of betrayal. Well-mannered words passed between husband and wife found stilted conversation fall away to silence, until Archie burst into a spontaneous revelation. Barely able to meet Agatha's gaze, her husband confessed that he had fallen in love with another woman, and wanted an immediate divorce.

Divorce. Upon hearing the word, red and white blotches like oilcloth gingham spread across Agatha's face, as anger replaced disbelief. This was not happening, *could not* be happening.

"Her name is Nancy Neele," he said. "You remember her," he said. "She's been in our house," he said. It was all so rushed and unexpected, the words hardening into a wall of denial structured by her refusal to forsake a happy ending.

Agatha was sick, her stomach an acid swirl of recrimination and self-doubt. She begged for time; she *would* be different; she *could* change. Panicking, she asked for three months; he gave her four. Sixteen weeks of polite pirouettes, circling rather than crossing paths, saying words but skipping thoughts. He skillfully avoided the real issues by arranging schedules of separate play, biding time, nothing more.

The morning of Friday, December third, began the same as any other in Sunningdale. Cook had served eggs, beans, sausage, and tomatoes, a proper English breakfast. It was Agatha who spoke first, announcing her intention to spend the weekend resting at a bed and breakfast in Yorkshire three hours away, and invited Archie to join her. He was unavailable, he said, having already made plans to meet his friends, the Jameses, for a weekend at their lodge in Hurtmore near Godalming. Her disappointment roiled in her mind, poisoning her mood. She was the one who shouted first, for volume was all she had left now. Meaningless words and one idle threat. If he would not be spending the weekend with her, she threatened, she would not be at home when he returned.

Archie's reaction was cold and prepared. Worse still, he was in control. The louder his wife shouted, the less need there was for him to respond at all. He only had to tell her the truth. Slowly, without emotion, he did. He had waited long enough, he said, and had tired of the charade they were playing. He was leaving the house—and her.

Agatha squinted her eyes in real pain, or perhaps to prevent the flow of tears. Yet even as she moved her hands to her face, she heard him say he would seek a divorce regardless of her cooperation. Having spoken his mind, he picked up his newspaper and left the room. It was over that quickly. White heat and then nothing.

She did not actually see him leave the house, but rather knew he had gone when she heard the sound of his Delage touring car reach the end of the drive, spinning pieces of cinder into the road as he drove away.

She instinctively pulled her hair back from her face, the way she did when she was nervous, rolling the curls against her index finger, staring into space, as if concentration alone could control the future. She was in the same spot several hours later when the ringing of the telephone startled her, breaking the spell.

Her immediate thought was of Archie, but the caller was not her husband. Rather, her neighbor, the ever-eager Mrs. DeSilva, was on the phone inviting her for tea and bridge. She declined the offer, somewhat weakly, since she had no actual plans and could not imagine an excuse that sounded sincere. Days earlier the two of them had been in London shopping on Albemarle Street, dashing from one store to the next, giddy with the excitement of the holidays. At M. Goodson Lingerie, Agatha purchased an elaborate white satin beauté nightgown to wear as a surprise for her husband during her planned weekend interlude. She would look beautiful, she thought. *And lost love would find its way home.* It all seemed so silly now, brushed away by the coarse broom sweep of the morning's enmity.

Her natural instinct was to drive to London, to speak to Archie, to apologize. But his final stare across the breakfast table had been so filled with hate she could barely bring herself to remember it. There was little doubt that he was upset, but perhaps her imagination was amplifying the extent of the damage. If only she could weigh his mood, she thought; only then she would know if the rift between them was irreparable. That afternoon, Agatha gathered up Rosalind and the child's teddy bear and, bundling them against winter's chill, drove the twenty-five miles to Dorking to visit Archie's mother, Peg Hemsley. Agatha had never really liked her, but Archie and his mother had always been close. Surely Peg would know just how bad things were.

Surprised and delighted to see her granddaughter, Peg set out tea, scones and gooseberry jam from Alice Biddle's shop in London. The jam had been expensive, but Peg loved serving a proper tea. Agatha, however, barely noticed the food. She leaned in as her mother-in-law's conversation buzzed and darted around subjects with the manic behavior of a fly about to die. She chattered in circles with no destination—the sound of her voice apparently its own reward.

Defeated, Agatha returned home and sat alone that night at the dinner table. The scene of that morning's confrontation replayed itself in an endless loop, always ending with the same bitter threat.

Desperate, yet hardly without resources or the determination to save her marriage, she began to craft a plan worthy of any Agatha Christie mystery. The plot was subtle, yet obvious enough for those who knew where to look for clues. Only the ending was left to fate.

After packing a valise with several dresses, her new nightgown, two silk scarves, and two pairs of shoes, Agatha carried the case to the front door and then returned upstairs to wait. There was always the chance that at any moment, Archie might still return. It was, of course, the foolish dream of a woman who refused to give up hope, and by ten p.m., she knew as much.

Placing the letter to Carlo, and another to Archie, on the inlaid table in the dark foyer, Agatha put on her favorite muskrat fur coat, velvet hat, and leather gloves, stopping only to glance briefly in the hall mirror and button up her dignity. Hugging her dog for luck, she picked up her valise and, without looking back, left the security of the house and the only world she knew.

The night sky was crisp black. The air felt cold against her skin, flushed as she struggled with the weight of the valise, her steamy breath leaving a vapor trail for her passion to follow. The gravel under her feet sounded like a knife scraping burnt toast as she walked slowly to her car, a polished Morris Cowley. She was relieved when the car started immediately. Agatha knew nothing of cars, except the excitement she felt when driving them. *This is it then,* she thought, fear and determination pressing her foot on the accelerator. A moment later, she was gone, disappearing into the darkness.

The following morning, a fifteen-year-old gypsy boy named Jack Best was walking toward the village of Albury, along the lane crossing through Newlands Corner. Beanpole thin with a thatch of light brown hair standing at attention, Jack was smiling. More than just the bracing weather and the dramatic vistas of the North Downs, the teenager was excited by the prospect of work. He had gotten a job with a hunting party shooting game that day on the grounds of the nearby estate of the Duke of Northumberland. The sweeping grasslands stretched as far as the horizon, interrupted only by thick shaws of ash and maple trees that thrived in Surrey County.

This particular section of Newlands Corner had many roads still unpaved, many suddenly reduced to lanes that struggled to find passage through rough brambles and thick underbrush stretching for several hundred acres. This was harsh country, miles removed from the convenience of city life, and it was the place that Jack Best now called home.

When Jack saw what he thought was an automobile far down the scarp, partially hidden in boxwood, his curiosity drew him to the rutted path through the undergrowth some three hundred yards from the road. "Near the chalk pit I saw the hedges broken and the hood of a car sticking up," he said. "I looked inside the car and saw clothing on the floor. There was no one about. The car was covered in frost and the wheels had become fast in the hedge. I ran back to the road and told a policeman."[v]

Frederick Dore, a mechanic at the Thames Ditton plant of AC Car Group, was enjoying his breakfast at Alfred Luland's refreshment stand not far away. Dore, too, had seen the car minutes before on his way into town. Now overhearing the excited Jack Best, Dore left his porridge, rasher of bacon, and sliced tomatoes topped with sugar to trek through the underbrush along the edge of the chalk pit to closely examine the Morris Cowley for himself. "I noticed the windscreen of the car above the bushes," he said. "All the lights were out then. I found the current given out, suggesting that it had been abandoned in the darkness when the lights were burning. It certainly looked to me that it had been scuttled downhill empty, for there were no skids marks on the slope to indicate that the brakes had been applied," he later told reporters.[vi]

The flush of whispered excitement had leaked through the village by the time Dore climbed back to the road, where curious onlookers had gathered. Leaving Luland to watch over the car, Dore raced to the Newlands Corner Hotel on Clandon Road, where he telephoned the police, providing a complete report of the vehicle and the scattered clothing inside.

Two hours later, a little after ten thirty a.m., several officers from the Surrey County Police Headquarters in Guildford made their way to Newlands Corner, by which time the news had spread to the neighboring villages of Albury and Shalford. Given that the North Downs were pastoral and normally isolated from mystery or excitement, the abandoned Morris Cowley was an instant source of speculation. According to their official report, what the police uncovered, in addition to the car, was a fur coat, two pairs of black shoes, a gray jumper, evening "frock," and an expired driver's license belonging to Mrs. Agatha Christie, of Sunningdale, England.

In less than an hour, a pair of policemen arrived at Styles asking to speak with the Christies. It was left to a very nervous and upset Carlo to explain that neither Mr. nor Mrs. Christie were home—Mr. Christie presumably in Godalming; Mrs. Christie on a spontaneous excursion via motorcar.

It is not always the unexpected that causes the most disruption in our lives. Having worried all night over Agatha's absence, Carlo now waited in dread for the policemen's news. Whatever Carlo had expected to hear at that particular moment, the extraordinary tale of a ditched car and missing driver in a remote stretch of Newlands Corners was not it. As her face took the color of fireplace ash, Carlo sank slowly into the faded damask of an easy chair, shrinking within its folds.

Her hands were shaking as she reached into the pocket of her dress and extracted the note Agatha had left for her the previous evening. "I shall not be home to-night," Agatha wrote. "I will let you know to-morrow where I am."[vii] Agatha went on to request that Carlo cancel her weekend reservation at a boarding house in the Yorkshire village of Beverley. Several hours earlier, Carlo had done as instructed, sending a telegram through the Ascot exchange: "Regret cannot come— Christie," it read.

Several miles away at Hurtmore Cottage in Godalming, Mr. and Mrs. Sam James were preparing to sit down to lunch when they heard the sound of insistent rapping on their front door. Seconds later, their butler, Wills, whispered in Mr. James's ear that the police were waiting in the sitting room. "We don't normally receive visits from the police," he later explained to a reporter from *The Daily Mail.* "Very disturbing...very disturbing. Especially when we were told Mrs. Christie was missing."

Just as they were hearing the news, a relaxed Archie Christie entered the room with Nancy Neele. He wore casual golfing attire—a sport coat over wool breeches. Nancy's hand released his as the policemen rose to greet them. When told of the discovery of his wife's car, abandoned on the slopes of Newlands Corner, Archie looked like a man more annoyed by the interruption than concerned about his missing wife.

While claiming no knowledge of Agatha's whereabouts or even her exact plans for the weekend, Archie mentioned her recent depressed state, attributing her condition to her "highly dramatic nature" and "a nervous breakdown of sorts." Archie agreed to accompany the police to the North Downs, now the site of a widening search party. He requested a few moments to proffer his appreciation to his bewildered hosts.

As it happened, however, Archie Christie did not travel immediately to Newlands Corner. By all accounts, he journeyed first to his home in Sunningdale to discuss the situation with Carlo Fisher. Lilly, the housemaid, opened the door for her returning master, taking his hat and coat with nervous apprehension. Ever since the arrival of the police earlier in the day, the staff had been buzzing with that odd mixture of gossip and foreboding that arises when servants anticipate disaster.

Archie found Carlo in the study, visibly upset. She never had much sympathy for Agatha's husband, whom she considered to be self-absorbed and emotionally absent from the family. That impression was strengthened by his attitude of irritation and frustration.

Far from sensing any danger in his wife's disappearance, Archie seemed to suggest it was the performance of a desperate woman. The worry plainly etched on Carlo's face did little to dispel Archie's annoyance at the disruption of his weekend. He was unmoved by the discussion of the letter Agatha left for her secretary. It was only after Carlo produced the sealed note with Archie's name scrawled on the envelope that his mood altered, at least momentarily.

Carlo was eager to know its contents, certain it would put an end to the mystery surrounding her employer's disappearance. Snatching up the envelope, Archie ripped at it like a raptor, deliberately shielding it from Carlo's view with broad shoulders and turned back. She noticed only a brief flash of anger, covered by the impulsive toss of the note in the fireplace, where both watched the evidence dissolve in flames. Shaking his head, he uttered the word "Nothing."

Nothing? Carlo thought. *So why destroy it?* she wondered in silence.

When Archie eventually arrived at Newlands Corner with Carlo in tow, there were over a dozen policemen assembled at the point where Agatha's car had veered off the road. He was met by Deputy Chief Constable William Kenward from the Surrey Police. Kenward, a stout, middle-aged career officer, saw the Christie disappearance as a quick recipe for career advancement and the potential for international publicity.

Two years earlier, in 1924, Kenward was given a commendation for his help in the arrest and capture of Jean Pierre Vacquier in Byfleet. The dandyish Vacquier (ironically, a physical duplicate of Agatha's famed Belgian detective, Hercule Poirot), was convicted of the strychnine poisoning of Blue Anchor pub owner Alfred Jones—the husband of his paramour, Elsie. It was a case that generated enormous public interest. Now, eager to be back in the press spotlight, Kenward began to weave a tale of intrigue in the isolated thicket of the North Downs.

Not far from the spot where Agatha's car was being towed up the rutted hill to the nearby Guildford Garage on Epson Road, Kenward directed his search party to the mysterious waters of Silent Pool. A favorite of Alfred, Lord Tennyson, the pool was said to hold the ghost of a maiden drowned by King John in medieval times. Unfortunately for Kenward, what it apparently did *not* hold was the body of Agatha Christie. Unwilling to admit defeat, Kenward ordered that Silent Pool be dredged by a team of experts the following day.

In Torquay, three hours south on the English Channel, the local police visited Ashfield after Archie suggested Agatha might have traveled to her childhood home. That lead, too, proved fruitless after it was discovered that the house was deserted. "Autumn leaves were still lying thick in the doorway, the windows were fastened, and there were no footmarks in the carriage drive or on the footpaths."[viii]

On Sunday, while Archie remained cloistered inside Styles with his daughter and Carlo, Kenward called upon the Special Constables, a force of volunteers who rallied to comb the underbrush and wild hedges growing across acres of remote land.

The weather that evening had turned brutally cold, dropping to a record minus two degrees Fahrenheit and partially freezing parts of Silent Pool. Thick sticks were used to break the ice, yet the dredging produced no sign of the missing writer. Schoolchildren, taking to the fields in the hope of uncovering clues missed by the police, giggled in delight at the fun, making up singsong rhymes that echoed across the downs. As dusk burned the winter sky gold-orange, Kenward returned to his office in Guildford and decided to throw the net wide to expand his search.

The deputy chief constable issued a missing person's bulletin to over four dozen police departments in surrounding communities. Using a description and photo furnished by Carlo, Kenward also alerted the nation's press, headquartered in London, to the sinister implications of the breaking story.

MISSING

From her home "Styles" Sunningdale
Mrs. Agatha Mary Clarissa CHRISTIE
(WIFE OF COLONEL A. CHRISTIE)
Age 35[1] years, Height 5 ft. 7 ins. Hair Red (Shingled),
Natural Teeth, Eyes Grey, Complexion Fair, Well Built.
DRESSED—Grey Stockingette Skirt, Green Jumper, Grey and dark
Grey Cardigan, small Green Velour Hat, may have hand bag
containing £5 to £10. Left home in 4 seater Morris Cowley car at
9.45 p.m. on 3rd. December leaving note saying she was
going for a drive. The next morning the car was found abandoned
at Newlands Corner, Albury, Surrey.

As expected, there were numerous false sightings from locals attempting to be helpful or hoping for fame. Fuet, the porter at Milford Station, south of Godalming, reported on Sunday morning that a woman looking like Mrs. Christie asked him the time of the next train to Portsmouth. A woman named Mrs. Kitching was certain she saw Agatha in Little London the same day. John Buckner spotted her having tea in Petersham near Richmond. Ralph Brown offered her a lift in Battersea, claiming that she "seemed to be in the kind of mood when she did not care what happened."[ix] The woman declined the ride.

What seemed to be the most reliable tip came from a farmhand named Ernest Cross, who reported to the police that he had started a Morris Cowley for a stranded woman at daybreak on Saturday. "It was about 6:30 on Saturday morning as I was going to work, I came upon a woman in a frenzied condition standing by a motorcar near the top of Newlands Corner hill, a few yards from Newlands Corner Hotel," Cross swore in a police affidavit. "She was moaning and holding her hands to her head and her teeth were chattering from the cold.

"She was wearing only a thin frock and a thin pair of shoes, and I think she was without a hat. The lights of her car were full on and I asked if I could be of any assistance."[x]

When she saw Cross heading toward her, the woman trilled a cry for help, asking him to please attempt to start her stalled car. With the gallantry of a laborer, Cross removed his

---

[1] Agatha Christie was 36 years old at the time.

jacket and handed it to the shivering woman, before giving the crank two swift turns and sparking the engine to life.

Helping the stranger into her car and retrieving his coat and her thanks, he turned to leave. "As she climbed in, I noticed the engine was running very smoothly, and thinking she would be all right, I walked on down the hill," he said. "At the time, it was quite dark, and I thought it funny that a woman should be out in such thin clothes and at such an early hour, but concluded she had lost her way but was distressed because she could not get her car to start. The last I saw her was as she drove along the road round by Newlands Corner in the direction of Shere."[xi][2]

Believing the farmhand's account, Kenward hypothesized that Agatha was so exhausted that she drove the car off the road. Leaving the car without engaging the emergency brake, she started to walk toward the hotel when her car rolled down the embankment, eventually becoming caught in the scrub on the edge of the chalk pit. Arguably it was not a particularly convincing story, but it was his and, as such, immediately accepted.

"It is believed that she tried to find her way in the dark but lost her bearings and stumbled towards the woods, since then nothing has been seen or heard of her."[xii]

By Monday, newspapers in France, Spain, and Germany carried the story of Agatha's disappearance. Even the venerable *New York Times* featured its coverage on its front page under the headline "Mrs. Agatha Christie, Novelist, Disappears in Strange Way from Her Home in England."[xiii]

Mrs. DeSilva, convinced by her bridge group to speak with the police about her conversation with Agatha the day she disappeared, positively fluttered in her devotion to her missing neighbor, whom she described as "beautiful."

> Mrs. Christie is one of the sweetest women who ever lived. But to those who knew her well, it was clear that she suppressed her emotions rather than cause distress to anyone. I think that she had been working too hard, and for some months she had said that she could get no ideas for her work, could not write a line.
> I think the climax came when her mother, to whom she was greatly attached, died in the early

---

[2] Press accounts of the incident in the *Surrey Advertiser* and the *Daily Express* identified the man as a gravel worker named Edward McAllister.

part of the year. That distressed her very much, but she still went bravely on. Her doctor told her that she must have rest, and things would right themselves.

Some months ago, I think it was in June or July, she had been away and came back to Sunningdale to arrange about the disposal of her mother's furniture. She came on to me and was obviously so ill that I sent her straight to bed. Next morning she seemed quite fit again, and she said to me, 'You have saved my life.' She had been ailing for some months, but recently seemed better.

I played golf with her a week ago yesterday—she played a very good game of golf and tennis and also went in for riding—again on Monday. On Wednesday, we motored up to London together. She was then full of an idea she had of taking a furnished house in town, so that she could be more with her husband, and of letting Styles furnished.

We met some friends and all lunched together at the Carlton, where we discussed arrangements for spending a few weeks in Portugal early in the New Year. Mrs. Christie said she could not go before Christmas because of her little girl, and we decided to go about the first week in January. My husband has a house there, and we were going to spend three or four weeks together. Mrs. Christie was delighted with the idea.

During Wednesday afternoon, we went shopping, and when finally I left her, she was going on to the Forum Club, where she proposed to spend the night as she had a dinner engagement in town.[xiv]

The publicity swirling around Mrs. DeSilva apparently appealed to her sense of theater, as she held court in her home, Lindsay Lodge. "Friday, I telephoned asking her to come round for tea and bridge," she cooed, "but she sent a message that she could not as she was going out or had someone coming. I do not remember which. That was the last I heard of her. I am sure that Mrs. Christie's disappearance is a case of absolute exhaustion—loss of memory or something like that."[xv]

The illusion of some mysterious memory loss had been introduced the previous day by Archie himself, as a suggestion for his wife's unusual behavior. Speaking to a reporter from the *Westminster Gazette*, Archie mused, "I cannot hazard even a guess as to what has become of my wife. The only explanation I can offer for her disappearance is that she had a nervous breakdown and is suffering from loss of memory."[xvi] It sounded believable enough. Now, if only Archie could convince himself.

He was neither talkative nor particularly present when, on Monday morning, he drove into London with Carlo to speak to inspectors at Scotland Yard in an effort to enlist their aid. Agatha's secretary later described him as being "lost in his thoughts." And while officials at the Yard were accommodating, other than confirming details received from Kenward, they declined to become directly involved without a special invitation from the local police.

Sending Carlo back to Sunningdale via train, Archie moved anonymously through the streets of London, a man at odds with his life. He thought of war and of flying again. No longer in uniform, but no less handsome, he felt suddenly disappointed.

The sounds and decorations of Christmas formed a discordant backdrop to his malaise. Spirited shoppers, carolers, the vibrant crisp of the season mocked him. He was supposed to be enjoying London with Nancy now, not being drawn into a mystery. Archie Christie knew more than ever how he felt: deeply in love with a woman he could not have, and at the whim of a wife he did not want.

He had not seen Nancy Neele since Saturday—two days, a lifetime for lovers. She had returned to her parents' home on Crosley Green in Ricksmansworth, north of London, keeping in touch with Archie discreetly via telephone. The need to stay apart now was evident; any hint of an improper relationship would prove damaging.

While he had managed to keep her existence from the press, he knew that his involvement with the twenty-six-year-old beauty was far from a secret. They frequently golfed together at the Prince's Club in Sandwich and ate dinner together at restaurants in London. And perhaps most important at the moment, his mother, Peg Hemsley, was an encouraging supporter of his affair. She loved gossip, and at the first suggestion of intrigue, was thrilled to share what she knew with the press.

"My daughter-in-law seemed depressed about her work," Mrs. Hemsley told *The Daily Mail*'s special correspondent when he located her in Dorking to ask about Friday afternoon tea. "[It was a] story she was engaged in writing."

> She frequently referred to the death of her mother who died earlier in the year, and it was obvious that she was still grieving at her loss. For some days following her death, Mrs. Christie went about very depressed and seemed at a loss to account for some of her actions.
>
> On one occasion, while driving away from a friend's house, her little dog Peter was knocked down. She thought the animal was dead and lifted it into the car. She became frantic with grief, and according to her own statement, never quite knew how she got home. She declared that she drove in a frenzied condition for miles, and did not know what roads she was taking.
>
> When she arrived home, her servant discovered the dog was quite well and sitting up in the back seat. Mrs. Christie had declared that the dog was dead, and when the servant took the dog out of the car to show Mrs. Christie, she refused to believe it was alive.
>
> I feel certain myself that something of a similar nature must have happened on Friday. She was devoted to her husband and child, and she would never willingly have left them.
>
> It is my opinion that in a fit of depression and not knowing where she was going or what she was doing, my daughter-in-law abandoned her car at Newlands Corner and wandered away over the downs.

"When she left me, she seemed a little brighter," Peg Hemsley said, "but sat deep in thought for a few moments in her car before starting away."[xvii]

In an effort to attract readership and maintain the circus that had become Agatha Christie's disappearance, *The*

Daily News offered £100 as a reward to "the first person giving information leading to the discovery" of the author—"if alive." [xviii]

Aerial biplanes in the sky joined bloodhounds on the ground as over a hundred police combed the vast countryside, divided into quadrants by the increasingly determined Kenward. However, the deputy chief constable was not with them. While continuing to insist Agatha would be found among the pools and brambles of the North Downs, Kenward was faced with explaining away a dramatic new clue that had surfaced overnight. It was a letter received by Archie's brother, Campbell Christie, postmarked on Saturday at 9:45 a.m. from London SW1—three hours *after* the Morris Cowley was discovered. The letter was written by Agatha Christie.

Campbell had opened the letter the previous day, read its contents and placed it aside on his desk at the Royal Woolwich Military Academy, seeing nothing unusual in its contents. Agatha had written that she was not feeling well and was going to a healing spa in Yorkshire to rest. Campbell was unaware that Agatha was missing and only learned of it on Monday, when he read about her disappearance in the newspaper. By that point, he was unable to locate the actual letter, but he did find the envelope bearing the postmark and sent it to his brother, who in turn passed it along to Kenward.

Now faced with the very real possibility that Agatha was alive and well in London, outside of his jurisdiction, Kenward called for the services of a psychic, Miss Rice-Johnson, who spent the better part of Tuesday morning speaking privately with Kenward in his Guildford office. Armed with the psychic's cosmic revelations that Mrs. Christie was to be found "among the tortured branches of the desolate pools," Kenward emerged from seclusion and held a press conference in which he suggested a rather convoluted timeline.

> [Mrs. Christie] left home in her car about 10 o'clock, drove to London, posted either directly or indirectly the letter to Captain Christie, her brother-in-law, which bore the 9:45 Saturday morning postmark.
>
> Then she drove back to Surrey in the small hours, passed through Shere, on the Dorking-

Guildford road below Newlands Corner where she
was seen...by a carman at 3 a.m. going in a westerly
direction.

Eventually, she arrived at Newlands Corner,
where she abandoned the car and wandered off.[xix]

By Tuesday afternoon, special correspondents from
London's *Times, The Daily Mail, The Daily Express,
Westminster Gazette, Surrey Advertiser* and *Daily Sketch* had
established a press tent at Newlands Corner under a temporary
tarp quickly erected for protection from an intermittent drizzle.
Several dozen reporters were now stationed in Berkshire in
front of the Christie house, where neighbors began to complain
of the growing disruption created by all the traffic and noise.

Berkshire Constabulatory Superintendent Charles
Goddard, headquartered in the nearby parish of Wokingham,
had ordered a police guard outside of Styles, as well as
assigning a plainclothes detective inside the residence at
Archie's request. Unlike his Surrey counterpart, Goddard
projected mild amusement at the ongoing spectacle, convinced
that Agatha was very much alive and simply in need of some
time away from her husband.

Goddard was not, however, inactive. He quietly
observed Archie's increasing nervous and defiant behavior,
provoked, it seemed, by the cauldron of gossip that continued
to swirl around him. A volunteer had found a shoe "similar to
ones worn by Mrs. Christie" in the area near Silent Pool.
There was talk that Agatha carried a gun and perhaps had
contemplated suicide. Her passport was missing, as was a large
sum from her bank account. Worse still was the passing
mention of his liaison on page one of the *Westminster Gazette*,
buried within extensive coverage of the disappearance.

"Colonel Christie," the reporter wrote, "was a guest on
Friday night at Hurtmoor [sic] Cottage, the charming solitary
house of Mr. and Mrs. James, some two miles from Godalming.
The only other person there was a Miss Nield [sic], a young
woman friend of the family who pays them frequent visits."[xx]

There it was, for all to see. In the tiniest print, but
screaming at Archie as if it were a headline, here was the first
hint of impropriety. Parting the blinds with his index finger,
Archie glared at the throng gathered outside the gates of

Styles, pacing, staring, unpredictable. Far worse than not knowing how much they knew was not knowing what they would write.

Feeling obligated to meet their demands for a comment, Archie handwrote a statement and asked the plainclothes detective to reveal its contents to the press. "I have no news from my wife," he wrote, adding that he was feeling sick and harassed. Denying that his wife ever owned a revolver and never mentioned suicide, he noted that her passport had been located inside the house and that no money had been removed from her bank accounts—either in Sunningdale or Torquay.

By Wednesday morning, Kenward had ordered three hundred police and special constables to be added to the search party on the Downs. "Tangled heaths were beaten down by men walking ten yards apart armed with long sticks, and in some cases assisted by dogs. At times, they could be heard calling to each other through the dank drifting hill-top mists, while overhead sounded the drone of the planes as they cruised to and fro."[xxi]

A reporter from the *Daily Chronicle*, acting on the information in the letter sent to Campbell Christie, traveled to Yorkshire and began canvassing the resort hotels in the area around the wealthy spa town of Harrogate. The all-day search discovered "no trace" of the missing writer.

Thursday, by press count, there were four hundred to five hundred men peppering the land, now trodden flat. Despite his lack of success, Kenward insisted that "the solution of the mystery lies in the vicinity of Newlands Corner, where Mrs. Christie's car was abandoned."[xxii]

Archie secretly joined the search party, bringing Peter, the Christie's wirehaired terrier, to the North Downs in an effort to pick up Agatha's scent. Unfortunately, the only thing Peter managed to pick up was a new name. "Patsy [sic], the pet dog of Mrs. Christie, the missing novelist, was brought to Newlands Corner today to join in the search for his mistress," according to the *Daily Chronicle*.

Little knowing the purpose for which he
had been brought, Patsy scampered joyfully over the

open country, and thoroughly enjoyed this
afternoon's freedom. Colonel Christie joined Deputy
Chief Constable Kenward, and, for nearly three
hours, helped in the search. With Patsy, they worked
right down the valley from the spot where Mrs.
Christie's car was found, and tramped around by the
Silent Pool.

Few people knew that Colonel Christie was
taking a personal part in the search, or that the dog
belonged to the missing woman.

High hopes had been centered on today's
intensive hunt. Two aeroplanes skimmed as low
over the ground as they dared; a tractor was used
to break down bushes and copses otherwise
impenetrable, and men had waded through marshy
ground and clambered into pits and hollows. Not a
trace of Mrs. Christie was found.[xxiii]

Returning to Sunningdale and Styles, Archie roamed
the large home, trapped by the press and the increasing
speculation that he had played a part in his wife's
disappearance. Fed by the Christie's cook, Lillie, who spoke of
a quarrel the morning Agatha had disappeared, the reporters
read Archie's irritable disposition as a sign of guilt rather than
one of worry. And Lillie casually mentioned another letter—
the one written by Agatha to her husband, the one he
destroyed, and the one the police never knew existed.

Deputy Chief Constable Kenward and Inspector
Sidney Frank Butler (representing Superintendent Goddard)
met at the Bagshot Police Station Thursday night. An hour
later, Archie Christie was brought in for official questioning.
Disgruntled, he struggled to explain why he had destroyed
evidence he had failed to reveal. With every effort he made to
clarify, Archie's aura of culpability grew.

"Her letter referred to a purely personal matter and
had no bearing whatsoever on her disappearance," he stated.
"She had something to tell me, but I cannot discuss what that
was. I feel convinced that it was written long before she
decided to leave home and the way she apparently did."[xxiv]

Upon leaving the police station, Archie was surrounded
by reporters, all of whom were unaware of the discussion that

had just taken place. Pushing past the probing correspondents with a wave, he said only that Kenward would be issuing a statement. For his part, the deputy chief maintained an atypical silence, refusing to comment on the late-night session.

On Friday, December 10, London's *The Daily Chronicle* published what it regarded as a "frank statement" from Archie concerning his wife's disappearance. "There had been no quarrel between us," he lied, eager to dismiss the rumor of marital discord. "My wife and I had never quarreled over any of my friends, all of whom were quite well known to her. I had not stayed at the cottage where I spent last weekend for three months previously. She knew quite well where I was going."[xxv]

Oh yes, Agatha knew, he thought. He brooded over it, his conviction festering until silence was no longer an option. Pushing buttons and daring their marriage to shift beyond rueful acceptance. "Things were fine; there was nothing," he said again, as if repeating the thought with different words might make it more believable. Yet, the more he spoke, the less credible Archie Christie looked. He was a man more interested in public perception than in uncovering the truth— or so it appeared. Fleet Street could read the signs, and the signs read murder.

"It is inconceivable to me that [Mrs. Christie] should have deliberately left her little girl, Rosalind, of whom she was extremely fond," a friend said to the press. "And if she has lost her memory and is wandering, how is it that she has not been seen? People with or without memory must eat and must have shelter at night in this weather." [xxvi]

London businessman Sebastian Earl, who worked with Archie in the Rio Tinto Building,[3] shared an elevator ride with Agatha's husband that week. "He was in a terribly nervous state and told me the police had followed him up Broad Street and all the way to the office and were now waiting outside. 'They think I've murdered my wife,' he said."

Prolific British crime writer Edgar Wallace, still six years away from writing the story that became "King Kong," had his own theory. "Agatha Christie's disappearance seems to have been voluntary," Wallace wrote in an exclusive article for *The Daily Mail*. "Her act was the culmination of a long period of depression, obviously due to some cause other than worry

[3] The Rio Tinto Company was a copper-mining concern, headquartered in London. Archie Christie worked for Austral Ltd., an investment company with offices in the Rio Tinto Building.

over her work. The disappearance seems to be a typical case of 'mental reprisal' on somebody who has hurt her. To put it vulgarly, her first intention seems to have been to 'spite' an unknown person who would be distressed by her disappearance."[xxvii]

Mystery writer Dorothy L. Sayers, a casual friend of Agatha, leapt into the case by writing her own theory while on special assignment to *The Daily News*.

> In any problem of this kind, there are four possible solutions: loss of memory, foul play, suicide or voluntary disappearance. The first—loss of memory—is bound to present us with a baffling situation, because it implies an entire lack of motive, and it is an axiom of detection that where there is a motive there is a clue. But a voluntary disappearance, also may be so cleverly staged as to be exceedingly puzzling especially if, as here, we are concerned with a skilful writer of detective stories, whose mind has been trained in the study of way and means to perplex.[xxviii]

Arriving on the scene at Newlands Corner with no small degree of fanfare, Sayers took one look at the Silent Pool and the surrounding hills with the howls of bloodhounds in the distance and declared, "No, she isn't here" with beatific certainty.

There were those who disagreed, including Deputy Chief Constable Kenward. Far from giving up on his belief that Agatha's body would be found on the desolate downs of Surrey, he redoubled his efforts in the area, asking for the public's help in searching over three hundred acres of wilderness.

"Great Search Today by Public for Mrs. Christie" headlined the *Sunday Pictorial* on December 12. Like a company picnic in which everyone from the cleaning staff to the chairman are invited, thousands of curious people responded to the plea, costumed for the hunt with boots and walking sticks.

The Daily Mail placed the count at five thousand, while *The Daily Chronicle* estimated triple that amount. "15,000 People Search for Mrs. Christie" its front page screamed in bold type, adding "Three Thousand Cars Bring Up Helpers."

The mist-laden countryside was scoured by thousands of men and women on foot, and by scores on horseback. Six bloodhounds were used in the hunt, but they were not the only canine helpers. Alsatians, collies, terriers, and even the smallest of pets accompanied their owners through dense, dim woods, and thick brown bracken, across lonely moorlands, and up hill and down dale, from dawn to dusk. The cost of the search to the Surrey police up to the present is estimated at about £1,000.[xxix]

Sir Arthur Conan Doyle, creator of the Sherlock Holmes mysteries and devout spiritualist, requested and received a single glove once worn by Agatha in an effort to divine the woman's location. Appointed as an honorary deputy-lieutenant of Surrey in 1902, Conan Doyle had been driven to the world of spiritualism after the death of his wife and eldest son. He toured the world giving speeches on the subject with his channeler Horace Leaf.

Leaf was given the glove and asked to use his psychic powers to determine if Agatha was still among the living. Writing a letter to London's *Morning Post,* Conan Doyle stated with certainty that Leaf had predicted Agatha would be found—and soon. "I gave him no clue at all as to what I wanted or to whom the article belonged," he stated. "He never saw it until I laid it on the table at the moment of consultation, and there was nothing to connect either it or me to the Christie case. The date was Sunday last. He at once got the name Agatha.

"There is trouble connected with this article," Leaf prophesied. "The person who owns it is half-dazed and half-purposeful. She is not dead, as many think. She is alive. You will hear of her, I think, next Wednesday."

By Monday, December 13, scuba divers from the London firm of Siebe Gorman and Co. on Westminster Bridge Road offered to "sound every pool in the district"—a proposal readily accepted by Kenward. In addition, eighty members of the Adlershot Motor Cycling Club volunteered to "scour the Downs at their own expense." If not exactly news, it nevertheless passed for such, as the deputy chief constable began the day by updating the press in his daily briefing.

Disappointed by the failure of the Great Sunday Hunt to turn up anything relevant beyond some muddied boots and an elderly volunteer who nearly drowned in quicksand, reporters began to spin intrigue through the creative use of imagination. There were suggestions that Agatha was now dressing as man or assuming various disguises, though the rationale for such behavior defied conventional wisdom.

An empty "shooting lodge" discovered in a desolate part of the moors suddenly became "one of the most secret and fantastic woodland cottages one could imagine—a kind of eerie Hansel and Gretel house in the loneliest part of the Surrey Hills." The three-room bungalow, known to its owner Major Williams-Ellis J.P. as Stapledown, was dramatized as the perfect hide-out for the missing novelist. According to the reporter writing the front-page headline story of the *Westminster Gazette,* the cabin contained a "blue empty 20 oz. bottle labeled 'Poison, lead and opium'; a postcard, the contents of which are unknown; a woman's fur-lined velour coat; a box of face powder, end of a loaf, and a cardboard box with East Clandon and Twyford addresses; children's books titled 'Sunbeam' and also the 'Velvet Rabbit'; and log ashes in the fireplaces and other evidences of recent occupation." Adding a bit of hyperbole, the writer labeled it "the loneliest back-wood habitation in all Surrey, so secreted in a labyrinth of woodland paths that it must be impossible to direct a stranger there."[xxx]

Kenward continued to insist for no apparent reason that "Mrs. Christie is not in London. She will be found on the Downs. It is not a theory. I am convinced from what I know."[xxxi]

Even as the heavily mustached investigator said the words, he wondered if they were true. Though dozens of acres of barren downs remained to be searched, Kenward knew that the most obvious areas had already been combed in a methodical foot-by-foot examination that had yielded nothing. More worrisome still was the telephone call from Superintendent Gilbert McDowall of the West Riding Police, suggesting that Mrs. Christie had perhaps been found.

Calls to report sightings of Agatha Christie were hardly unusual, having increased to a dozen per day. The previous morning, a woman traveling via train from Waterloo to Egham had been positively identified as the missing novelist. Upon closer examination, the woman's hair color turned out to be blond, not red; her age was twenty-two, not thirty-six; and her height five feet five inches, not five feet seven inches. Mable Crust, the female in question and the daughter of a local tradesman, threatened to sue the constabulary of Runnymede for harassment.

And so it was that when McDowall called Kenward to ask for assistance in identifying a possible match with the missing Mrs. Christie, the deputy chief constable paid it little attention. The spotlight in which he found himself was far too bright to be shared, particularly with someone from the effete resorts of North Yorkshire.

It was in the North Yorkshire town of Harrogate that a part-time saxophonist named Bob Leeming and a sometime drummer named Bob Tappin, working nights playing in the Harry Codd Dance Band, noticed a familiar face among the guests in the Winter Garden Ballroom of the Harrogate Hydropathic Hotel. Certain that they had located Agatha Christie among the hotel patrons, the two Bobs reported their information to the West Riding Police, hoping to collect the £100 reward offered by *The Daily News*.

Known since the 1500s for the healing properties of its sulfur springs, Harrogate was the playground of the rich and royal, society's darlings who valued their privacy and expected it to be respected. Fearing the potential disaster of a misidentification, McDowall requested help from Kenward. It was only after receiving a second call on the morning of December 14 that Kenward deemed it necessary to alert Carlo Fisher, who in turned telephoned Archie Christie at his office in London.

Convinced to take the 1:40 p.m. train from King's Cross to Harrogate, Archie arrived just after the sun had set, as dusk washed the large, formal gardens of the elegant Hydro in tones of winter blue and mauve. Met by Superintendent McDowall, Archie entered the hotel's stylish lobby, decorated with potted palms and Belgian carpet. He sat alone in a far corner, an open newspaper partially hiding his face. The beads of sweat forming on his upper lip were concealed by the front-page picture of the very woman he sought to identify.

There was the slightest rustle as a tall, spirited redhead descended the stairs from an upper floor. Dressed in a satin evening gown of pale salmon georgette, a delicate silk shawl covering exposed shoulders against the night air, the woman was neither camouflaged nor shy as she moved with the refined grace of a debutante. Looking as lovely as he had ever seen her, Agatha Christie glanced across the lobby and stared directly at her husband.

As he rose, she moved confidently in his direction, gliding past other guests about to enter the dining room. Extending her hand, she took his in hers. "Hello," she said. "My name is Neele. Mrs. Teresa Neele."

ONE

Mrs. Miller
Has a Baby

*One of the luckiest things that can happen
to you in life, I think, is to have a happy childhood.
I had a very happy childhood.*

Agatha Christie:
An Autobiography

FEBRUARY 21, 1890. WHEN MRS. FREDERICK ALVAH Miller, Clara to her friends, discovered she was pregnant in the winter of 1890, the very first thing she did was announce to her cook that cow's cream should be served with every meal. Clara knew about being pregnant. Eleven years earlier, she had given birth to her daughter, Margaret, whom she called Madge. Her son, Louis Montant, nicknamed Monty, had been born a year later. And each time, cow's cream had eased the discomforts of pregnancy and eliminated complications, or so Clara thought. At thirty-six, she was, after all, no longer young, and had the wisdom that experience brings. Yes, it would be cow's cream at every meal.

Her own mother, Mary Ann, had given birth to five children, of whom she was the only girl. When her father, Army Captain Frederick Boehmer, died after falling off his horse and left the family with little income, her mother sent nine-year-old Clara away from her home in the West London suburb of Bayswater to live with her rich aunt, her mother's elder sister Margaret.

Margaret had just married an older widower, a successful American businessman named Nathaniel Frary Miller, who now lived in England in a large home in Cheshire, south of Manchester. While Nathaniel had a grown son, Fred, still living in the United States, he loved the idea of having a young child around the house again and enthusiastically agreed to accept Clara as his own.

For the naïve youngster, the move was a rather tumultuous one, thrust as she was into strange surroundings with a new uncle and an aunt with whom she had precious little history. Despite the luxury of her Cheshire home, she longed for the warm and familiar world of her own family, now nearly two hundred miles away. While it was the custom of the times to relocate children to ease families' financial burdens, it was small consolation to the young girl. As months became years, Clara escaped her reality in an imagination that was fueled by loneliness and a lost sense of security.

There were moments of joy, to be sure, particularly during those special weeks around holidays when Nathaniel's seventeen-year-old son, Frederick Miller, visited. Frederick was eight years Clara's senior, and was, without doubt, the most engaging storyteller she had ever met. He was bright as a 110-volt bulb plugged into a 220 circuit—racing through anecdotes as if being timed. Handsome and seized with an energy that Clara thought bordered on magical, he would share tales of his life in New York, California, and the wilds of Paris with the charm and assurance of a boy without a care in the world, for indeed that was who the affluent Fred Miller was.

Educated in a Swiss boarding school, he returned to his grandparents' home in Manhattan and was invited to join the exclusive Union Club, where he shared cigars with William Blackhouse Astor Jr. and other members of society's elite. While showing no particular talent for work, he pointed to his inclusion in the Social Register as if it were a badge of honor. He had the thick arms of a farmworker, less from exercise than genes, for he favored sleeping late and greeting the day in a gradual fashion, not unlike his contemporaries blessed with wealth in the Victorian age.

Young men of his class were not expected to support themselves, since their families provided all the necessary money to cover expenses and pay for a life of gentlemanly leisure. Life was lived at a casual pace, timed precisely from party to party, and guest house to cottage. Fred owned four tuxedos by his sixteenth birthday, dated his first debutante the following year, and spent weeks visiting at Bathgate, the country estate of millionaire stockbroker Leonard Jerome while romancing the "King of Wall Street's" daughter Jennie (later to become Lady Randolph Churchill).

Yet, over the years, he maintained a touching long-distance relationship with his young cousin, twice removed, culminating with a gift—a bound volume of poetry written by Robert Southey—inscribed, "To Clara, a token of love." Love. The word made Clara's heart soar with a child's hope of gallantry and affection. She had read about, even dreamed about, this kind of love. From that day forward, Clara began to write in a journal of the special fondness she kept in her heart for *"mon cousin merveilleux."* For seven years, she proclaimed her fondness for Fred in sonnets and poetry, occasionally binding her writing with hand-embroidered covers featuring the name FREDERICK in gold.

For much of that time, her cousin remained in the United States, flirting with society's daughters and polishing his reputation as a charming raconteur. It was not until Fred turned twenty-two that he gave any thought to settling down, and then only after having a sobering conversation with his father, who was terminally ill with a heart ailment. It would take eight more years, until September 1877, for Frederick Miller to finally propose to Clara Boehmer; she promptly declined the invitation to marry with the startled look of one who feels she is unworthy, announcing that she was "too dumpy" for the philandering playboy.

If only I were beautiful, Clara thought. She wanted to say yes, to throw her arms around this man she had fantasized about marrying for over a dozen years. Instead she shook his hand and disappeared into her room to dissolve in tears.

While Fred could hardly conceal his astonishment, the rebuff fueled his desire and purpose. There were several more clumsy attempts to capture her hand before Clara became convinced that Frederick was being authentic in his feelings and could be genuine in his promise to "protect and love my most darling one."

The pair married in April 1878 in Cheshire, and after a monthlong honeymoon in Switzerland and several more months living with the widow Margaret, they settled into

family life, choosing to rent furnished accommodations in
Torquay, a popular seaside resort on the south coast of
England. Central to the area called the British Riviera, Torquay
was the lounging ground of bored aristocrats and ultra-rich
foreigners who wore excess time and wealth as a proud fashion
accessory.

Rudyard Kipling, writing to his friend Charles Eliot
Norton, a Harvard art history professor, described Torquay as
"such a place as I do desire acutely to upset—by dancing
through it with nothing on but my spectacles. Villas, clipped
hedges and shaved lawns; fat old ladies with respirators and
obese landaus—the Almighty is a discursive and frivolous
trifler compared with some of 'em."[i]

That first house, the one young marrieds never truly
forget, had as its most distinguishing feature a rather long,
narrow conservatory that overlooked Tor Bay. Little more than
a glassed-in porch, lightly furnished with potted palms and
rocking chairs, the conservatory was Clara's favorite place to
spend her days while her husband played whist at the Royal
Torbay Yacht Club downtown.

Several months after the birth of Madge, or "Mudge"
as Frederick occasionally teased, Clara found she was again
pregnant and insisted on traveling to America to meet her
husband's family and tour the extensive real estate holdings
he had inherited from his father. Manhattan was, as Clara
remembered, "a noisy place with quaint stores," her favorite
being the dress shops on the opulent "Ladies' Mile" around
Broadway and Twentieth Street. She lunched on watercress
sandwiches under the great mansard roof of the flatiron Lord
& Taylor store, where Frederick's gaggle of society friends
marveled at the ease with which she juggled pregnancy,
motherhood, and shopping. But Clara had proven to be well
suited to all three, as shown when the family, including the
newborn Monty, returned to Torquay in September 1880.

Almost immediately upon setting foot in England,
Frederick was called back to New York for business, leaving
Clara to look for a new rental in Torquay, their previous house
now being occupied by a rather large Russian opera singer and
her timid husband. Her aunt Margaret traveled from
Manchester by train, and together the two women canvassed

nearly three dozen properties, all of which were dismissed as being inadequate for one reason or another. All, that is, except for a property known as Ashfield, sitting high above the seaport on Barton Road.

The house was an oversize villa of stucco and wood, owned by a Quaker family named Brown, who had lived in it for several dozen years. With their children gone, the Browns had decided to sell Ashfield and move into the city. The asking price was £2,000, which Clara agreed to and promptly paid from an equal amount bequeathed to her by Nathaniel Frary Miller upon his death, and conveniently held locally in trust by her aunt. Determined to have her way, she eliminated any chance of her husband's disapproval by not telling him until after having taken possession of the house.

"I am happy to think of thee and thy children living here, my dear," Mrs. Brown is reported to have said, which was to Clara the next best thing to an ecclesiastical beatitude.[ii]

The property was set well off the road, with sweeping vistas and rolling lawns that ended in a forest of ash trees, adjacent to the tennis and croquet grass. There were potted daffodils, tulips, and marigolds in gardens edged with gravel, and an enormous porch shrouded in creeping fig, which shaded the interior from the afternoon sun. A large conservatory was built across one side, and a smaller greenhouse on the other— this used more as a shed than a place to grow flowers.

In addition to a drawing room, sitting room, library, dining room, billiard room, and ballroom, the ground floor of Ashfield featured a butler's pantry, larder, and kitchen, which was rather large even by Victorian standards. It was here that Jane Rowe ruled. Jane was Clara's inspired discovery. She was a cook who could not only routinely prepare meals for eight or ten guests without complaint, she also had an endless supply of inventive and delicious recipes to do so. The coal-burning stove had room for six pots, a boiler for hot water, and an oven that was excellent for baking rock cakes—so called because of their shape, not texture.

By the time Frederick arrived back in Torquay, Mrs. Miller had moved a surprised Mr. Miller into a large separate bedroom with its own dressing area on the second floor. Madge and Monty each had rooms of their own as well. Down the hall, their playroom was hardly bigger than an oversize closet, but upstairs on the third floor, the school room with its piano and tables was routinely turned into forts or palaces as the day's fantasy suggested.

By far the largest bedroom on the second floor belonged to Clara. It was here, ten years later, that she spent the first two weeks of September 1890, supine on her feather bed in the final days of her pregnancy. Aunt Margaret had traveled from the city to help with the preparations for birth, which were overseen by a midwife named Mrs. Shelton-Price, who, according to her bill, charged one crown and two shillings to deliver Agatha Mary Clarissa Miller at 2:14 p.m. on Monday afternoon, September 15. Clara chose the name Clarissa to honor herself, Mary for her mother, and Agatha after the heroine in Dinah Maria Mulock Craik's *Agatha's Husband*, Clara's favorite book at that time.

While the children were rather nonplussed by the arrival of a new baby in their midst, to their father, it was an occasion for grand celebration. Ashfield was opened for visitation from the neighbors, the clergy, and several of the headmasters from the private schools flourishing that year in Torquay. Fair-haired and chubby, with pale blue-gray eyes, baby Agatha became the instant darling of Clara's world. So much so that for the first month and a half, Clara refused to hire a nurse to care for the infant, nurses being quite common among upper-middle class families in England.

When "Nursie" finally arrived, Agatha was just under two months old and Clara was freed of the more physical aspects of motherhood and found her niche in playing with the child every afternoon at three. This would be a ritual that continued until Agatha was nearly five years old, because structure and efficiency were essential to Clara, and grew even more so as the years unfolded.

Because of this, as Agatha first learned to walk, and subsequently to play, it was always Nursie, with her heavily starched cambric cap atop a broad, wrinkled face, who encouraged the child in the earliest forms of exercise. Together they shared the excitement of running through the rolling lawns of Ashfield. That is to say, Agatha would run; Nursie, being rheumatic, would sit watching her charge with experienced eyes. While Agatha's body grew spindly and tall, there was always the safety of vast grounds, full of adventure found in the smallest discoveries—a knothole in a tree, a ground turtle missing its tail, the first blooms of summer.

At the age of twelve, Madge left home for boarding at Miss Lawrence's School in Brighton, and eleven-year-old Monty went away for classes at Harrow in London. It was then that Agatha discovered that being the only child remaining at Ashfield had unexpected rewards. Far from being lonely, she was doted on by the servants, her father, and a mother whose ability to create stories came as naturally as her ability to speak. And speak she did. The long-winded conversations between mother and daughter took the form of fantasies acted out in full regalia—only to be continued, and expanded, by Agatha during her extended periods of solitude.

While most children develop imaginary friends, Agatha Miller created entire families of them. According to her biography, "The Kittens" were the first she could remember, assigning different human names and characteristics to feline characters. There were also gladiators, based on Viking lore, and knights of tables round and square.

Pets, as well, held a rather elevated position in Agatha's small world—her first being a bright yellow canary named Goldie, who, in her imagination, became "Master Dickie." Goldie was soon joined by George Washington, a four-month-old Yorkshire terrier that Agatha received as a gift from her father on her fifth birthday. George Washington was nicknamed Tony for convenience and was alternately costumed in ribbons and bows, or caps and hats, depending on the crusade or exploit.[iii]

There was a low, round bowl of fish in the billiard room—more decoration than functioning pets. Agatha referred to them all collectively as Mrs. Fish, the exact identification of moving carp made all the more difficult because their numbers seemed to expand and then unexpectedly decrease, a by-product of natural selection.

The senior pet in the household was Monty's dog, Scotty, a low-slung Dandie Dinmont whose proximity to the floor aided in dusting the seldom-used sitting room. When Agatha was born, Scotty was nearly ten, living another five years before being struck by a careening cart owned by a tradesman selling pots and brushes. While upsetting to Monty, who buried his dog in the backyard pet cemetery, the death of Scotty sent Agatha into a period of dramatic mourning in which she insisted all the servants wear black armbands.

The previous year, Frederick had hired local artist N.H.J. Baird to paint Scotty's portrait—a portrait Agatha now required to be draped in black fabric. While Baird would return to Ashfield to paint portraits of the remaining family members, including Nursie, it was the one of Scotty that held special significance. A loved one lost. The first family death. Tragedy. Remembrance.

Agatha's nightmares started then as well—a repeated dream of a stranger with clear blue eyes and an enigmatic smile who carried a gun. "The Gun Man," Agatha called him, and he terrified the small child to such an extent that Nursie was asked to keep the gas lamp lit in the nursery all night, necessitating the window to be left open slightly to refresh the oxygen in the room.

It was also during this period that Agatha developed a fondness for what she labeled "alone time," so called because she was free to frolic in her fantasy world in the garden without adult supervision. Less prone to mischief than introspection, Agatha would select a perch in one of the large trees that populated the lawn. By far, her favorite was an enormous fir known as Madge's Tree, her sister having laid claim to the conifer in her own youth. Hidden deep within its boughs was a thick bench-like branch, carpeted in fallen needles and bracketed by pinecones.

Thus clothed in the magnificence of the large fir, Agatha was free to explore the magic of her mind, creating tales of intrigue and adventure, always with an underlying theme of conquering unknown frontiers and new worlds. That she had little direct knowledge of anything outside of the limits of Torquay did not matter. Her life was one filled with the potential of imagination, and in that world, she was queen. Her mother had seen to that.

Ever since her birth, Agatha had been regaled with the most fantastic of stories, some true, most not, but all with a decided moral that dictated that goodness prevails over evil. While Nursie had her stock of a half-dozen tales that she repeated with regularity during walks and at bedtime, Clara was purveyor of constant joy through stories that were consistent only in their continued uniqueness. Never one to repeat a tale—in fact, she forgot her made-up sagas as soon as they had left her mouth—Clara took inspiration from the moment: the spider walking across a table, the candle burning in the window, a mouse, an orange, the door that could read minds!

With each telling of a different story, the little girl quivered with anticipation of the next sentence—no, the next word, for Clara would often stop mid-thought to decide exactly where she wanted her tale to go, Agatha tugging on her mother's skirt, begging her to continue. By the time it was completed, Agatha was bursting with questions and assumptions that only mutated into grander versions of the story during her "alone time" excursions among the boughs.

With her older siblings away at school and no neighborhood children with whom to play, Agatha turned her imagination into her best friend, confidant, and ally. She also accomplished something rather remarkable for a child of five. She taught herself to read.

For a reason now lost in history, Clara had determined early in her youngest daughter's life that she would not learn how to read until she was at least eight. A woman known for being influenced by her instincts, which she thought clairvoyant in nature, Clara was now convinced that reading too young was harmful to vision. Clara held this belief despite having insisted that both of her older children be taught to read as soon as they were able to hold a book.

The decision to outlaw reading was only one of a number of rather spontaneous revelations that occurred to Clara while lying on her fainting couch in the drawing room soon after Agatha's birth. There was, in fact, to be no educational instruction of any kind given the child, who was never to be permitted to attend school. Additionally, she was to wear high-buttoned shoes to strengthen her ankles, soft-corseted gowns to allow for growth, and a large "straw or clothed brimmed hat" whenever she ventured outdoors as protection from the sun.

Nursie was instructed to keep all books out of Agatha's reach, a harder assignment than one might imagine, given the hundreds of books that lined shelves throughout Ashfield, especially in the library, where Frederick's love of the classics was evident. It was in a small crawl space off of the school room on the third floor that Agatha discovered what was to prove the most delicious of contraband—a copy of *The Angel of Love,* a girl's romance written by Mrs. L. T. Meade, a gift to Madge from her brother on Christmas Day, 1885.

Removing the book and hiding it underneath her long wool jacket that barely cleared the floor, Agatha crept through Ashfield, an operative on a mission. Skirting the nursery, and, further down the hall, the room where her mother lay sleeping, Agatha tiptoed through the door that bordered the scullery, scampered swiftly across the lawn, and made good her escape by climbing into the safety of Madge's tree. Her only witness was her little Yorkie, Tony, who raced after her to the base of the tree, thinking this a new game to be played. But Agatha was *not* playing as she opened the two-hundred-page book. Following along with her index finger, she struggled to understand the words.

What started as a secret would likely have remained as such, had it not been for Nursie's unexpected arrival at the base of the fir tree one afternoon several months later. To her surprise, she heard Agatha reciting what seemed to her to be a story about a schoolgirl. Calling up through the branches to her charge, she was startled when a book dropped from the tree, with Agatha close behind. The guilty look on the little girl's face was laced with excitement as she hopped in a circle, exclaiming, "I can read! I can read!"

It fell to Nursie to break the horrible news to her employer that very afternoon. "I'm afraid, ma'am, Miss Agatha can *read*," Nursie announced to Clara, handing her the now-tattered copy of *The Angel of Love*.[iv] First astounded, then resigned, Clara raised her arms in defeat and ordered that the school room must be *filled* with books—old and new. If Agatha was reading, she declared, she should be reading *everything*.

Now freed from her mother's reading restrictions, the five-year-old rushed forward into the adventure of learning with abandon. There were so many books and so many stories that the challenge became less about learning new words than it was about finding time to discover them all. Bypassing the children's books, she devoured Charles Dickens, Edgar Allan Poe, Lewis Carroll, Rudyard Kipling, and anything written by Mrs. Molesworth. Known as the Jane Austen of the nursery, Mary Louisa Molesworth quickly became Agatha's favorite writer as she read and reread Molesworth's *Tell Me a Story*, *The Cuckoo Clock*, *The Tapestry Room*, and *The Carved Lions*.

It was a small progression from reading to writing the alphabet and numbers. Nursie, she found, could only help so much, her movements too deliberate and sentences too slow when Agatha needed to rush. Her father, therefore, was soon recruited as tutor. He was convinced by Agatha to work an hour of classes into his day, right after breakfast and before his club. She would dutifully climb up into his lap, now round with middle age, and smell something akin to wet chrysanthemums in his beard, the lingering odor of his tobacco.

Eventually, Frederick inherited the task of teaching penmanship and math, precision being his forte. He was quite good at both writing and calculation, inspiring his youngest child with examples from everyday life as common-sense illustrations. Hand-copying bills from the J.O. Donoghue home furnishing store, Agatha soon added accounting into her classroom mix.

When Madge returned home from nine months in Paris—sent there for "finishing" after completing Miss Lawrence's School, she brought with her *Le Petit Précepteur (The Little Tutor)* as a gift for her baby sister. Madge, who had always had a dramatic bent, added equal proportions of grace and charm to her outgoing personality during her time abroad. She reentered the Torquay social world cultured, cultivated, and soon in demand by single young men who found her witty and attractive. The transformation was not lost on Agatha, who saw in Madge her own future.

"I remember the excitement of seeing her alight at Ealing from a four-wheeler cab. She wore a gay little straw hat and a white veil with black spots on it, and appeared to me an entirely new person."[v]

Peppering her English with bon mots in French, Madge started to refer to Agatha as *ma petite poulette*, and threw herself into instructing her sister in her new language, using *Le Petit Précepteur* as her guide. It was the beginning of a camaraderie that would thrive for the rest of their lives.

By the convention of the time, Madge's coming of age
included being properly introduced into society, which to her
father's mind meant *New York* society. It was an expensive
proposition, but it was an investment in his daughter that
Frederick Miller was prepared to make, and the reason why
the Millers spent part of early 1896 in America. With Clara
orchestrating and Frederick funding, Madge's world was a
whirl of balls, parties, formal dinners, and evenings spent at
the opera and theater.

During that period, Agatha was shuttled to Clara's
Aunt Margaret, whom Agatha called Auntie-Grannie. Soon
after her husband's death in 1869, Auntie-Grannie had moved
from Cheshire to a grand house in Ealing, then a chic suburb
of London. Agatha had been to Ealing occasionally, typically
visiting for weeks at a time with her mother, lavishing attention
on Auntie-Grannie, who constantly complained of one
infirmity or another. For Agatha, it was a timeless place, where
days slipped into weeks in a monotony that offered security by
way of its utter predictability.

Auntie-Grannie welcomed Agatha along with the sun
into her bedroom every day at seven a.m., the heavy draperies
pulled back in low-hung swags to reveal a four-poster bed
piled high with pillows. Thick with the aroma of lavender and
stale smoke from an oversize marble fireplace, the room was a
catchall for knickknacks and stacked paperwork. If not the
normal child's playground, it was a fun house of sorts, every
cranny an unexplored frontier. What was a castle one day
became a galleon the next, in a world where escape was
limited to illusion in a house Agatha said had "all the romance
of a foreign country."[vi]

Auntie-Grannie always wore black, as was the fashion
for widows—long, cinched gowns buttoned to the neck and
barely containing her ample flesh. Each Sunday, she was
joined by her sister Mary, whom Agatha called Grannie B. and
who also wore black, for an elaborate afternoon meal. Over the
years, Grannie B. had added weight to her already stocky
frame, and the vast excess that graced the Sunday dinner table
only added to her girth.

"An enormous joint, usually cherry tart and cream, a
vast piece of cheese, and finally dessert on the best Sunday
dessert plates" was typically served, according to Agatha in
her autobiography.[vii]

The meal arrived at the dining room table promptly at two thirty p.m., and then only after Agatha's two grandmothers had finished discussing their weekly business—Margaret doling out coins to her sister for services rendered and goods purchased during the previous seven days. Mary was still struggling with her widow's pension, adding to her income by doing simple errands for Margaret and providing needlework for her neighbors in Bayswater. While Margaret had the wealth, Mary had the family—her sons Ernest and Harry would often accompany her on Sundays (her eldest son, Fred, was stationed in India), and together with Agatha, the assembled clan would gorge for several hours before drifting into various parts of the house and falling fast asleep.

It was at moments like these that Agatha was free to roam the great rooms filled with heavy mahogany furniture, the sun casting webs of light through expensive hand-sewn Nottingham lace draperies, every table cluttered with trinkets, books, picture frames, and bronze statues of unverifiable origin. She could also be found in the kitchen, where Auntie-Grannie's cook Hannah taught her how to punch dough and bake bread and spin delicate crystal candies from boiling water and sugar.

It was a time of abundant leisure, an extravagance that found most children playing outside with a gaggle of friends. But Agatha did not have friends, save imaginary ones, whose circle had now expanded to such an extent that she made a point of dividing her nursery room into sections to allow them all their appropriate space. It was here that twilight fell, underscoring her vulnerability and opening the specter of a new emotion—abandonment. It would never be far from the surface for the remainder of her life, a natural spring that flowed unnoticed under the surface, only to emerge when least expected.

When the Millers—Frederick, Clara, and Madge—returned from New York in the summer of 1896, Agatha met them at the port of Southampton, going back to Torquay with her family in three rented carriages—one for passengers and the other two for the trunks filled primarily with ball gowns purchased in America. While the women chattered about their expectations of the summer season on Tor Bay, Agatha's father remained mute, stoic, and preoccupied with the realization that the Millers' life in Torquay would never be the same.

There are few things in life as unsettling to a man as the realization that he is a failure. Despite the outward appearance of financial success, Frederick Miller was unwise in business and investments. Perhaps *unwise* is too harsh a term, since he was never expected to have any knowledge of business, wasn't trained for it, and never cared to listen to updates about it. He was, like many in his class, a gentleman of leisure. There were others to count pennies, collect rents, sell property, and reinvest the capital. Unfortunately, the "others" that Agatha's father had selected were not much better at the game than he was. On this last trip to America, he had verified that as a fact.

The H. B. Chaflin Company, a well-known New York dry goods merchant in which Nathaniel Miller had been a partner, had been facing increasing financial difficulties ever since its founder, Horace Brigham Chaflin, died in 1885. The Chaflin concern had been investing Frederick Miller's money for him with diminishing returns. And while the firm offered a variety of reasons why, the fact remained that Frederick's principal was shrinking, and he was in serious financial trouble.

The news of his dwindling empire was followed by advice from his late father's business partners that Frederick Miller should consider looking for a job. It was a foreign concept, and one which Fred never intended to seriously entertain. Those in his class did not *do* such things. What he *was* capable of instigating were certain economies of scale, beginning with making arrangements to rent Ashfield fully furnished and completely staffed for a period of one year.

The decision to leave Ashfield, albeit temporarily, was not taken lightly, but once it was made, the entire household participated in the process of preparing the house to be occupied by strangers. The good dishes, silver, and personal items were wrapped and sent into storage; closets were emptied; books were counted and labeled with identification tags; and dozens of trunks and suitcases were opened, and the packing process began.

Clara, in her usual dramatic fashion, turned the entire event into a party of sorts, having explained the unexpected process to Agatha as an "adventure." This was, after all, a word her daughter knew well. The exact reason for the adventure was less clear to the six-year-old. When she finally grasped that her father was having financial difficulties, Agatha offered to give him her purse full of copper coins and her most valued possession—her dollhouse.

Although Agatha had two dolls, including a fancy porcelain one named Rosalind bedecked in a silk gown and ribbons, it was her dollhouse over which she obsessed for countless hours. Completely furnished, one piece at a time, with miniature sofas, beds, chairs, tables, silverware, glasses, plates, utensils, and artificial food, the toy house was Agatha's pride. Her willingness to give it up suggested the concern she felt over her father's plight and her devotion to him.

Clara pulled Agatha close, stroking her hair and pulling her long curls through her fingers. It had a calming effect on the six-year-old, as it had for as long as she could remember. There, wrapped in her mother's arms, Agatha was reassured. Through the tightly bound corset of her mother's dress, she felt the beat of Clara's heart—steady, comforting. Surely there was no emergency here, no need to part with possessions. Her mother said so, and her mother always told the truth.

Even as Frederick made arrangements to lease Ashfield to a rich American family for a considerable profit, Clara diminished the impact by giving several lavish dinner parties and afternoon teas. Newly famed British author Rudyard Kipling was invited with his wife, Carrie, along with Lady MacGregor, the widow of Sir George MacGregor and society doyenne of Torquay, who lived in the great house Glencarnock.

Carrie Kipling, whom Agatha had seen riding in tandem with her spouse on Torquay's newly constructed cinder bicycle track, was the subject of local gossip after it was discovered that she was *older* than her husband. Lady MacGregor made certain everyone knew. Kipling's friend Henry James visited for tea as well, upsetting Clara by his insistence on splitting his sugar cube in two. It was, she lamented, an "affectation, as a small knob would do quite as well."[viii]

Amidst the swirl of chatter and packing, Nursie created her own drama by announcing that she was retiring to live in a small cottage on an estate in Somerset, one county over, but for Agatha, a lifetime away. Her absence translated into a daily letter-writing campaign in which Agatha poured her loneliness into notes that helped fill a void that would be felt for years. "Dearest Nursie," she wrote. "I miss you very much. I hope you are quite well. Tony has a flea. Lots and lots of love and kisses. From Agatha."[ix]

With toys and books and her beloved dollhouse now packed away in storage, Agatha wandered the large yard and invaded Kai Kai, the nickname given the small greenhouse on Ashfield's west side. From among the spiderwebs, old croquet mallets, and broken lawn chairs, she found a bedraggled Mathilde, a rocking horse brought from America for Madge. The tattered toy had long since lost its mane and tail, but refused to give in to the passage of time when called into action by yet another child who would mount its worn wooden back and command its rusted springs to perform. Mathilde's "splendid action" threatened to catapult her rider into space, if only to prove that she was able.

In the simplicity of her metal hoop, a common plaything of the period propelled forward with a wooden stick, Agatha created entire worlds. "My hoop was to me in turn a horse, a sea monster, and a railway train," Agatha remembered in her autobiography. "Beating my hoop around the garden paths, I was a knight in armour on a quest, a lady of the court exercising my white palfrey, Clover (of the Kittens) escaping from imprisonment—or, less romantically, I was an engine driver, guard, or passenger, on three railways of my own devising."[x]

Agatha also loved riding TrueLove, her brother Monty's horse-and-cart tricycle. Minus its pedals, TrueLove was still capable of providing a lesson in the pull and dangers of gravity through seemingly endless runs down grassy slopes in the backyard, before crashing into the large monkey tree. The thrill was enough to excite screams of laughter and fear, and almost enough to salve the way back to normalcy.

In Agatha's ever-changing world, however, "normal" was never a constant. And certainly not in 1896 as the Millers left Torquay for a year abroad. There were tears, of course, particularly when Agatha discovered that her little Yorkshire puppy was not to be taken along on the trip. For his part, Tony was only too happy to be left with a former housemaid named

Froudie, who showered the dog with copious treats and heated his meals over her coal stove.

Clara and Frederick, like many in the upper classes, traveled with abundant luggage—on this trip, eighteen pieces, including several four-foot-high trunks with drawers and fold-down shelving. Due to the bulk of the baggage alone, an entourage of carriages was required to move the Millers from Torquay to their paddle-wheel steamer, the newly christened PS *Duchess of York*, docked in the seaside resort of Folkestone, Kent.

Madge and Clara, long prone to seasickness, had followed the advice of their local pharmacist and carried a bottle of Elixir of Terpin Hydrate and Heroin with orders to take "one to two dessert spoonfuls at first sign of distress." They did as instructed and immediately upon boarding their steamship went below to their staterooms and fell fast asleep.

Agatha and her father watched as their baggage was counted and boarded and then charged along the promenade to the forward turtle-back deck, where they remained, heads to the wind, for the entire two-hour crossing to Boulogne, France. Once there, the family was transferred to their wagon-lit cabins for sleeping on the overnight train to Pau, where they would live for the next six months as the guests of the Hotel Beausejour.

Pau sits in a picturesque valley along the edge of the Pyrenees Mountains in southwest France, a dramatic departure from the sea-resort setting of Torquay. Dominated by the classic Chateau de Pau castle, birthplace of France's Henry IV, Pau initially found fame for its alpine skiing and dramatic views—though Agatha remained unimpressed, calling her first sight of the Pyrenees "one of the great disillusionments of my life." To her, the mountains appeared like "a row of teeth standing up, it seemed, about an inch or two from the plain below."[xi]

Such was the economy of traveling in France compared to that of the British Riviera that Frederick Miller was actually able to make a great deal of money on the holiday, while Clara took advantage of the local culture to immerse Agatha in the French language on her first trip abroad. Mademoiselle Mauhourat, a large, fragrant woman from nearby Gelos, was engaged for Agatha's lessons. Mademoiselle instructed Agatha in *Français parlé* for three hours a week in the hotel lobby. The thought of being overheard by complete strangers as she struggled with the phonics of a foreign language inspired Agatha to stage a hunger strike wrapped in the guise of the flu, effectively casting Mademoiselle Mauhourat into outer darkness.

Despite the failure of teacher and pupil to bond, Clara was not about to give up on her determination to see her youngest daughter fluent in French, or as she preferred to call it, "the language of love." She called upon a young dressmaker's assistant named Marie Sijé to accept the newly created post of teacher-nanny-seamstress. The twenty-two-year-old Marie, dark hair piled in a chignon and smelling of rose water, spoke no English, forcing conversation into a guessing game of intention and meaning.

Agatha was helped through her confusion by two newfound friends, Dorothy (nicknamed Dar) and Mary Selwyn, whose late father had been a bishop in the Church of England. Perhaps encouraged by the umbrella of devoutness that shelters those whose families are "of God," Dar and Mary, seven and five, respectively, engaged in the harmless mischief that seems the province of young girls trapped within the confines of hotel living—sugar surreptitiously placed in salt shakers, toilet-paper dresses hung on statuettes.

It was not until Dar and Mary took Agatha on an excursion that included an escape from a fourth-floor dormer window and a carefully balanced walk across the hotel's parapet that Clara restricted her daughter's freedom and remanded her to her room to "reflect on the danger of trespassing." A horrified Mrs. Selwyn took to her own bed after being redressed by the Beausejour's management.

Agatha found the entire event entertaining, failing to admit to any sense of calamity amid the excitement of play. The real thrill was friendship. She delighted in the camaraderie of playmates, the joy of the actual over the imagined.

Looking back later, Agatha declared the winter of 1896 nearly perfect. *Absolument incroyable de chaque manière*, she was pleased to say. There were the usual embarrassments that seemed to follow her everywhere, though they were less faux pas than a result of her tender age. She had suffered through a growth spurt and was now more willowy than ever, taller than either of the Selwyn girls. Her shoes were always too tight, as she had inherited the thick ankles of the Millers, and as hard as she tried to be inventive in buttoning them, she was in constant discomfort.

With the arrival of June, however, the cool, thin mountain air took on the heavy humid quality of summer, leaving starched crinoline sagging under its own weight, and the sky scrubbed clean of clouds as if an overzealous housekeeper was helping God. Frederick had begun to spend his afternoons alone on the hotel's long terrace, staring blankly into the distance as if trying to read a faraway sign. He had not been feeling well for weeks and blamed the changing weather for his lethargy.

On the advice of a doctor, he made arrangements for his family to move to the sea, choosing the colorful village of Argelès-sur-Mer on the Golfe du Lion. It was called a "holiday from the holiday," with the festive street vendors loudly caroling their wares of cheese, fish, nuts, and vegetables, plus an assortment of handmade crafts and clay pottery.

Agatha found Argelès much like Torquay, though with fewer grand villas and without the therapeutic spas or healing tonics then commonplace on the British Riviera. The same could not, however, be said about Lourdes, where the family traveled the following week.

The Millers joined the mass pilgrimage of the faithful, the infirm, and the curious who journeyed to the Sanctuary of Our Lady of Lourdes to pray in the Basilica of the Immaculate Conception and drink from the healing grotto spring. The water, Agatha would later say, tasted "remarkably normal," unaware that the trip was anything more than a sightseeing excursion in the Pyrenees. Ever since Bernadette Soubirous, the teenage daughter of an impoverished miller, reported having eighteen or so visions of the Virgin Mary, the area had been overrun by the devout and those expecting divine intervention. Frederick Miller was one of them.

Neither Agatha, Madge, nor even Clara was aware of the chest pains that Frederick had been experiencing with increased intensity since their travels began. Fifty years old, overweight, and unexercised, Frederick had settled into middle age with the casualness of one who felt entitled. He was encouraged by his doctors to rest and reject physical activity, unfortunately compounding his condition and increasing his angina. The waters of the grotto in Lourdes provided hydration but little else, and even as he and his family left the village, his mood was a mix of fear and frustration about his future and that of his family.

From Lourdes, the Millers traveled to Cauterets, some thirty minutes away and famous for its healing thermal baths. To Agatha's surprise, they were joined again by the Selwyn girls, whose corrupting influence on the six-year-old had only intensified with absence.

At the base of the 7,600-foot Cabaliros summit, Cauterets provided Agatha and her friends endless hiking trails and hills "to toboggan down through the pine trees on the seat of [their] pants," much to the horror of Marie, who had been left to supervise the children.[xii] The girls routinely followed the elderly, mimicking their hesitant walk, laughing gleefully in mock horror if caught mid-impersonation.

Their noisy pranks and rowdy horseplay stood out in Cauterets. Protected like a jewel surrounded by undeveloped mountains, Cauterets lingered in time, finding no particular reason to hurry through the seasons. It was in that placid place that Frederick found comfort, horseback riding in the hills, sharing in the tranquility of nature through solitary meditation.

By August, the family had moved on to Paris, which Agatha thought disappointing, later remembering her first glimpse of the nine-year-old Tour d'Eiffel only in the vaguest terms. Automobiles, which she termed "bewildering," were not so easy to ignore. "They rushed madly along, smelling, hooting, driven by men with caps and goggles, and full of motoring equipment."[xiii]

Continuing north, the Millers wound down their year abroad with several months at the Grand Hotel in Dinard-Saint-Enogat, Brittany, overlooking the River Rance where it flows into the English Channel. It was the kind of ethereal beach resort that invited thoughts of God. Or at least it did for Frederick, who had learned from a local doctor that he was suffering from kidney disease and now felt certain that his death was imminent. By coincidence or fate, no sooner did he receive his sobering diagnosis than Frederick began to feel markedly better.

He joined his wife in their suite to watch nightly performances staged by their daughter in the little alcove created by a bay window. Exercising her recently discovered flair for dramatics and with Marie as her costar (a costar who still only spoke French, at that), Agatha went through her nightly repertoire of fairy tales, ending with a hour-long version of *Cinderella* in which she played Prince Charming and all the ugly stepsisters.

For her seventh birthday, she received swimming lessons and three caged exotic birds, who traveled with the family to the Isle of Guernsey as they made their way via ferry back home. Their days in St. Peter Port on the island's east side were hectic, shopping for small gifts to give to the servants at Ashfield, and more expensive ones for Auntie-Grannie and Grannie B., who each received Baccarat perfume flasks.

The sudden death of the smallest of Agatha's birds— the one she had named Kiki—plunged her into a period of mourning, though this was more out of duty than sorrow, since the delicate finch had been such a recent addition to the family. Even so, an appropriate funeral had to be arranged, and with Clara's help, a shoe box lined with satin ribbons was used as a ceremonial casket, into which Kiki was laid to rest. The actual burial was performed by Frederick, who accompanied his wife, daughters, and Marie for a two-mile hike into the hills, carrying the coffin while singing a version of "Onward, Christian Soldiers." Each day thereafter while on Guernsey, Agatha insisted that Marie join her to reenact the processional now labeled *"visiter la tombe de Kiki."*

It was late October 1897 when the Millers moved back into Ashfield, an occasion marked by a six-course meal prepared by Mrs. Rowe, who had worked all the previous day on the elaborate recipes. The entire family, including Auntie-Grannie, visiting from Ealing to welcome them home, feasted in the dining room, where the only family member not welcome was Tony. The Yorkshire had put on a great deal of weight, courtesy of Froudie's treats, and Agatha decreed that her favorite pet was to be placed on a diet—one that was to be rigorously enforced.

The worry over money was evident, witnessed more via hushed conversation than in any particular economization.

The Millers were entertaining less extravagantly, but had no fewer parties. What previously had been grand dinners and balls now turned into afternoon teas, lawn events with petite sandwiches replacing full-course meals.

Garden parties in Torquay were lavish, formal affairs where social standing and class determined who was invited and who ultimately attended. The women dressed in long muslin gowns sashed with pale ribbon, their oversize flowered hats casting their faces in shadow; the men were attired in three-piece suits, their vests barely able to contain ample bellies. Lingering over fruit ices and lemonade, these were gentle, charmed moments in time, marked by the sounds of gracious laughter and the *thunk* of croquet mallets against colorful wooden balls.

These were the ideal events for teenage girls like Madge to be introduced to eligible boys from neighboring towns. With her cultivated personality and handsome features, Madge was enormously popular, receiving boys in the drawing room at Ashfield, where Clara carefully positioned herself between them. It seemed to Agatha that Madge made a point of not choosing a favorite, preferring to allow the boys to compete for her favor, with her younger sister keeping track of the order via a diary in which Agatha rated the various gentlemen callers.

With increasing frequency and in seeming defiance of her husband's strained bank account, Clara took Madge on extended shopping trips to London, visiting dressmakers and assorted seamstresses who were talented enough to copy any style gown that had slipped into favor, or redesign those that hadn't. With her father traveling back to New York in an effort to recharge his finances, Agatha spent much of that winter and early spring in the care of Marie.

During this period, she began to learn to play the piano under the tutelage of Fräulein Üder. The German virtuosa who had had a short-lived concert career was now living in Torquay "and accepting the tonics" while making herself available for instruction to "unique and special pupils of outstanding skill."[xiv] While Agatha had yet to prove herself to be outstanding musically or in any other way, the small yet imposing Fräulein accepted her new pupil with excitement and a four-week advance payment.

Clara also insisted that Agatha learn to dance. Each Thursday, Marie would take Agatha by the hand and walk with her the mile-and-a-half to the class held above Callard's Confectionary Shop and Restaurant. Just opening the door of Callard's was a sensory experience, the waft of hot, sugared air filling the nostrils with joy.

Mrs. Callard sold Agatha's favorite toffee, and every Thursday, she would never fail to purchase two—one for herself and one for Marie, who anointed the taste *"magnifique."* After consuming the candy, the pair would climb the side stairs at 44 Fleet Street to the Athenaeum Room located directly over the shop. It was there, in the stark hall lined with wooden chairs along the north wall, that Miss Florence Eva Hickey gave instruction in dance, having learned it herself from Madame Ernesta Rinaldi, who preceded her in the school. Agatha learned to waltz to Johann Strauss I and polka to Johann Strauss II, dancing with the other girls and Miss Florence Eva Hickey. Boys, it seemed, were at a shortage, at least in dance classes in Torquay.

They could, however, be found in abundance playing cricket in the summer months, and Agatha found herself openly ogling them during matches, thinking them "heroic" in their all-white uniforms. For several years after returning from France, Agatha accompanied her father to weekly matches where he was the official scorekeeper in Torquay. As part of her lessons in mathematics, Agatha became his assistant, methodically tracking every scored run and lost wicket. Of all the moments she would later remember spending with her father, those days at the cricket matches were among the fondest—predictable and exciting and theirs alone.

In the spring of 1899, Frederick began to experience renewed chest pains, mostly during the night. In April be began to keep a journal of his "heart attacks," noting fifteen episodes through June 1901. In an effort to appease Clara and keep Agatha from seeing his distress, he often sought the opinions of London doctors rather than his own in Torquay, which is why Frederick was in Ealing with Margaret on January 22, 1901, when they received the news that Queen Victoria had died. On the throne for sixty-four years, the longest reigning British monarch, Victoria had been enormously popular, and her funeral turned into a public spectacle. Margaret and Mary immediately made plans to secure rooms from which they might watch the funeral procession, while Frederick wrote to his "Darling Clara," offering comfort to his wife, who was extremely fond of Britain's Queen. He made mention that all the stores and banks were closed "except those in poorer quarters," and described his visit to a new doctor "specializing in foul elixirs."[xv]

Frederick had assumed his health would improve during the summer months, his favorite season in Torquay. The misty, salty breeze coming off of the bay refreshed him every time he stopped to inhale that wonderful air. In his journal that summer, he made no mention of the sea or the salt water. Instead he noted thirty attacks of angina pain between June and October, including several so severe that he was barely able to attend the Regatta, Torquay's largest annual event. Held each August since the mid-1800s, the Regatta attracted several dozen yachts and sculls for two days of races past Haldon Pier, amusements, fireworks, and a grand ball in the evening.

Marie took Agatha to the Regatta that year to see the fortune teller Madame Arenska, with her oversize turban the color of a blue jay; the enormous fat man with a missing front tooth; and a lady with tattoos up and down both arms. Together they rode the merry-go-round and bought large cuttings off the nougat block from the candy vendor, who talked so fast, he never seemed to breathe.

Clara coaxed her husband into taking her to the Sunday night dance, never realizing his chest felt as if it were bound by an iron strap underneath his tuxedo jacket and wing-tip collar. The stabbing pain was ice-pick sharp, but gradually disappeared during the carriage ride back to Ashfield.

The following month, Fred returned to Ealing, this time to consult a new heart specialist named Sansom. "He says most positively that my heart is not dilated and is of normal size & there is nothing valvular [sic] wrong but that it is weak & irregular," he wrote Clara. "I have felt wonderfully better the last two days—better in fact than I have for three weeks— scarcely any breathlessness and splendid nights. I don't know whether this is owing to a prescription of Taylor's with digitalin in it or to my doing much less walking."[xvi]

He traveled back to Ealing two more times for consultations, and then, in late November, he consented to have a job interview with a government official lunching at Boodle's, the London gentlemen's club. It was one of those senseless efforts, offered and accepted more out of politeness than intent. Yet, as he took a carriage back to Ealing, his mind was not on work, but on Clara. He was, he thought, still in love, and very, very fortunate.

The slightest tickle of a cough that had begun in Torquay several weeks before had grown into a lingering cold, then bronchitis. By the time Frederick's stepmother sent for a doctor, the bronchitis had progressed into pneumonia. Rest was prescribed, along with coltsfoot, a natural herb thought to prevent coughs.

Clara rushed from Ashfield when she received the telegram that suggested her husband had slipped into delirium. His sheets were drenched from sweat despite the frigid weather that had lingered over London for days. By the time Madge and Agatha were sent for two days later, Clara knew her husband was dying.

It was afternoon and Agatha was standing on the landing outside of her father's bedroom when her mother rushed from the room, hands to her face, her eyes covered. One of two house nurses on duty followed behind her just as Auntie-Grannie came up the stairs. "It's all over," she said to Frederick's stepmother. And indeed it was. Frederick Alvah Miller was dead at fifty-five. And for his youngest daughter, Agatha, life would never be the same.

TWO

Coming of Age

I see thee not, and yet I see
As though mine eyes drew solace from thy face

Clara Miller
on the death of her husband

NOVEMBER 1901. CLARA MILLER WAS INCONSOLABLE IN HER grief. The days following her husband's death were passed in the hushed tones of darkened rooms and quiet footsteps, as if sound and light were responsible for her sorrow. She rarely lifted her head from the pillow or rose from her bed, able to move but unwilling to challenge days where death was the plot and pity its star.

Agatha was sheltered from most of the activity surrounding preparations for her father's funeral by Auntie-Grannie's cook Hannah, who kept her occupied in the kitchen, burying Agatha's face in her skirts when the child felt the need to cry. She was not allowed to see her father in repose, or attend the funeral ceremony. Desperate to see her mother, Agatha finally was allowed into her bedroom at twilight the night of her father's death, and then only briefly.

Clara gave what comfort she could, but saw her late husband in Agatha's heavy-lidded eyes and in her questions, which unfortunately now all centered on the funeral. Frederick's body was placed in a coffin and moved into the dining room, where it rested under the lighted grand gas chandelier, casting graceful shadows over the polished wood. It had fallen to Auntie-Grannie to write letters on traditional beige stationery bordered with black announcing her stepson's death and extending invitations to the funeral. She accomplished this task efficiently and without any apparent emotion while seated in her favorite large chair, adjacent to the body over which she kept watch. That weekend, Frederick Alvah Miller was buried in the Ealing cemetery not far from the house. His stepmother had seen to all the arrangements and paid all the fees.

Monty, who was always rather aloof and independent, remained true to form and did not attend his father's funeral. Having failed his exams at Harrow some years before, he had been asked to leave the school at sixteen, and eventually found work in a shipbuilding yard in Lincolnshire, on the North Sea. Charming but irresponsible, Monty was not particularly skilled at work, any more than his father had been. When it became clear that building ships was not to be in his extended future, Monty decided to make his calling with the Third Battalion of the Royal Welsh Regiment, in which he enlisted, sailing off in 1899 to fight the Boer War in South Africa. At the time, his father was relieved to have Monty become someone else's responsibility. Monty learned of his father's death by telegram, which reached him at his outpost in De Wildt, in an area now known as Transvaal. He sent no response.

Clara lingered in a deep state of depression and malaise in Ealing, a gas lamp turned down to its lowest setting. For two days, she refused to eat anything at all, preferring to be alone, reading and rereading a letter her husband had written to her just days before he died.

"You have made all the difference in my life," Frederick wrote. "No man ever had a wife like you. Every year I have been married to you I love you more. I thank you for your affection and love and sympathy. God bless you my dearest, we shall soon be together again."[i]

She had clipped a few strands of his hair and placed them carefully inside the envelope containing the letter, which she placed under her nightgown next to her heart. She also retrieved the remainder of his favorite Pear's Translucent Soap. Frederick always used Pear's, and smelling its crisp aroma brought immediate tears to her eyes, the flood of memory overwhelming. She carefully saved the soap as well, inside an envelope on which she had written, "I see thee not, and yet I see as though mine eyes drew solace from thy face."

The Ealing house became a bell jar of dulled whispers, muted even further by customary black mourning dress. While depressing attire to some, its layers of black offering little relief from the monotony, for Agatha the clothes provided an opportunity to play dress-up, complete with a lace mourning cap that made her feel very much part of the group.

For more than a month, Madge and Agatha read quietly to their mother, who continued to claim exhaustion and remained supine in her bed. Their Christmas was by necessity less celebration than ritual, affecting even the holiday meal. In deference to Frederick's passing, all liquor was removed from the recipes, leaving the stuffing inside the Christmas goose without its signature beer-soaked onions—a specialty of Hannah, the cook. When the family finally returned to Ashfield in January, the front door was draped with black fabric, and all of Torquay was aware that Clara was no longer receiving visitors, preferring to be alone in her sadness.

Soon after, and upon the advice of her physician Dr. Huxley, Clara was sent to the south of France for three weeks as a "restorative," taking Madge along as her caregiver. Agatha was left under the watchful eye of the family cook, Mrs. Rowe, who thought it an excellent time to instruct her charge in the culinary arts. The doctor's five daughters—Mildred, Sybil, Muriel, Phyllis, and Enid—feeling particularly charitable, insisted that Agatha join them once a week on Tuesdays in their singing classes with Mr. Crow, who delighted in her "clear and gentle soprano throat." Soon, they added Wednesday classes in orchestra. Agatha played the mandolin, although she preferred the banjos she had heard at the minstrel shows on the pier, but no one she knew in Torquay even had a banjo.

Of the Huxley sisters, Agatha's favorite was blonde-haired Muriel, a year older than Agatha's ten and always giddy with laughter, her dimples pocketing her cheeks. The six girls were regular visitors to the strand by the bay, window-shopping and eating sweets, made all the easier because the Huxleys were rather notorious for not wearing gloves. "Oh, those Huxley girls," the nannies would gossip to each other, scandalized by their exposed fingertips.

On Thursdays, Agatha had progressed sufficiently in her dance classes to be considered for the excelled group taught by Miss Hickey herself. Not yet a teenager, Agatha was the tallest of the girls and had a body that had grown lithe and active. Still not particularly fond of the waltz, the camaraderie of friends *trying* to waltz made her deliriously happy.

It is in those awkward moments between childhood and adulthood that remembered happiness thrives, and so it was for Agatha, who began to keep a diary of her thoughts and experimented with early poetry. She was only eleven when she wrote:

> *I know a little cowslip*
> *And a pretty flower too,*
> *Who wished she was a bluebell*
> *And had a robe of blue.*[ii]

> *I know a little cowslip*
> *And a pretty flower too,*
> *And yet she cried and petted,*
> *All for a robe of blue.*[iii]

For a child still learning to spell, writing in rhyme proved an even greater challenge. Clara had introduced her to great poetry, including the work of Elizabeth Barrett Browning, who had convalesced in Torquay for a year in 1840. Instinctively, Agatha preferred romantic adventures and tackled Anthony Hope's *The Prisoner of Zenda,* rereading it with such passion that she memorized entire sections. "I fell deeply in love—not with Rudolph Rassendyll, as might be expected, but with the real king imprisoned in his dungeon and sighing,"[iv] Agatha said, admitting that she was transformed by her ardor into the lovely Princess Flavia, eager to save the fallen king.

It was easy to understand her preference, for summer came early to Torquay that year and brought with it lazy afternoons on the porch swing and sweet-sour pitchers of lemonade. Madge, who had turned twenty-three the previous January while in France, had blossomed into an intelligent, outgoing young lady who was actively being courted, upon her return, by no less than six suitors of varying sincerity.

Agatha found the ease with which her sister moved from beau to beau to be quite daunting. But then, *everything* that Madge did seemed so simple for her to accomplish. Just the previous year, her sister had written a series of short stories that were published in *Vanity Fair* magazine as part of their serial "Vain Tales." That had gotten all of Torquay talking about Madge's talent, and the gossip hadn't lessened now that she had managed to attract many of the eligible bachelors in the area.

The least likely to have made a positive first impression was James Watts, son of Clara's childhood friend Annie Brown, whom Agatha and Madge had known for years. James was a student at Oxford, rather quiet and unassuming, who lived in lavish style with his parents at Abney Hall, one of the largest estates in Greater Manchester.

He came from a highly creative, artistic family—his brother Humphrey managed his own local theater company, his brother Lionel was on the stage in London, and his late grandfather, Sir James Watts, was famous for his oratory as Lord Mayor of Manchester.

But young James had little time for any of that, having inherited his father's love of business—in this case, the warehouse business. W & J Watts and Company had erected an ornate building on Portland Street in downtown Manchester with grand staircases and crystal chandeliers. In all likelihood, it was not his pale blond hair or his low soft voice that attracted Madge. More probably, it was his flair with finances, for less than a year after they had first formally met, he came to spend the summer in Torquay and then proposed marriage to the eldest Miller child. Madge accepted without obvious surprise, as if marriage could be decided upon in a moment.

Ordinarily, Clara would have advised against such haste, but since her husband's death, she barely had the strength to argue, or even to give what passed as sage advice. Hers was a daily struggle to survive, made more difficult by limited finances. In his will, Frederick had left her his entire estate, which seemed to be generating more expenses than income. His pension guaranteed her £300 a year, while providing £100 a year for each of the three children. In today's dollars, this would equate to $30,000 annually for Clara and $10,000 each for Madge, Monty, and Agatha.

Madge watched as her mother finessed the budget, economizing on meals, and closing off portions of the house to save heat. Then she dismissed the gardener who had been with them for fifteen years. Seasoned maids were replaced with inexperienced, less expensive ones in a daily struggle to keep up appearances. "Yes, oh, yes," Madge said squeezing James's hand with the ease of one who had been planning the moment for months. James was the answer to their prayers.

Their marriage took place that September with a minimum of fuss. Clara, indeed all the family, was still officially in mourning, the accepted period of one year since Frederick's death not passed. Yet in Victorian England, young love trumped grief in the hierarchy of accepted behavior, with the new Mrs. James Watts emerging from her wedding at the old Tor Church looking every bit as lovely as any society debutante.

Agatha was her sister's maid of honor and, like all the bridesmaids, wore white with lily of the valley woven into the wreath on her head. Clara, still dressed in black, hosted a wedding breakfast at Ashfield. Guests included the Watts brothers—Lionel, the best man, Humphrey, and Miles, plus their sister Nan, a tomboy whose abilities to climb trees and handle a slingshot were legendary. Others in the bridal party included Madge's friends Norah Hewitt and Constance Boyd, plus James's adopted sister, Little Ada.

In addition to a union that would last a lifetime, the day produced a new best friend for Agatha in Nan Watts. Their personalities were as opposite as they were complimentary. One thing both girls shared equally was the love of a good prank, as they discovered when they poured rice in the honeymooners' suitcases.

The day after the ceremony, Clara walked through the halls of Ashfield feeling its size. What once was grand and comfortable was now a shell that echoed with memories, each room a reminder of her lost happiness. Just a year earlier, it had all been so different. Now, without her husband, there was an emptiness so vast that she was lost in the sepulchral tones of her own home.

Clara reached the conclusion it would be best to sell Ashfield immediately, not just for economy but her own rejuvenation. *Perhaps a move to Exeter, seventeen miles north, but a world away*, she thought. There, the rolling hills and crisp air were far more to her liking than the seaside of Torquay. And the *cathedral*. Clara loved cathedral towns, and the one in Exeter, built in 1400, had an incredible vaulted ceiling—the longest in all of England. And there were children there for Agatha. *Yes,* she thought. *Exeter.*

It was soon after Madge returned from her honeymoon that Clara spoke to her daughters about her plans. Madge, usually the dramatic one, reacted calmly but with determination. "If it is only a matter of money," she said, "perhaps James will help. I'm sure he will."

Agatha, normally the shy, silent one, was horrified. "Leave Ashfield? It's our *home*," she cried, breaking into tears. Her look was one of pleading, begging. As Agatha later said in her autobiography, it was the selfish act of a child. "I have never suffered from the absence of roots," she wrote, as an explanation.[v] But those roots were entwined around the only home she had every known. And so it was with a sigh and a consoling hug that Clara packed up her dream of a cottage by a cathedral in Exeter and stored it in some remote corner of her mind, wiping away tears that never seemed to dry completely.

There were few outward appearances of change at Ashfield. A new parlor maid was dismissed, leaving just one maid in the household plus Mrs. Rowe, who was told to economize in the kitchen. It was difficult for the elderly cook, who had routinely prepared lobsters for ten, to be reduced to finding inventive recipes for macaroni and cheese, but she tried as best she could, occasionally ordering eight filets where two would suffice.

The appearance of normalcy was little more than illusion. To Clara there would never be another carefree day, one without worry over money or health. As to the former, her bank account was barely adequate, nothing more, and always at the mercy of the generosity of her son-in-law, James. Where Clara's health was concerned, the stress of life had caused unpredictable pains to flair—chest pains diagnosed as heart attacks, stomach pains diagnosed as ulcers, and hip pains that were credited to either rheumatism or gallstones, depending on the doctor.

Now the center of her mother's world, Agatha moved into her late father's dressing room to be closer to Clara's bedroom in case she became ill during the night. Brandy and *sal volatile* were on her nightstand as remedies for Clara's increasingly frequent attacks, dramatized by Agatha as a prophecy of death.

"We were no longer the Millers—a family," Agatha wrote. "We were now just two people living together; a middle-aged woman and an untried, naïve girl."[vi] Agatha was naïve perhaps, but not unwise, as she redoubled her efforts to learn from books and the tales of others.

In that respect, Agatha was fortunate to have met the Lucys—Blanche, Reggie, Margie, and Noonie—whose father, Berkeley, had an uncle who owned Charlecote, a grand country house and deer park in Warwickshire. The Lucys *always* had a new story to tell, for their family came to England with William the Conqueror, so there was scandal throughout the family line. It was said that William Shakespeare was once caught poaching deer on their property, but Reggie Lucy swore that it never happened, while admitting it made a fine tale.

It was Margie and Noonie who taught Agatha—Aggie, to them—to roller-skate. The sport had just come to the pier, where the concert stage had been converted into a temporary indoor rink. For twopence, Agatha circled the wooden floor and the paved area that surrounded it, feeling the salty wind blow through her hair, and casting off the pall of her mother's sadness.

And then there was the musical stage. Looking back on the beginning of her teenage years, Agatha marked her performance with the Huxley girls in a local presentation of the Gilbert and Sullivan operetta *The Yeoman of the Guard* as her most triumphant moment. Cast in the lead as Colonel Fairfax, she became the epitome of an Elizabethan gentleman—albeit one with a soprano voice. It was her first legitimate stage performance, since one could hardly count the evening amateur hours in Dinard with Marie as legitimate. Agatha was a huge success, absorbing praise from the audience with little of the shyness that up until that point had proven to be the bane of her existence. But then, of course, she was in front of *friends*. She felt that to perform the same lines in front of total strangers would have been impossible.

Yet, just as things were returning to normal, Madge visited Torquay from her own new home, Cheadle Hall, an estate built by her father-in-law as a wedding gift. Stepping from her carriage, she burst forth with news that would completely change the family dynamic. Madge revealed, with no small degree of drama, that she was pregnant and hoped for a son. Clara Miller was thrilled at the prospect of a grandchild—a new baby to generate the magic that only babies can. And Agatha, while not quite sure how babies arrived, nevertheless promised to be the "very best auntie in the world."

The following August, both Madge and Agatha were true to their words. Baby Jack Watts was born, and Agatha leapt into her role of devoted and attentive aunt. It was as if a window had opened and the manteau of motherhood had been draped upon her shoulders. She fussed about the baby, dabbing at his mouth and chin, and cooing words that seemed to make perfectly good sense to Jack and Agatha, but to no one else.

At Christmastime, Agatha and Clara joined the elder James Watts, his wife, and extended family at Abney Hall, the family estate in Cheshire. Built in 1847, and enlarged by Sir James Watts, the baronial home was Gothic by design and furnishing, with swords and shields granted equal wall space with Renaissance oils and sketches. Massive staircases soared skyward around an enormous entrance hall leading to dozens of bedrooms, while the gilded library and ballroom set the tone of opulence and splendor.

There were fifteen servants standing at attention amid holiday decorations as Agatha and Clara stepped from their carriage in fancy dress. It was a scene that would repeat itself annually for years, as the Watts and Millers celebrated in time-honored tradition with a six-course feast that included oyster soup, fillet of turbot, roast turkey, beef sirloin, plum pudding, mince pie, and trifle—topped off by an even half-dozen desserts.

Showing an appetite that would become legendary in a few years, Agatha staged eating contests with her brother-in-law Humphrey, and regardless of how much she ate, she would claim to always leave the table hungry. Somehow the display worked well within the confines of Abney Hall, which was all about excess and privilege. It was not, however, the way properly finished ladies behaved, and Clara made arrangements to polish her daughter's more rustic edges by

sending her twice a week to Miss Guyer's school in Torquay
for classes in grammar, elocution, and mathematics.

Mary Guyer was a cultured spinster who ran the Girton
Hall Ladies' School on Meadfoot Road in an organized and
strict fashion, which lent itself perfectly to the precision of
math, a subject in which Agatha was well grounded and found
continuously fascinating. There was a right answer and a
wrong answer—all quite straightforward.

When it came to the arts, however, Miss Guyer was
reluctant to give her girls the freedom needed for self-
expression and found Agatha's energy "exhausting," according
to an early evaluation. Miss Guyer was ill-prepared for the
child's rush of creativity, which took form during her first forays
in composition. While writing an assignment on the theme of
autumn, Agatha moved from the lyrical falling of golden leaves
into a story about a pig named Curlytail who rooted acorns in
the forest. Agatha's essay did not muse on autumn, Miss Guyer
explained. This, she said, was something else altogether, and
deemed Agatha's attempt at writing "too fanciful."

After nearly two years of Girton Hall Ladies' School,
Agatha's twice-a-week formal education in Torquay came to
an abrupt halt when Clara, in typical spontaneous fashion,
declared that mother and daughter were off to Paris as soon as
an appropriate, conveniently well-funded tenant could be
found for Ashfield. Trunks were brought out and packed, the
dog was taken back to its temporary home with Froudie, and
the good china was moved into storage to prevent accidental
breakage—again.

For Agatha, the preparations for travel took on all the
earmarks of adventure. Since neither she nor her mother had
any real need to handle the more laborious elements of
packing, the servants having now become expert in the task,
the Millers were free to set their itinerary and make
arrangements for Agatha's continuing education in France.

Clara decided that she would live at the Hotel d'Iena,
in the sixteenth arrondissement, the most fashionable in all of
Paris. The hotel was surrounded by dress and hat shops,
always an essential, and convenient to a number of museums,
including the Musée Guimet and the private Musée d'Ennery.

An American family named Patterson arrived in Torquay and, like Clara before them, formed an attachment to Ashfield the moment they were shown it by the house agents R. Nicholson & Son. As soon as the Pattersons proved their worth by prepaying their rent in cash, Clara and Agatha, now flush with funds, sailed for the continent and the excitement of 1904 Paris.

When Madge had her season in the City of Lights, she attended Mademoiselle Cabernet's *pensionnat,* and although Clara heard that Mademoiselle had fallen on hard times, she nevertheless placed Agatha in her care to learn the history of the French provinces and correct deportment. There were also piano lessons, at the instrument of Madame Legrand, who taught Agatha the intricacies of the third movement of Beethoven's *Sonata Pathétique.*

Her time at the school, Agatha later remembered, was "uneventful," primarily it seems because she failed to achieve the sort of notoriety her sister had during her nine-month stay. The girls at Mademoiselle Cabernet's all had heard about Madge's legendary leap from a second-story window on a dare, and her unceremonious landing atop a table where a trio of horrified society matrons were having tea with the headmistress.

Disappointed in Agatha's lack of progress in history and written French, but resigned to her daughter's disinterest, Clara removed Agatha from Mademoiselle Cabernet's tutelage and transplanted her to Auteuil, one of the richest areas of Paris and the home of Victor Hugo, Molière, and Marcel Proust. It was there, at the ultra-chic L'école Les Marronniers, run by a certain Miss Hogg, where Agatha was to learn how to "walk"—presumably the French did it differently. While the results at L'école Les Marronniers were not disastrous, Miss Hogg's tuition was. Sensing the need to economize on the educational aspects of their Paris holiday, Clara ultimately settled on Miss Dreyden's School, owned by a relative of Auntie-Grannie's physician, Dr. Barwood, who highly recommended the place.

Dedicated to the arts, Miss Dreyden and her school exposed her dozen or so students to professional theatrical productions, including an outing to see Sarah Bernhardt in what was one of her last performances, playing the golden pheasant in Rostand's *Chantecler.* Yet it was Gabrielle Réjane, the classically trained French actor, who made the largest impression on the *very* impressionable child. "I can still hear now, as I sit quiet a minute or two with my eyes closed, her voice, and see her face in the last words of the play, *'Pour saver ma fille, j'ai tué ma mere,'*[4] and the deep thrill this sent through one as the curtain came down,"[vii] Agatha remembered in her autobiography.

It was at Miss Dreyden's that Agatha was allowed to explore her musical talent unencumbered by lessons in grammar and science. Under the monocle of Austrian maestro Charles Füster, she advanced her piano training, performing Tchaikovsky, Strauss, Fauré, and Chopin. Practicing five hours a day, Agatha became so proficient that she considered becoming a concert pianist, playing the great stages of Europe. Encouraged by the optimistic Maestro Füster, at fifteen Agatha saw her future.

Her vocal teacher, Monsieur Boué, who had quite a devoted following in Paris, saw the potential for an entirely different kind of stage career and suggested Agatha train for the opera. "Ah, mademoiselle. Her voice is like a bird," he warbled to Clara, who remained unconvinced. While her daughter's soprano voice was not particularly powerful, it nevertheless had a certain enchanting quality that Boué felt might develop into a professional instrument. Whether naïve or dedicated, every day Agatha ventured from Miss Dreyden's School with a chaperone (for teenage girls were not allowed alone on the streets in Paris) to Boué's studio in a fifth-floor walk-up just off the Place D'Iena. Once there, she would sing arias in Italian, German, French, and Latin, exercising her voice box and conditioning her cords, methodically following the instructions of Maestro.

After completing her courses at Miss Dreyden's in 1905, and considering herself a "finished lady," Agatha packed up her music and returned with her mother to Ashfield, where she was greeted with enthusiasm by the Lucy sisters, who claimed that Torquay had become "ever so festive" in her absence. There were now evening dances by the sea at the Bathing Saloon, and afternoon concerts by the Royal Marine String Band. Outdoor roller-skating had expanded to the length of the pier, and horses were now stabled on South Street

[4]"To save my daughter, I killed my mother."

for riding along the beach where boys and girls were still segregated from each other while swimming.

For females, the bathing process was a rather involved one: Not only was most visible skin covered with some sort of fabric, including woolen stockings, but the bathing costume itself was not permitted to be worn on the street. This regulation of polite society meant that the actual transformation into bathing gear had to be conducted in the privacy of a bathing shanty, the size of an outhouse, colorfully painted and literally rolled into position into the water on wooden wheels similar to a stage coach. Having reached an adequate depth, the back door of the small changing room was opened on the water side, with the female's entrance into the water guarded from the peering eyes of curious males.

Swimming in the bay was one of Agatha's favorite pastimes, enjoyed daily in the summer months. It was during one such outing, in the company of her nephew, Jack (still young enough to be allowed to visit the Ladies' Bathing Cove), that Agatha nearly drowned in rough surf. She was rescued by the old man who operated the mobile bathing houses, after he noticed her flailing in the choppy surf. She remembered the incident less for its near fatal consequence than for her indignation over not seeing her entire life pass before her eyes.

Agatha Mary Clarissa Miller had grown into a lovely, shy teenager who became aware of the attraction she had for the opposite sex for the first time in her life. If her ankles were a bit thick and her hair now grown so long that it reached to her waist, she was still quite lovely in a classic sense, where beauty was judged more for lithe lines than upturned noses.

A year after Agatha returned to Torquay, she was invited to Florence as the guest of Clara's friend May Sturges, who had traveled from America to the Alps to be operated on for a disfiguring goiter, which hung rather obviously from her neck. After successfully enduring the surgery, May traveled with her nurse Stengel to Italy, where she asked Agatha to join her for several weeks while she recuperated.

It is said that Italian men are born with the ability to flirt. It certainly was the case in 1906, for Agatha found herself pinched and followed as she toured the cathedrals and visited Brunelleschi's dome at the Santa Maria del Fiore in the Piazza San Giovanni. She viewed Michelangelo's *David* at the

Accademia Gallery and found the Uffizi Museum so
spectacular that she returned multiple days in a row just to sit
among its splendor. Full of the *romanzesco* of Italy when she
returned after a month in that country, Agatha began to gush in
Italian as if she spoke the language. She had, it seemed, *arrived.*

Her mother thought otherwise, of course, since no girl
was ever fully finished until she had "come out" to society,
much as Madge had done in New York. Given the depressed
economic circumstances of the household, Agatha would
neither be presented at court nor have a ball dedicated in her
honor. What she would have, however, was three months in
Egypt, where the winter was seasonally perfect, and the bills
were paid, yet again, by renting Ashfield at an extraordinarily
high price.

The particulars were handled by Clara, who looked
upon organizing the trip as a diversion from her continuing
string of health problems, which remained unresolved despite
a seemingly endless round of examinations by local doctors
and specialists. After months of bickering, she finally
succeeded in booking adjoining rooms facing the Nile at the
Gezirah Palace Hotel in Cairo. Clara and Agatha sailed on the
SS *Heliopolis*, which had just been launched by the Egyptian
Mail Steamship Company, and embarked on a vacation that,
over the next ninety days, would find both mother and
daughter reevaluating their lives.

For Clara, the time away from Ashfield gave her the
long-delayed opportunity to write her will, boring enough
under ordinary circumstances, but in the harsh glare of the
Egyptian sun, made all the more torturous. For Agatha, at
seventeen, there were five dances a week—one at each of the
grand hotels lining the Nile—plus months of lazy afternoons,
where swatting flies while sitting on the veranda was the most
exertion expected from refined British girls being courted by
officers in His Majesty's Service.

None of it was serious, of course, since Clara had no
intention of allowing any soldier, sailor, or military policeman
to corrupt her daughter's virtue. She was, however, not above
suggesting that Agatha *think* about marriage, preferably to a
man from a family with either a peerage or funding "unrelated
to speculation."

For the moment it was all harmless fun, underwritten by the obvious need for ready cash. The economics of the moment underscored each and every appointment and expense, from polo matches to picnics, croquet tournaments to games of badminton. Any thoughts of education came through experience in the classroom of life, and Agatha was *living,* or at least as far as her personality would allow.

During her three months in Cairo, she met some two dozen men, curiously finding several in their late thirties or early forties to be the most interesting. Those closer to her own age, or in their twenties, held less appeal, for they lacked the life experience she longed to absorb, preferring to live vicariously through the anecdotes of others.

Still uncertain of her looks and shyly reticent about conversation, she allowed those around her to control the mood and the moment. Perhaps most important, these months in Cairo provided Agatha the opportunity to hone her skills as an observer of life, creating an inventory of stories and characters from which to draw in the future. It did not, however, make her an active participant.

One of her dance partners, an army captain named Craik, suggested as much as he escorted Agatha off the dance floor and over to her chaperoning mother. "Here's your daughter," he said to Clara. "She has learned to dance. In fact, she dances beautifully. You had better try to teach her to talk now."[viii]

It was a criticism wrapped in a compliment, and quite a good example of her dilemma. Prepared with all the essentials of an outgoing adult, Agatha was saddled with a personality that was only truly comfortable when left alone. Clara responded with her usual impulsiveness, redoubling her effort to thrust her daughter into social settings where isolation was not an option.

Their homecoming to Torquay was cause for family celebration, with visits to the Cheadle house and Abney Hall. It was also the beginning of spring and long weekend trips to the country houses of acquaintances from Cairo.

Mr. and Mrs. Park-Lyle, who had made their fortune in sugar, had rented an estate in Windsor, where they invited several dozen guests for hunting and boating. Agatha, of course, did neither, but Clara insisted she attend, assuring her of spontaneous fun.

Early on in the weekend, an Army gunner made his attraction obvious to the teenage girl. His ardor showed ingenuity as he finessed his way into tennis matches, lobbied to fill her dance card, invited her for walks around the lake, and even maneuvered his way into driving her to the train station for the trip back to Torquay.

Just as the train was about to pull from the station, and Agatha exhaled relief at being rid of her unrequited suitor, the man hopped on the train and invaded her compartment. Taking the seat directly across from her, he glared intently at Agatha before blurting, "I meant to put it off until I met you again in London. I can't wait. I have to tell you now. I am madly in love with you. You must marry me. From the moment I first saw you coming down to dinner, I knew you were the one woman in the world for me."[ix]

Now it was Agatha's turn to glare. It was not supposed to be like this. When she dreamed of her first marriage proposal, it was *always* by a knight, or at the very least, a duke. She longed for someone with charisma, charm, and a stable of horses. Certainly *not* wanted was a gunner in the army, and certainly *not* a gunner who insisted on following her all hours of the day and night. Embroidering her answer with a rush of polite words did not make the impact of "No!" any less stinging. And the silence that followed for the remainder of the trip was as awkward as any Agatha ever endured.

Perhaps inspired to find her prince, or at least to enjoy the summer, at the age of eighteen Agatha launched into a whirlwind of social activities specifically selected to maximize her exposure to potential suitors. It was, in fact, a flirting ritual that she later labeled *le pays du tendre*. This may have played out to a romantic conclusion had it not been for the sudden illness that placed her in bed for several weeks and under Dr. Huxley's care. Thus confined to her bedroom and certainly not receiving suitors, she entertained herself by drying pieces of bread that had been shaped like tops and painting them with varied colors and friends' names, to be given later as gifts. It was, as Agatha remembered, a rather boring way of passing time, which, in turn, prompted her mother to suggest perhaps her daughter might try writing.

This was hardly a novel idea. Clara had previously suggested exactly the same concept to Madge during one of her convalescences, and she produced the stories that ended up in the prestigious *Vanity Fair* magazine. Thus challenged and eager to outdo Madge in *something*, Agatha borrowed her sister's antique Empire typewriter and began pecking out a thirty-page story she titled "The House of Beauty," using the pen name Mack Miller, Esq. Written around the themes of madness and the occult, the storytelling was better than most teenagers could imagine, though not good enough for publication, as Agatha quickly learned upon sending it to various magazines and receiving rejection slips in return.

Other stories followed as time allowed, including "The Call of Wings" and "The Little Lonely God" among them. Each was labeled with a different nom de plume and dutifully sent off to magazine publishers, who just as dutifully returned them with their own versions of the rejection letter.

Knowing well that writing would never be more than a pastime, Agatha continued to train her voice, certain that opportunity would find her, even in Torquay. In an effort to help burnish her luck, Agatha followed local custom and arrived at dinner parties "with music," a fitting tribute to her hosts in this era before radio and when the photograph was in its infancy. While it was not Royal Albert Hall, it was *performing*, and as long as it was confined to small parties among friends, Agatha was comfortable enough to revel in the attention and gushing compliments, reinforcing her fantasy of a life on the stage.

Her fantasy was amplified in the fall of 1909 when Madge invited her sister to experience an evening of Wagnerian opera at London's Covent Garden Theatre, with Karl Richter conducting American soprano Minnie Saltzman-Stevens in her European debut. Neither sister was prepared for the event, as Saltzman-Stevens was so triumphant that even the orchestra gave her a standing ovation that left Madge mesmerized and Agatha in tears.

She exited the theater shaking with the excitement of the moment, dreaming of a future in which she would sing *Isolde*; the roses tossed onstage would be for her! Returning to Torquay, she exercised her voice, coaxing it to a range she had thought impossible to achieve. Finally, purely by chance, a friend of May Sturge with connections to the Metropolitan Opera in New York arrived in Torquay and agreed to hear her sing. The resulting critique innocently set the stage for one of the greatest non-musical careers in history.

"The songs you sang tell me nothing," the woman observed. "But," she added quickly at the first sign of Agatha's disappointment, "the exercises *do*. You will make a good concert singer, and should be able to do well and make a name at that." This, however consoling, was not what the girl who had just given Madame Saltzman-Stevens a standing ovation needed to hear. In that second, Agatha Mary Clarissa Miller knew she would never be a professional singer.

"I came back to real life," Agatha wrote in her autobiography. "I pointed out to Mother that she could now save the expense of music lessons. I could sing as much as I liked, but there was no point in *studying* singing. I am sure there be nothing more soul-destroying in life than to persist in trying to do anything that you will do badly and in a second-rate manner."[x]

Denied her dream, Agatha withdrew once again into herself, falling back on her writing with increasing frequency, less from skill than boredom and a need to produce something, *anything*. Egged on by her sister and encouraged by Clara, Agatha began to draw on her months in Egypt, the aroma of the desert and its people still vivid in her memory. It was in this moment of desperation and determination that *Snow Upon the Desert* was born.

A comedy of manners, *Snow Upon the Desert* was a poorly constructed tale in severe need of editing, but despite it all, still managed to demonstrate the writer's unique ability to create memorable characters and plots. Combined from several unrelated false starts, this novel succeeds in part because it established her potential. Certainly novelist Eden Phillpotts, a neighbor of the Millers in Torquay, saw that possibility.

In 1910 Phillpotts was the most famous author residing in Devon. A friend of the Millers for twenty years, his novels and plays were known for their country settings and included *The Farmer's Wife*, later to be turned into a feature film starring

Michael Wilding. When prompted by her mother to send Phillpotts her novel, Agatha reluctantly acquiesced and received a letter in response.

It was a heartfelt, genuine appraisal of the work of a fledgling writer, one who would have been easy to dismiss. "I can hardly express the gratitude I feel to him," Agatha wrote in her autobiography. "He could so easily have uttered a few careless words of well-justified criticism, and possibly discouraged me for life. He realized (instead) how shy I was and how difficult it was for me to speak of things."[xi]

> Some of these things that you have written are capital. You have a great feeling for dialogue. You should stick to gay natural dialogue. Try and cut all moralization out of your novels; you are much too fond of them, and nothing is more boring to read. Try and leave your characters *alone*, so that *they* can speak for *themselves*, instead of always rushing in to tell them what they ought to say, or to explain to the reader what they mean by what they are saying."[xii]

Perhaps more significant than his advice was Phillpotts's offer to introduce Agatha to his literary agent, Hughes Massie. A legend among British writers' representatives, Massie was an elderly curmudgeon well known for putting authors on notice with his opinion of their work. To Agatha, he was a "large dark swarthy man" who found *Snow Upon the Desert* to be a provocative title—"suggestive of banked fires." Unfortunately, he found the writing less than enticing, returning the manuscript with some solid advice attached: Try again with a different subject.

Agatha, though terrorized by the man, took his advice willingly, and next produced *Vision*, a tale that liberally borrowed from Gaston Leroux's *The Mystery of the Yellow Room*, which had been recently published in French. Leroux's book is perhaps the finest example of a locked-room mystery, in which a crime is committed in a space bolted from the inside. And while *Vision* was rejected as well, Agatha persevered, writing additional poetry and short stories.

Still completely uncertain that writing was her future, Agatha paid equal attention to her other pastime—romance—encouraged by Clara, who was never far from the center of any relationship. Most were little more than innocent flirtations until Agatha traveled to her mother's friends, the Ralston-Patricks in Warwickshire, for a weekend of riding, sidesaddle. During her visit, she was introduced to a colonel in the Seventeenth Lancers, thirty-year-old Bolton Fletcher. Rather tall, though not the slimmest of men, Bolton escorted Agatha to a formal ball, during which she was radiant in white brocade.

It took the Colonel only days following Agatha's return to Ashfield to write his first letter of love. It was followed by another, plus flowers, chocolates, an enameled brooch, and then a proposal of marriage. Agatha was easily flattered by the attention, saying she was "charmed like a bird." Her mother, in contrast, was alternately worried and curious at the continuous assault of affection toward her twenty-year-old daughter. She advised caution and a period of separation, which ultimately ended six months later when Bolton sent Agatha a telegram: "Cannot stand this indecision any longer. Will you marry me yes or no?" Agatha's one word answer: "No!"

It took several long months and an Indian summer before another suitor entered Agatha's life—this time in the form of an old acquaintance, Wilfred Pirie, whom she had last seen in passing thirteen years earlier while on vacation in Dinard. Then he had been a young midshipman in the Navy; now he had been elevated to the rank of sublieutenant on a submarine that docked frequently in Torquay.

Wilfred's father had been a friend of Agatha's father, both men now long deceased. Their memories were periodically refreshed when Clara and Mrs. Lillian Pirie reminisced over tea and scones. Agatha would listen with the intensity of a cat stalking a wren, not so much to hear reflections of the past as to watch Mrs. Pirie conduct herself. She was obviously bright. Moreover, she was poised, moving easily from discussions of opera to interior design to art history without pausing to collect her thoughts. Mrs. Pirie was, to Agatha, everything she could hope to be.

Unfortunately, Wilfred was not. Despite his claim of undying devotion and proposal of marriage on their third date,

Agatha could not think of him as a lover. He was simply too nice, too kind, and, well, unromantic. He was the first to offer to wash the dog and the last to think of sending flowers. While she accepted his offer to have "an understanding," the equivalent of a ringless engagement, it took only his request to spend his following holiday not with her but on an expedition to South America looking for gemstones, to convince her that their understanding was over.

These "events," as Agatha later called them, were certainly no more than harmless crushes and would have been discarded as such had they not taken away from her writing. If nothing else, they inspired her to compose some love sonnets, more experimental than successful.

In September 1911, she celebrated her twenty-first birthday at a party hosted by the Lucys, who invited what seemed to be every eligible bachelor in Torquay to witness the event and learn a new dance called the tango, judged "incredibly naughty" by the girls in attendance. It was at that moment that Agatha took a new look at Reggie Lucy. Reggie had just returned to Torquay after having served as a major in the Gunners, and looked, well, *different*. He was certainly handsome. But Reggie had always been handsome. To that, in her eyes, he seemed to have added something else— experience perhaps, she could not quite decide. Whatever it was, Agatha Miller suddenly found herself developing "an understanding" with Reggie as well, after an impromptu proposal on the Torquay Golf Course. He had just demonstrated how to use a wooden driver and was standing behind her, clasping her hands around the club's grip, when he whispered in her ear, "Would you like to marry me?" This, to Reggie, qualified as a definite proposal, while leaving room for further adjustment to the offer if the need arose. Agatha had no sooner said yes when Reggie placed provisos on his promise. "Just bear me in mind, and, if nobody else turns up, there I am, you know," he said.[xiii] This was apparently not a romance for the ages, or even for the moment, for soon after Reggie returned to his regiment, Agatha began to realize that perhaps she needed something more.

While Reggie and she communicated by post for over a year, these were not torrid letters of passion. Reggie was interested in Agatha more as a sister than a wife, pledging his love, but always reminding her that she was available for another if something better came along. That something appeared in the ballroom of Ugbrooke House, the vast manor home of Lord and Lady Clifford of Chudleigh, on October 12, 1912. On that date in the grand halls of the nine-hundred-year-old castle, the Cliffords held a gala ball to celebrate the gallantry of the Royal Field Artillery at Exeter.

Handsome in their tan dress uniforms with assorted medals, ribbons, and high laced boots, the soldiers swaggered among the women, feeling very proud of themselves and their brigade. Agatha was invited and attended with family friends, all of whom knew Arthur Griffiths, a lieutenant in the garrison. This particular evening, Arthur was ill and could not attend, but he passed along Agatha's name to a friend, suggesting he look after her.

Agatha was not hard to spot, lissome and lovely in a peach gown, her light hair pulled into a chignon with white lilies of the valley. She held a small beaded bag, twisting the strap between her fingers as she gazed across the dance floor. She was standing alone when he walked toward her and introduced himself as Second Lieutenant Archibald Christie. He was taller than she by half a foot, with a complexion that reminded her of roses. His hair was slicked down and parted perfectly on one side, his blue eyes sparkling as he looked into hers. And right then, in that very second, Agatha Miller fell madly, completely, impossibly in love.

THREE

Mrs. Archibald Christie

A is for Angel, by nature (?) and name
And also for Archibald, spouse of the same

Agatha Christie
The AA Alphabet for 1915

OCTOBER 12, 1912. AGATHA MILLER HEARD NO BELLS THAT evening in Chudleigh when she danced with Archibald Christie. She had expected bells, or at the very least to see a galaxy of stars, when face-to-face with true love for the first time. Surely that was how Mrs. L. T. Meade explained the process in her romance novels. But for Agatha it seemed to be more of a progression that moved logically in small steps through a labyrinth constructed of information and emotion.

As they danced that first dance and then another, Agatha learned that Archie Christie was born in India, the son of a judge who had died years earlier in a fall from a horse, a death not unlike that of her own grandfather. Archie's mother, Margaret (who was known as Peg), lived with her second husband, William Hemsley, the headmaster of the excellent preparatory school Clifton College, in Bristol—a school Archie had attended with his brother, Campbell. While learning all this in Archie's arms, Agatha also discovered that he was a wonderful dancer.

He held her lightly, almost shyly, as they waltzed and shared bits of stories from their lives, spontaneous recollections laced with easy laughter.

The relationship might have ended there, for when Agatha left Chudleigh Castle and took the train home from Newton Abbott, she never expected to see him again. That did not, however, mean she didn't think of him and wonder if he thought of her as well.

Shortly after Christmas 1912, she received her answer. It was mid-afternoon during a badminton game at the home of her next-door neighbors, the Mellors, when her mother summoned Agatha home. *Unannounced* a suitor had called, which, to Clara Miller, was *totally* unacceptable. Her daughter was to return to their home immediately and handle the situation.

The twenty-two-year-old woman who stormed across the street and into the drawing room at Ashfield was not the same woman Archie Christie remembered. No longer demure, she looked out of breath, irritated, and disheveled. Archie stood up to greet her, his face flushing the color of pomegranates as he blustered a feeble excuse about finding himself on a motorbike in Torquay and impulsively deciding to stop for a visit.

It was now Agatha's turn to blush. When her mother had telephoned, she assumed her uninvited visitor was a "dreary young naval lieutenant"[i] whom she had been trying to avoid for weeks. Seeing Archie, Agatha felt her features soften into the instinctive smile of young love. "Archie," she heard her lips speak, extending her hand before she took a seat next to the piano.

The conversation was light and sparked with laughter, much of the humor coming from Agatha regaling her suitor with stories of her exploits on roller skates, in bathing houses, and her five-minute ride on an airplane for which her mother paid five pounds at a fair the previous year. Caught up by the mention of flying, Archie leapt to his feet, words positively tumbling from his mouth: *He was a pilot*, having just received his Royal Aero Club Aviator's Certificate from the Bristol School at Larkhill. "I'm the two-hundred-forty-fifth pilot in all England," he bragged, as Agatha's eyes widened in anticipation of their first flight together. The romance of that vision quickly faded, however, when he continued with the news that he had applied for acceptance into the newly formed Royal Flying Corps.

It was as exciting as it was dangerous, and they both knew it. But Archie continued to beam with pride at his accomplishment, and Agatha smiled too at the spirit and determination of her wonderfully animated new friend. He was invited to stay for dinner that evening—Christmas leftovers straight from the larder. Archie in his own enthusiasm invited Agatha to travel up to Exeter the following Sunday to attend an afternoon concert and promised to escort her later to the Redfield Hotel in nearby Bristol for tea.

Even as Agatha was gushing acceptance, Clara shifted in her seat at the dinner table and addressed their guest. "My daughter does not accept invitations to travel to concerts *alone*," Clara said, "and most certainly would never take tea with a man in a hotel." The embarrassed silence that followed was interrupted when Archie included Clara in his invitation. She could come with her daughter and join them, he added.

While appealing in intent, the gesture placed Clara in the uncomfortable position of playing chaperone for her adult daughter, and committed Clara to attend a concert in which she had no interest. It was time for a compromise: Clara agreed to allow Agatha to travel to Exeter alone for her date, but remained adamant about the Redfield Hotel. Tea, if any were to be served, could be enjoyed in the very public setting of the Exeter central railway station before Agatha's return trip home. It was an unusual concession for Clara to allow, and its importance was not lost on her daughter. Clara liked Archie Christie, and later, as Agatha watched his motorbike backfire down the driveway, she wished that he could stay forever.

Before Archie left, Agatha invited him to attend a New Year's Eve ball at the four-month-old Torquay Pavilion, scheduled to take place just three days later. Designed by architects Edward Rogers and H. C. Goss, and later revised by Torquay Borough engineer Henry Augustus Garrett, the Pavilion was known as the "Palace of Pleasure" for its elegant combination of soaring, ornately plastered ceilings with an exterior tiled in white Doulton stoneware.

The ball was a festive affair, crowned by the unveiling of a sparkling chandelier that had been ordered from France and had arrived several days before the event. It would have been the highlight of Agatha's entire year had it not been for Archie's strange behavior. In the course of those three days, he had changed from being an attentive, somewhat humorous, always handsome suitor into a withdrawn, sulking, and very distant escort—one Agatha said looked like a "sick sheep." He refused to dance the entire evening and barely touched the food on his plate.

Agatha's immediate assumption was that she was the cause of his distress, and she found herself chattering and laughing in a magpie monologue, as if talking twice as fast would make up for the fact that her escort was not speaking at all. It took another forty-eight hours before Archie could bring himself to confess the cause of his malaise. His application to the Royal Flying Corps had been accepted. Second Lieutenant Archibald Christie was now officially a military pilot, one bound for training in Farnborough, thirty-four miles southwest of London, before being shipped out to destinations unknown.

Though their relationship was still only weeks old, Archie could not imagine himself going a single day without the companionship and support of the woman before him, and he told Agatha so—asking for her hand in marriage. Her reaction was properly guarded, the result of years of seclusion and indulgence. Yet even as she remained noncommittal, there was a scenario playing out in her mind. *Happily ever after. Til death us do part.*

When Agatha finally exhaled, her words spoke not of Archie Christie but of Reggie Lucy. She was, after all, engaged—after a fashion, but engaged nevertheless. Reggie Lucy needed to be informed.

Dismissing Reggie as irrelevant, Archie again declared his love for the girl he called "Angel" and, as Agatha Miller rolled the image around in her mind, she smiled the look of one who has just been granted a dream come true. It would take several weeks before Agatha told Reggie that she had fallen in love with a flyer, and when she did, he accepted her decision with the same nonchalance with which he had embraced their friendship and betrothal.

In the Royal Flying Corps, Archie reported directly to Major Robert Brooke-Popham, who had been placed in charge of RFC Squadron Three. Brooke-Popham liked Archie's aggressive approach to flying a plane, seeing in his second lieutenant the makings of a great fighter pilot. Meticulous in both his appearance and record keeping, Archie dutifully recorded his various training flights, noting the date, range, and time in a diary he would continue to keep for his entire life.

What his diary did not reflect was the freedom Archie felt when taking to the air. The profession of pilot fit perfectly with his personality, as it called for split-second decisions and non-wavering commitment. Flying fed his need to control and slowly, but obviously, altered his personality.

At the moment, however, the only thing Agatha chose to acknowledge was the fear she felt mixed with love. She worried about her fiancé, fearing he would crash, certain he would be injured or killed. The stress transformed her from a girl who thought of flying as a romantic lark to a woman determined to persuade her fiancé to avoid planes completely.

In several letters written at the start of 1913, Agatha pleaded with Archie to give up flying and find "something safer" within the service. She was particularly horrified when Samuel Franklin Cody, a legendary showman and aviator who was then manufacturing planes for the military, crashed his Cody biplane in a tree, falling four hundred feet to his death. Archie responded to her fear with carefully worded letters aimed at appeasing her concerns without acquiescing to her requests.

"Can't give up flying yet," he wrote in a letter late in August 1912, pointing to the instability of the Cody plane. "I am taking no risks and feel pretty confident that no harm can come to me."[ii]

Clara offered absolutely no consolation to her daughter on the subject of flying or marriage. Agatha's mother thought the former was akin to blasphemy. "If God intended man to fly...," she ranted, on more than one occasion. To her, the only thing worse than dating a pilot was marrying one, pointing to his lack of a satisfactory income and no possibility of promotion in the future.

Nevertheless, Agatha had made up her mind that hers would be a marriage of love, and she wanted to marry Archie "dreadfully." She was, she said, prepared to wait a lifetime. For the next two years, it seemed as if that might be a distinct possibility, since the pair barely saw each other, and then only in rushed encounters during Archie's military leaves.

The separation was emotionally debilitating, a trawler dragging a full net, pulling at the heart and leaving little room for common sense. At first Archie, then Agatha, logically contemplated their relationship, each determined that it was unlikely to succeed. Archie was concerned about Agatha's lack of money and his emotional and physical unavailability;

Agatha wracked with concern for his safety and worry over the health of her mother.

For all the uncertainty in the Miller household, life in Torquay was still a refuge of civility and leisure, with its beaches, concerts, regattas, and dinner parties. The rich and royals continued to travel there, now more than ever, as much of Europe became increasingly restive and on edge. There seemed to be arguments everywhere: Women were fighting to win the right to vote, protesting in the cities; rebellions were beginning in Ireland between the Catholics and Protestants; Germany was taking Britain to task over its colonization policies—and vice versa; and the Balkan states were quarreling over conditions real and imagined.

When Archduke Franz Ferdinand of Austria and his wife, Sophia, were assassinated on June 28, 1914, in Sarajevo by a member of the secret Serbian society known as the Black Hand, the news was barely mentioned in Torquay. There was neither official mourning nor the cancellation of a single party. In London, however, the mood was far more turbulent. There were reactionary speeches in the House of Commons and the House of Lords, where the prospect of war between the Austrian-Hungarian alliance and Serbia was condemned.

In another month, on July 28, 1914, the Austro-Hungarian throne declared war on Serbia, and this time not even the tranquil beaches of Torquay remained unaffected. Auntie-Grannie called with the news and spoke to Clara, who in turn spoke to Agatha, who rightly predicted that England would be quickly drawn into the conflict. On Saturday, September 1, Archie was placed on alert and told that he would soon be deployed to France. Knowing very well that he might not return, his one thought was to see Agatha before he left the safety of Salisbury.

It would take two days and any number of favors asked and received before Agatha and her mother were able to book seats on a train to get them to the Third Squadron, by which time Archie had been moved into transit quarters at his training base. While the couple had only a few hours together before Agatha was remanded to Torquay, they were, for Agatha, hours she would always remember and treasure.

On the return train ride, Clara was saying a silent penance while fingering an imaginary set of rosaries. Agatha leaned into the cold glass window: This was, she realized, a time of profound loss. The world as she knew it had taken a step off a precipice and was now falling into darkness. Wherever it landed, it would not be the same place it had been, and she missed that place already.

According to his diaries, Archie departed his base camp on August 5, and England itself on August 12. Every day following England's declaration of war against Germany, there was news of killings and bombings. The threat had left its smell in the air, though in England it seemed to have acted as an elixir, for an unprecedented number of volunteers crammed into halls across the country, seeking to enlist.

Agatha herself joined the Voluntary Aid Detachment (VAD), a group of nurses' helpers who paid for their training in wound care, sanitation, and hygiene. Having no proven talent, Agatha felt that the VAD was her only opportunity to help the war effort, and in doing so, support her fiancé at least in spirit. "I wanted to have a part in it," she said in a recording made for the Imperial War Museum.[iii]

It was tedious, tiring, and unimaginable work for a young woman whose greatest challenge up until that point had been keeping her stockings in place while swimming in Tor Bay. She worked alongside one doctor and eight nurses, extremely short-staffed professionals who looked upon an extra set of hands—even inexperienced ones—as a valuable commodity. An emergency hospital had been set up in the old Torquay Town Hall, where soon boatloads of wounded soldiers began to arrive from the harbor and others arrived by train.

At first Agatha was assigned to be a ward maid, polishing brass, cleaning floors, and carrying out other general housekeeping chores. After five days, however, she was promoted up to the hospital ward where the most seriously injured soldiers lay wounded and dying.

Young men without legs or arms or with missing sections of face and skull became commonplace. Her apron blood-drenched, she carried the stench of death and dying home each night on her long walk up to Ashfield. It was a horrific plunge from the protected life she had long enjoyed.

For many of her contemporaries, the sights and sounds were too horrendous to endure. Of all her friends, Agatha alone found the task at hand inspiring, for she was at last contributing to society in a way that would have made her father proud.

"From the beginning, I enjoyed nursing," Agatha wrote in her autobiography. "I took to it easily, and found it and have always found it, one of the most rewarding professions that anyone can follow."[iv] In addition to being rewarding, it was the perfect occupation to keep Agatha from worrying about the dangers Archie was facing in the field.

By the time her fiancé had earned his first leave in December 1914, he had seen combat in the Miracle of the Marne, so called because it ended with a Franco-British victory over Germany—halting that country's monthlong offensive to overtake Paris. As the Germans retreated, Archie returned to the air in the First Battle of the Aisne, attempting to keep the enemy from entrenching themselves along the French river. He was proficient enough in his flying skills to be named flight commander and captain (temp.) in November.

When Agatha received a "Dear Angel" letter from Archie in December announcing that he would be coming to London in several weeks, she launched into her own campaign to welcome him home in patriotic style. First, she asked their cook to make a dense fruitcake with marzipan icing—Archie's favorite—then she started packing her most alluring gowns, planning on spending every waking moment at his side.

On December 21, Agatha and her mother traveled by train to London for what was to be an emotional reunion. Clara spoke of Agatha's need for patience with her fiancé. He had now *seen war*, after all. Things would be different, she suggested. As usual, Clara was sensitive and accurate in her advice. Seeing Archie for the first time in four months, Agatha found him nervous and unable to meet her eyes. "Both of us had lived a large tract of experience on our own. The result of it was that we met almost as strangers. It was like learning to know each other all over again," Agatha recalled. "His own determined casualness and flippancy, almost gaiety upset me."[v]

There was a part of him that looked right through her, the sort of look fortune-tellers use when gazing into a crystal ball, as if seeing another time and place. Perhaps he was, because when Agatha suggested that it might be time for them to consider getting married, he did not answer her right away. He paused like an actor on the stage, waiting for an audience reaction before he spoke.

He said something about it being the wrong thing to do. The timing was wrong, what with the war and the shelling of aircraft. "You stop one, you've had it, and you've left behind a young widow," Archie added with the smile of someone making a joke about death, pretending it would never happen yet unable to stop thinking about its inevitability.[vi]

She suddenly wanted to hold him, allow him to cry on her shoulder and release his fear. Instead, she found herself awkwardly pleading to spend the rest of her life with a man she hardly knew. After several minutes of stalemate, she abandoned her argument, determined to enjoy their brief time together, reacquainting herself with her flyer, handsome as ever in his freshly pressed uniform.

Unfortunately for Archie, he selected that exact moment to present his fiancée with her Christmas present—an expensive Louis Vuitton dressing case, costing nearly an entire year's salary. While no doubt it was worth every penny, the case was completely unappreciated by Agatha, who deemed the gift inappropriate and told him so. It seemed a frivolous expense at a time when the Millers were struggling with finances to such an extent that earlier in the year they considered ending the perpetual care of Nathaniel Miller's gravesite in America. The argument that followed flamed brightly and then sputtered like wet fireworks, with both Agatha and Archie feeling slightly embarrassed, uncertain how their love could have become so easily sidetracked.

On December 23, Agatha and Archie saw that Clara got safely on the train back to Torquay, after which they boarded one of their own to Bristol, where Archie's mother and stepfather were awaiting their arrival. The journey was arduous, with overcrowded compartments filled to capacity with passengers, many bearing gifts. By the time Archie's brother, Campbell, met their train several hours later, Agatha was frazzled, irritated, and confused. The trip had done nothing to bring the pair together and now the thought of enduring Archie's overbearingly happy mother was more than she cared to tolerate.

Begging exhaustion, Agatha went immediately to her room and had just settled into the too-soft bed when she heard a knock on the door, followed by Archie's voice asking to be let inside. Cracking open the door just wide enough for a sliver of hall light to cut through the room, Agatha saw yet another incarnation of her fiancé—this one announcing his intention to marry her the very next day, on Christmas Eve. He was now every bit as certain that they must marry *immediately* as he had been just hours before that any thought of a wedding was ridiculous.

As Agatha opened the door allowing Archie to enter, the whiplash of emotion that she felt was made all the more intense by his eyes. Rather than the soothing, compassionate gaze of a man in love, they held the erratic excitement of a person about to open a surprise present. Even as she listened to the hasty litany of reasons that supported his decision, she felt her own body collapse on the bed under the weight of an emotional overload.

Archie was suddenly a runaway train, and there was little Agatha could do to stop his momentum. She knew that this impetuousness was pure Archie, and to love him, one had to accept this about him. Common sense aside, Agatha Mary Clarissa Miller was getting married.

The day that followed held none of the romance that poets ascribe to weddings or that Agatha had dreamed for hers. No custom-written wedding vows or hand-selected music. No nave full of invited guests straining to catch a glimpse of a beautiful bride gowned in white, walking down an aisle. No post-ceremony luncheon or rice-tossed getaway. It was also to be a wedding with no family in attendance.

Given that the day before a holiday is never calm, the nearly impossible task of generating an instant marriage license took on even more urgency as bureaucrats were hurriedly called upon. After several false starts involving clerks and the courts they ran, a kind registrar, who recognized Archie as a local resident, decided to bypass the normal two-week waiting period and issued the needed document on the spot.

Fortunately, Bristol's Emmanuel Parish Church, with its distinctive bell tower and gothic design, was available. So too its vicar, who was quickly located at a neighbor's house down the street, and then the church's organist, practicing inside the church for Christmas services.

A few hours later, as dusk began to fall over the sleepy village with its grand homes and manicured gardens, Agatha walked up to the church door alone. Just as she was about to enter, she spotted a local acquaintance named Yvonne Bush and asked her to serve as witness to the marriage ceremony.

For his part, Archie's stepfather, William, represented him. When she received news of the impending nuptials, Peg Hemsley had hysterically taken to her bed, where she remained for days.

Agatha, remembering the moment, wrote, "No bride could have taken less trouble about her appearance. No white dress, no veil, not even a smart frock. I was wearing an ordinary coat and skirt with a small purple velvet hat."[vii]

While admittedly rushed and disorganized, the wedding of Mr. and Mrs. Archibald Christie was legal and binding, of that Agatha was absolutely certain as she clutched her marriage certificate on the four-hour trip the newlyweds took from London to Torquay later that Christmas Eve.

Agatha took the precaution of telephoning her mother to warn her in advance of their hasty wedding and pending arrival. Given the reaction of Archie's mother, Agatha was certain that her own would take it no less dramatically. Fortunately, it was Madge who answered the telephone that Christmas Eve, having come to spend the night with Clara in Ashfield before escorting her to Abney Hall for Christmas Day, as family tradition dictated.

After the initial shock and feigned outrage at missing her little sister's nuptials, Madge inhaled a deep breath like a scuba diver about to submerge and suddenly giggled at the absurdity of Agatha's wedding day. Madge promised to sooth ruffled feathers and hurt egos as best she could before Agatha joined them at Abney, and after rushed good-byes hung up the telephone.

Archie had managed to book a small room at the Grand Hotel in the center of Torquay, just across the road from the train station, for a one-night honeymoon. The Grand Hotel is a Victorian palace that sits on Tor Bay Road, holding court over the village and its harbor. The newlyweds walked the half-block from the train station and entered through the hotel lobby decorated in holiday garlands and lights, with an enormous Christmas tree standing proudly near the Grand's library. It was an impressive show that dazzled with its blend of simplicity and grandeur, both understated and sophisticated. It was also barely appreciated by the twosome as they were shown to their room and fell into an exhausted sleep.

Clara was celebrating Christmas with Madge and the extended Watt family at Abney Hall when Agatha and Archie walked into the drawing room of the manor house to be joyfully welcomed with applause. The holiday reunion became a double celebration as the family welcomed Archie as one of its own. It was only Clara, her clairvoyance always active and sensitive, who picked up a quality from her new son-in-law that seemed at odds with the festivities. She later labeled it "ruthlessness," and it would be a feeling that never left his aura in her presence for the remainder of her life.

Agatha could see nothing but love when she looked at her husband, and that day in that place she beamed with pride at the man by her side. The celebration was, by necessity, short-lived, with the pair returning to London that evening so that Archie could travel back to France—six months of uncertainty and horrors of war were his only guarantee before he could hold his bride again.

Agatha returned to the hospital, where her days were a mélange of bloody bandages, severed limbs, psychiatric nightmares, and the constant smell of death. In the evening, Torquay, like much of the coastline, was now blacked-out against enemy attack, and Agatha spent her evenings reading to Auntie-Grannie. Her grandmother's cataracts had diminished her eyesight, leaving the now-elderly widow unable to care for herself or her home in Ealing. Clara was the first to suggest that her aunt move into Ashfield, where she could be properly cared for. Margaret Miller looked upon the offer as the loss of her independence and remained obstinate to the move right through the moment the carriages carrying her heavy mahogany furniture were making their way up the Barton Road hill in Torquay.

Secretly, Clara welcomed her aunt's company. With Agatha gone for much of the day, Ashfield loomed large and deserted, even the foundation shrubbery leaned away from the house as if reaching for an escape. Most days her daughter typically arrived home after sunset and then left the dining room table the following morning to run errands long before breakfast. For Clara, even Auntie-Grannie's domineering presence was preferable to her own loneliness.

Archie continued to write letters to his Angel, professing his love and complaining of the terror and hardships of waging war, though his own involvement in any heroics or ambushes was only casually mentioned and then with the minimum of danger implied. When, at last, he was given his next leave in mid-1915, Agatha rushed to see him in London, and again their time together was disjointed and uncomfortable.

Archie had not revealed to his new wife that because his high-altitude flying had acerbated his asthma, he had been temporarily reassigned to a desk job organizing pilots in a depot where recruits were assembled for initial classification, preliminary training, and assignment to active units. Regardless of how well Archie performed his assignment, handling the more mundane elements of administration did not suit his temperament. His melancholy mood barely hid his disappointment that his direct involvement in helping to fight the war had been reduced. Agatha found that his aggressive personality would flare and wane more unpredictably now. At those moments, nothing she said or did was remotely adequate or endearing, the resulting discussion amplified out of proportion to the situation.

Even as she returned to Torquay after only three days with her husband, she began to wonder if their rush into wedlock had been as wise in retrospect as it had seemed in the excitement of the previous Christmas. Clara attempted to remain positive for her daughter's sake, while privately having conversations with Auntie-Grannie about the inappropriate haste of the nuptials and her total lack of trust in Archie Christie, whose only consistency seemed to be thinking of himself first and foremost.

When Agatha became ill with a rather severe case of influenza in August 1915 and was sent home from the hospital for extended weeks of recuperation, she unboxed her sister's Empire typewriter and began to write—at first more poetry and then, on a dare from Madge, she decided to write a murder mystery so clever that her sister would be incapable of guessing the killer.

Three weeks into her writing and recuperation, Agatha regained her health enough to return to work and was invited by the wife of Dr. Clarence Ellis to join the staff of the newly opened hospital dispensary, which could make good use of Agatha's precise accounting skills and ability to organize. The dispensary was the antithesis of the ward floors, with their frantic pace and agonizing screams. Under Mrs. Ellis and her counterpart, Agatha's friend Eileen Morris, the dispensary was a logically arranged and methodical place that specialized in efficiency. To some it would have been a boring assignment, but to Agatha it was a font of information outside the grasp of general knowledge, thus making it even more fascinating.

There were few places on earth where a discussion of the effects of a particular poison could last all morning and peak sometime around afternoon tea. The dispensary in Torquay was one of those places. As with all things Agatha, she launched into the project with enthusiastic verve, hoping to eventually study for and pass the difficult tests at Apothecaries' Hall, which certified licensed dispensers. This was heady stuff for a girl without so much as an elementary school education, and Agatha was determined to achieve her diploma even if it meant giving up what little free time remained to her at home at Ashfield.

As a result, what little writing Agatha produced in the latter part of 1915 centered on letters to her husband. Archie was extremely fortunate not to have encountered "so much as a splinter" during his time on foreign soil, and during his rare three-day leaves back in England he enjoyed spending nearly every minute satisfying his physical need to be with his wife. Unlike most women of her generation, Agatha actually enjoyed making love, as she would later express in her poetry, where she could freely wrap her words in sensuality.

Her basic nature was inclined to shy devotion, and in Archie Christie, Agatha had married a man who needed constant reassurance and attention—two items that his wife supplied in abundance. Spending their first anniversary apart, the couple wrote affectionate notes, Agatha longing to spend more than a few minutes a year with her husband and Archie promising that his love would remain strong. "You were rather a dear last year entrusting yourself boldly to me, but you will never regret it and I will love you as much as then."[viii]

In the course of their first year of marriage, the Christies spent a total of six days together. It was not, however, for lack of interest or wont of trying for more time off. Archie had actually accomplished the impossible during wartime and received more leave than many, a reward for his skills as an ace fighter pilot.

Agatha routinely searched the military gazette for mention of her husband's exploits in Squadron Three—she was both concerned and excited when she found his name in the newspapers and proudly clipped it out and saved it. She made mention to him of her work as well, though Archie failed to acknowledge her accounts of working at the dispensary. He was preoccupied with torture and death on the ground and engine failure and firefights in the sky. Even as Agatha's knowledge of medicine grew, her ability to share her accomplishment decreased, absorbed into his talk of sorties and bombing raids, about which she knew little.

She returned to writing stories in the middle of 1916, more from frustration and boredom than any pressing drive to create. She did, however, find a new approach to the mystery she had begun the previous year, reworking it to be centered around poison. It was a rather amusing way to utilize the esoteric information she was learning in the dispensary, and in her own mind, a glamorous way to occupy time between filling orders.

As Agatha later wrote in her autobiography, she knew she would need to create a detective to solve the crime she had concocted for her new story, someone unique and as far away as possible from the most famous detective of the day, Sherlock Holmes. "I settled on a Belgian detective [and] allowed him slowly to develop into his part...a tidy little man, always arranging things, liking things in pairs, liking things squared instead of round. And he should be very brainy—he should have little grey cells of the mind—that was a good phrase; I must remember that—yes, he would have little grey cells."[ix]

She named her detective Hercule Poirot for no particular reason. "Whether it just came into my head or whether I saw it in some newspaper or written on something— anyway it came," she said.[x] And Poirot's assistant, his Dr. Watson as it were, was named Captain Hastings—tall, thin, and angular, whose general way of looking at life was as vague as Poirot's was specific.

Agatha centered the plot of her new book in a manor house she called Styles in the historic county of Essex, in the east of England. It did not matter that Agatha had never traveled there. She knew that it was known for its marshes, oversize cattle, and a remoteness that seemed to have been tailor-made for mystery.

Bits and pieces of the plot began to assemble themselves in her head as she presided over the bottles of arsenic and digitalis at work. Yet, the story remained a scattered effort that became more frustrating as it became more complete. "As I began to be enmeshed in the middle part of the book, the complications got the better of me instead of my being the master of them," she later wrote.[xi]

Sensing her daughter's frustration, demonstrated by constant forgetfulness and daydreaming, Clara suggested that Agatha should take a break—to Dartmoor. Though that was akin to suggesting Siberia to a Russian, Agatha embraced the concept of a fortnight in Dartmoor with a tourist's eager spirit.

Dartmoor is desolate, tranquil, and utterly unique in the nearly spiritual serenity that transcends the vast moorland. It is dotted with stone-circle remnants of round houses used by farmers in prehistoric times. Clara booked her daughter at the Moorland Hotel in Haytor, which Agatha described "large and dreary." Her room was cold and stern, much like a convent, with a solitary picture on the wall of sheep grazing in tangled grasses blown by an invisible wind.

Her twin bed was covered with a worn orange spread that had lost much of its nap, and muslin encased a blot of feathers that was too thin to be called a pillow. Directly opposite the bed was a surprisingly comfortable reading chair with lamp, the room's real center, while along the far wall stood a simple wooden desk—the kind that might otherwise be in a child's room.

It was dreary, yes, and outside, the damp cold weather no doubt furthered that impression as Agatha settled into a daily routine of rising early and writing in longhand for several hours in the morning, until her fingers ached and cramped round her pencil, and the lunch bell finally pealed the call to the dining room.

It was in the afternoon, just as the sun began to move shadowed lines across the moors and the cattle huddled into tight herds, that Agatha found her greatest peace. Having accomplished her writing for the day, she took off across the moors on foot, away from the village and into the grasslands, running her hand through her hair, still thick enough to base a marriage on.

As she walked with long strides, breathing in the moist heavy air, she was reminded how she loved to hike. Hiking was her favorite means of exercise, second only to swimming, and as she was lulled by its pace and expended energy, she rehearsed scenes from the next few pages of her book—the ones she would be writing the following morning—speaking all the lines for all the characters as if enacting a radio play with a single performer.

By the time her two-week vacation from the dispensary was finished, so too was *The Mysterious Affair at Styles,* the title she had given the book. The manuscript still needed some work, especially in the complicated middle section, badly in need of weeding out, like an overgrown garden. It was, Agatha decided, a good book—not great, but certainly far more entertaining than she had ever thought it might be. She had her handwritten pages typed professionally, with carbon copies prepared for mailing to publishers. Upon her mother's advice, she bound one copy and sent it to Hodder and Stoughton, the famous publishers of G. K. Chesterton's *Robert Louis Stevenson.*

In the evenings, she reread chapters to reassure herself that it was a fine piece of writing and, most important for Agatha, that Madge would never be able to identify the criminal. That was, of course, the best part and the reason for her smile as she stored the typed pages away in a large envelope in the top of her closet in Ashfield.

When Archie had his next leave, mid-1917, they spent it in the south of England, walking and talking in their first truly relaxed time together in several years. It was as if war had matured them to the point where they found the greatest joy in simply appreciating each other's existence. Merely touching reminded the young marrieds that they were alive and, more importantly, still together. So many friends had disappeared so quickly; overnight it seemed they were dead and gone.

It was in this quiet time that Agatha allowed Archie to read her manuscript, presented in its envelope just as she had sent a copy to Hodder and Stoughton. Archie liked the mystery and said so, in itself quite a revelation since he never paid compliments easily. He suggested that if Hodder eventually returned the manuscript, Agatha should consider passing it along to Methuen Publishing, where a friend of his from the military was a director.

Agatha agreed that Methuen, which published D. H. Lawrence, T. S. Eliot, and Henry James, was an excellent suggestion. When in fact Hodder did reject *The Mysterious Affair at Styles* the following month, Agatha submitted the manuscript to Methuen, enclosing a letter written by her husband's friend introducing the book. Within six months, the manuscript and the letter of introduction were returned, rejected again.

The effect on Agatha was less damaging to her ego than might have been expected, since she had never considered writing a career. It was, if anything, an interesting way to pass the time and to entertain a mind now full of formulations and antidotes for poisons. And even as she continued to send her book to another round of publishers, her mind was elsewhere, concentrating on the dispensary and passing her examinations at Apothecaries' Hall.

In early 1918, after three years of study, Agatha finally passed her last test and received her certificate qualifying her to dispense medicine. But any moment of celebration was tempered by the continuing influx of injured soldiers who needed their supply of pain elixirs and healing potions.

The time for celebration finally arrived, however, in August 1918, when Archie sent word that he was being transferred back to England as a colonel in the Air Ministry, based in London. There was no armistice for England, but Agatha felt as if the war had ended.

She immediately gave notice to the Mesdames Ellis and Morris and prepared herself for the start of married life. When her husband returned to England several weeks later, Agatha was there to watch him step from his plane, every bit a war hero—striking in appearance and impulsive in attitude. She was ever the worshiping wife, prepared to tend to her husband. Right away they began to set up their very first home together.

Housing was at a shortage throughout London, and Agatha thought them lucky to have found a pair of rooms on the second floor of a large, decaying house in St. John's Wood at Number 5 Northwick Terrace. The cost was two and a half guineas—a gold coin worth the same as a pound sterling—per week, payable to Mrs. Woods, who lived with her husband in the basement and dispensed advice on everything from cooking to shopping to raising babies.

As part of his Air Corps compensation, Archie was provided with a batman, a soldier who served as a butler to an officer, named Bartlett, who had previously worked for some time-honored Duke and was extremely efficient if slightly out of place among the faded chintz and worn furniture. In between taking classes in bookkeeping and shorthand, Agatha sewed pillowcases and draperies and attempted to apply a touch of Torquay elegance to St. John's Wood bland, not altogether successfully.

It was during one such bookkeeping class that the teacher dismissed her students with the news that the war had ended. The celebration in the streets of London was extraordinary. "Everywhere there were women dancing in the street. English women are not given to dancing in public: it is a reaction more suitable to Paris and the French. But there they were, laughing, shouting, shuffling, leaping even, in a sort of wild orgy of pleasure: an almost brutal enjoyment."[xii]

Archie's reaction was hardly what his wife expected. She was prepared for relief, joy, even jubilation. While all around them Londoners reveled in celebration, Archie remained calm and decisive. He would, he announced, be leaving the Air Ministry for a job in the private business sector. Perhaps real estate or money management would suit him. No future in the military, he said. And he refused to discuss it further.

The pronouncement left Agatha stunned—Archie had not thought to involve her in his decision, and she brooded over the abruptness of it, right through Christmas and into the new year. It might have gone on longer had Agatha not made a discovery of her own in January, one that she announced first to Archie, and then to the rest of her family while visiting Ashfield.

Having suffered with an upset stomach for several weeks, Agatha waited to visit a local physician in Torquay, a new doctor named Stabb who was married to an ex-girlfriend of her brother, Monty. It was the unfortunately-named Dr. Stabb who revealed the unexpected news that Agatha was two months pregnant, with a delivery date the following August.

Upon hearing the news, Archie matter-of-factly proclaimed that it would *definitely* be a girl (he thought that he would be jealous of a boy) and began spoiling his wife with food and cream—always cream, but then, it was her favorite, just as it had been for her mother. Chairs were held for Agatha at the table, special meals prepared for her dinner, and the mother-to-be tried—unsuccessfully—to make baby clothes.

Agatha did not have an obstetrician, such luxuries being deemed unnecessary for healthy young women in 1919. At that time a pregnant woman was expected to handle her growing size, her nausea, her general discomfort, and the birthing of a baby, aided only by her mother and a select group of friends, chosen for their experience with such matters.

Agatha's mother was three hours away, and with Auntie-Grannie in need of constant care, in no position to leave Ashfield. Agatha knew few people in London on whom to call for help. There was Mrs. Woods, certainly, whose wisdom on birthing extended as far as morning sickness. "Sickness means girls. Boys you go dizzy and faint. It's better to be sick."[xiii]

Her friend Nan Watts had married a man named Hugo Pollock and lived in Chelsea, but the two hadn't remained close. There was also the subject of money to consider: Nan had a lot of it, even after her husband left her for another; Agatha was struggling and felt strange not being able to casually go to tea and spend freely on scones with clotted cream.

When Archie left the Air Ministry, he went to work in the city for a corpulent financier who paid him £500 per year.

Agatha was still receiving the £100 legacy from her father's estate, and Archie had a military pension of £50 annually, so they were not poor. They were simply not rich, and that was a distinction never lost on Agatha.

She struggled with morning sickness, which seemed to extend through the afternoon and well into most evenings, and when she gave birth to a healthy baby girl in her old bedroom at Ashfield on August 5, 1919, at the age of twenty-eight, her first thought when she heard the news was, "I don't feel sick any more. How wonderful!"[xiv] Her mother and a midwife, Nurse Pemberton, helped her through her delivery.

They named their new child Rosalind, a compromise between Archie's preference for Enid and Agatha's favorite name, Martha. Eight-and-a-half pounds of joy with thick dark hair, she seemed to take immediately to Archie, who in turn delighted in spoiling his newborn.

Temporarily leaving Rosalind with the nurse at Ashfield for the first of many times, Agatha and Archie traveled back to London to locate a four-bedroom flat large enough to accommodate the new baby, a nurse, and a servant—a nurse and servant being the bare essentials of domestic help for even the poorest middle-class families.

They temporarily settled on a rather large furnished flat at 96 Addison Mansions in Kensington, not far from Holland Park, costing £90 a year. Agatha paid an additional £36 to Lucy, a servant who had worked years earlier for Clara at Ashfield, and hired a nanny named Jessie who had previously worked as a nurse in Nigeria. It was a satisfactory arrangement that found each element of the household keeping its own court—Jessie with Rosalind, Lucy with her housekeeping, and Archie and Agatha attempting to return to their pre-baby happiness and romance.

Despite her morning sickness, Agatha had gained weight during her pregnancy, and it was soon apparent that her body, so easily kept slim in her teens and early twenties, was no longer the svelte figure of an ingénue. Archie made comments in passing, though Agatha took no special notice of them. She felt her primary devotion should be to running the household and finding more permanent housing, which they could decorate as their own.

Archie left each morning, excited by his advancing career, returned at lunch to visit with the baby, and then spent much of the afternoon in investment meetings at his club, often returning late for dinner.

Despite passing her entire day at home, Agatha did not form a particularly close bond with her daughter; she checked in on her regularly, but little more. It was Rosalind's father who was clearly the baby's favorite—her cheeky smile never failing to appear when he would sneak his head into her room and call her name. They also spoke a baby language that, while amusing, Agatha did not understand.

Archie preferred reading his newspaper to sharing casual talk over lunch, labeling it research for his business. It therefore came as little surprise, when, in September 1919, he failed to notice the morning delivery of mail that Agatha brought to the table.

There, on top of the stack of paperwork, was an innocuous envelope bearing the logo of the Bodley Head publishing house. Opening it, Agatha found not the expected rejection letter, but rather an invitation to a meeting with Bodley Head founder John Lane in his London office to discuss her manuscript for *The Mysterious Affair at Styles*. She gasped for joy as she looked around for her husband to share in her excitement—but Archie had already left the room.

FOUR

The Mystery Writer

The true work, it is done from within.
The little gray cells.
Remember always the little gray cells, mon ami.

Hercule Poirot to Captain Hastings
in *Agatha Christie's* Murder on the Links

SEPTEMBER 25, 1919. JOHN LANE WAS VERY PLEASED WITH himself as he leaned into the mirror hanging over the sink in his bathroom and examined his beard. Using a small pair of manicure scissors, which he was barely able to handle with too-chubby fingers, he snipped at a few stray hairs. It was more for effect than actual trimming, for his beard was already evenly manicured with the precision of a putting green. Moving his head from side to side, he grinned with a smirk of satisfaction. Yes, he was very pleased.

When he first received the unsolicited manuscript titled *The Mysterious Affair at Styles*, he had placed it on a stack of similar submissions, certain it would prove as unimpressive as most. That's when he saw it—the word *affair*. As the founder of The Bodley Head Limited publishing house, the word appealed to him. The company had, after all, made its reputation by publishing books of "stylish decadence." Among them were the works of Oscar Wilde, the bon vivant wit whose passion for rough, working-class boys stood at odds to his sophisticated plays and short stories. When Wilde was prosecuted and ultimately convicted for "gross indecency" with other males, public outrage against Wilde sent a mob of Britishers armed with rocks to break every one of the front glass windows of The Bodley Head offices.

He therefore wondered about this *Mysterious Affair* and read the entire manuscript in one sitting, completely captivated by its contents. Not by any hint of scandal or lust—there was little of that. So little, in fact, that he should have been disappointed. Instead, what he found was a manuscript written with such intricacy and guile that he was fascinated by the mystery of it all. Carefully plotted and plumped with characters that positively jumped to life off the page.

His company had been playing with mysteries as a way to push The Bodley Head in a new direction—something it badly needed. Not that The Bodley Head was doing poorly. Lane had an adequate business, to be sure, just as he had had for the past twenty-five years since founding the firm and naming it after the bust of Sir Thomas Bodley that hung over the entrance to the library at the University of Oxford. But this manuscript was different. It was an entirely new type of mystery, set among the drawing rooms of the very rich, and peppered with enough plot to fool even the most avid of readers.

The writer was unknown to him, or anyone for that matter, apparently: a first-time authoress named *Mrs. Agatha Christie*. A wonderful name for a mystery writer, he thought, as he first sat down to dictate a letter inviting her to meet. Now, as he dusted imaginary lint from his shirt, that meeting was about to take place. Moving to sit behind his desk, he imagined what she would look like—this woman of poisons and plots.

Agatha had the advantage there. She knew of The Bodley Head company and its reputation.

It was not exactly her first pick for a publisher—a bit heavy on gossip and yellow journalism. Nonetheless, it did have some excellent writers in its stable of authors, which is why it took no small amount of courage for her to walk through the stately front doors on Zigo Street, sucking in her breath and wishing herself luck.

John Lane was a smallish man, with a pert little belly he kept well hidden inside a tightly cinched vest, and as he stood to face this writer/housewife/mother, his pale blue eyes were ill-prepared for what he saw. While he fingered her manuscript depicting a ruthless and elaborately clever poisoning by strychnine, he gazed across his desk at a young, willowy, attractive woman dressed in a navy suit with live violets on her lapel and a small white handbag grasped tightly within both hands.

Lane's inner office was crowded with piles of books and prints lying about on chairs and tabletops with seeming abandon. The chaos left Agatha with no place to sit and precious little room to move. Lane was not the sort of publisher who entertained much, either in his office or out, which explained his lack of preparation for a guest.

After quickly clearing a seat, he laid Agatha's manuscript on his desk, and proceeded to tell her that "some of his readers" thought it had potential. It was hardly a sure thing, he reminded her, and the risk he was taking was great. Agatha allowed her eyes to move toward her manuscript on his desk, the fingers of Lane's right hand beating a tattoo on its cover, and she felt her hands tighten their grip on her purse.

It was, as Lane had predicted, all so easy. Even as he opened his desk drawer and pulled out a completed contract, he kept that small bit of doubt hanging in the air between the two of them. "Your manuscript needs some work," he said, "particularly the last chapter." Originally written as a court scene, he suggested a simpler method to wrap up the dénouement.

"I think that should be easy enough to alter," Agatha said, attempting to keep the excitement out of her voice.

Lane raised his hand to cut her off, continuing his scene just as he had planned it days earlier. The publisher whom Agatha thought looked "rather Elizabethan"[i] was enjoying his role, tangling this human fly in his web and luxuriating in the moment. He was, he said, prepared to publish the book and to pay her a ten percent royalty on any copies sold over two thousand. In addition, he would agree to give her half of any serialization and magazine rights. It was, he assured her, a good contract, but Agatha had already stopped listening, just as he knew she would. The only words Agatha Christie heard were *I am prepared to publish the book.*

Lane did not mention that the contract entitled The Bodley Head to publish Agatha's next five books as well, or that it was unheard of not to pay *any* advance no matter how small, even for a first-time author. Instead, he slid the contract toward her, placing a pen on top of the paperwork, and waited expectantly.

Agatha signed her contract without reading a word, as he knew she would. And she was smiling and thanking him as he walked her to the door, her copy of the executed document safely folded away in her purse. As he shut his office door and returned to his desk, Lane smiled again. Mrs. Agatha Christie now belonged to him.

Even as she walked down the sidewalk outside The Bodley Head offices in Westminster, Agatha felt a slight hop in her step. She wanted to hug someone, or scream, or do something so wonderfully silly that everyone on the street would stop and stare in her direction. Instead, she boarded a tram and headed back to Kensington as if this day were no different from any other.

It was only later, after she told her rather astonished husband of her success, and produced the contract as proof, that they decided to officially celebrate with a night at the newly opened Palais de Danse. Located on Shepherd's Bush Road in Hammersmith, the Palais featured a live jazz band and an immaculately polished, large wooden dance floor, which was perfect for both the fox-trot and Castle Walk and every other dance they could imagine on the evening Agatha labeled as "perfect."

Immediately upon rising the next day, Agatha started writing changes to *The Mysterious Affair at Styles*, making small adjustments throughout, and completely altering the ending as promised. Though still not feeling like a professional writer, she did feel as if she was *working*—something entirely different from raising a child and keeping a home. Moreover, the work she was doing was well received. John Lane found her changes well crafted and immediately set about scheduling *The Mysterious Affair at Styles* for publication.

It was during Agatha's rewriting that Auntie-Grannie, ninety-two, caught bronchitis and died suddenly. Clara was devastated at the death of her adoptive mother and began obsessing over her own mortality. She begged Agatha to spend some time with her at Ashfield, and when her youngest daughter eventually arrived for her next visit, she brought with her a very special gift—the accepted manuscript to *The Mysterious Affair at Styles*, complete with its dedication: "To My Mother."

The book was serialized in the *Weekly Times* in England in late 1920, before arriving in book form in America in December of that year and in the United Kingdom in January 1921. It was favorably reviewed in the *Times Literary Supplement,* whose critic claimed that the "only fault in this brilliant story is that it is almost too ingenious."[ii]

Agatha clipped the book review and placed it in her memory book of souvenirs and pictures from her life, although not in a particularly predominant place. A single copy of both editions of her book was added to the shelves in the sitting room out of reach of the baby, and—as quickly as it had changed—life returned to normal.

Soon after her first meeting with Lane, Agatha had switched apartments within Addison Mansions, moving from her first floor furnished unit to a more permanent and similarly sized unfurnished unit on the fourth floor at number 96. Decorating the apartment became her passion, as Agatha's unique style transformed the rather sterile walls into a panorama of color and texture.

While Archie took command of papering the bathroom in a "brilliant scarlet and white tiled" pattern, Agatha chose shiny pink wall covering and a black background accented with a pattern of hawthorn for the ceiling in the sitting room, this over the decidedly pointed objections of her paperhanger. Rosalind's nursery was slightly more traditional, with a mauve frieze trim along the top edge of the walls, decorated with rhinos and giraffes.

It was a time of absolute domestic bliss when all things were possible and the world was at peace. "We never had such a happy time," Agatha later remembered. "I had married the man I loved, we had a child, we had somewhere to live, and as far as I could see, there was no reason why we shouldn't live happily ever after."[iii]

The small success enjoyed by *The Mysterious Affair at Styles* had little impact on Agatha's life. The Bodley Head had sold 2,000 copies of the 2,500 printed in England, which meant Agatha earned nothing in royalties, though she happily accepted a £25 check for her half of the serialization rights in the *Weekly Times.*

No one at Addison Mansions thought of her as anyone other than Rosalind's mother; and certainly there was no suggestion that she knew about medicines, poisons, or mystery tales as she pushed Rosalind's pram to nearby Holland Park each day, joining the other mothers with their children in the sun.

Her entire writing career might have ended as soon as it had begun if it were not for her husband and his constant thirst for capital. Archie's salary and the annuity Agatha received from her father's estate provided enough to survive, but little more. Given the mores of the time, there was no thought of cutting the household staff—a nurse and a maid were the minimum live-in servant essentials of civilized family life.

In addition, Clara was barely able to maintain Ashfield, even with the help she received monthly from Madge, and Agatha lamented that she wished there were *something* she could do to help. It was in this context that one day in mid-1921, Archie Christie suggested to his wife that she write another book, adding, "It might make a lot of money."[iv] Agatha was astounded, and not completely displeased, although it made her a bit uneasy that her husband was suggesting his wife work, quite unheard of in their set at that time.

Archie had never taken more than a passing interest in his wife's writing and certainly never suggested it was valuable. But now, he was complimenting her ability—albeit in a backhanded way—and suggesting it as a source of extra income. Always eager to please, and armed with his support, Agatha returned to her writing desk and set to work again.

This time out, there would be no Hercule Poirot or Captain Hastings to guide the reader through a maze of murder and treachery. Agatha had yet to develop an allegiance to her characters and sensed none from her readers, either. In her second book, *The Secret Adversary,* she introduced the literary equivalents of Agatha and Archie Christie in Tuppence Cowley and Tommy Beresford. Her two heroes were only loosely inspired by early pieces of the Christies' lives— Tuppence was in the VAD; Tommy in the RFC. The pair, old friends from childhood, hire themselves out as adventurers in what Agatha described as a "spy book, a thriller."

When John Lane received the manuscript of *The Secret Adversary,* he made no effort to hide his disappointment. The new direction of The Bodley Head Limited was mysteries, not intrigue, he reminded her, though he eventually did publish the book in January 1922,[5] and it sold slightly better than Agatha's first mystery.

The *Times Literary Supplement* labeled Tommy and Tuppence "refreshingly original."[v] The book's release might have been cause for celebration had events at home been less stressful. As it was, Agatha had no sooner delivered the manuscript to The Bodley Head than her brother, Monty, suddenly reappeared in her life. Monty—after living in Africa all these years—arrived in England in high dudgeon, attempting to settle down in London complete with a Negroid male servant named Shebani who insisted on calling Monty "Bwana."

Monty had gained little in the way of maturity from his years in the military in Africa. He seemed to possess an innate ability to become involved in schemes of questionable legitimacy. In addition, sometime near the end of the war, he had taken a bullet in the arm and, due to an unsanitary dressing, developed progressive septicemia. He was not expected to live long.

A specialist in tropical diseases in London restored him to relative health, at which point "Bwana" decamped to Torquay, Shebani in tow, having decided to move in with his mother at Ashfield. Once established there, he took to calling upon the servants day or night for meals and various domestic duties, and occasionally shot his pistol out the window at objects unknown, much to the horror of the neighbors.

Madge and her husband were frequently called in to manage Monty and keep the peace while Clara took to her bed, totally unable to handle the stress caused by her son's unpredictable behavior. The local gossip was replete with reports that Monty was a heroin addict, which he did nothing to dispel. His continuing misconduct only served to reinforce this scandalous notion.

Fortunately for Agatha, she was able to escape most of the drama thanks to Archie and the offer he received to travel around the world representing the British Empire Exhibition Mission with Major E. A. Belcher, a former professor at Clifton. Belcher was the assistant general manager of the Empire Exhibition, a world's fair of sorts, whose sole aim was to showcase products from the United Kingdom. The exhibition

[5] Dodd, Mead & Co., which had acquired John Lane, published *The Secret Adversary* in the U.S. in January 1922.

was planned for 1924, and Belcher was turned loose on the Dominions (Australia, New Zealand, Canada, and South Africa) to induce local businessmen to participate. In addition, Belcher had invited Archie to join him as financial head for the ten-month tour for a fee of £1,000, and Archie invited Agatha to come along. He estimated that his fee for services would cover any of Agatha's expenses not covered by the British Empire.

After hasty discussions with Clara and Madge, it was decided that a woman's place was with her husband—even if that woman had a two-year-old baby named Rosalind. The baby went to stay with Aunt Madge, Agatha went to shop for clothes, Archie wrote his letter of resignation to his employer, their London apartment was quickly sublet, and on January 20, 1922, the four of them (including Major Belcher's male secretary named Francis Bates) left England by ship. Their first destination: Cape Town, South Africa. Along for the first leg of their adventure were Mr. and Mrs. Hyams, family friends of Belcher. The Major described Mr. Hyams as "the East Anglia potato king."

The group set sail for Cape Town on the RMS *Kildonan Castle*, a rather large cruise ship with onboard entertainment, contests, and various dining opportunities. Almost immediately, however, the squallish weather sent Agatha to her cabin with seasickness so severe that she contemplated leaving the tour as it passed Madeira Island. She imagined herself jumping ship and working as a parlor maid in Madeira—tall parlor maids always being in short supply.

Fortunately, such a dramatic exit was not required and by the time the group reached Cape Town the first week of February, Agatha was delirious with excitement over seeing the country and exploring its beaches and exotic coastline. Belcher, on the other hand, had begun to show signs of his bombastic and controlling nature, waving his arms wildly as he complained nonstop to the hotel staff, with the overflow of his ire splashing on Bates, who often took the brunt of Belcher's wrath.

While Archie, Mrs. Hyam, and her daughter Sylvia visited Port Elizabeth with its famous Horse Memorial, Agatha joined Messrs. Hyam, Belcher, and Bates on the arduous train ride to the diamond mines of Kimberly before rejoining the group in Rhodesia.

At their own expense, Archie and Agatha took a private trip to Victoria Falls and stayed at the Victoria Falls Hotel, its lily ponds and mango-treed courtyard offering comfort from the intense heat. In a letter to her mother, Agatha wrote, "No road, only paths, just the hotel, primeval woods for miles and miles stretching into blueness."[vi] It was a romantic sojourn so intense that Agatha never dared return for fear of diluting the memory. Johannesburg was largely unimpressive to the Christies, but served their purpose in promoting the Exposition. Frequent quick trips to Muizenberg found the Christies on surfboards, "light, thin wood, easy to carry," as Agatha taught herself the sport, which she admitted was "occasionally painful as you took a nosedive into the sand."[vii] She was only thirty-one and still agile and fresh; a long, long way from cloistered swims in Tor Bay.

There was continued complaining from Belcher, who never seemed to be able to find a ripe peach and who altered their itinerary on a daily basis—sometimes several times in a day. (Agatha's glee at hearing that India and Ceylon would be added to their tour was dashed within minutes.) Bates had developed a phobia that convinced him that he was about to be consumed by snakes. And the Hyams had tired of the entire melodrama and returned to East Anglia and their potatoes.

Letters from home assured both Agatha and Archie that Rosalind was well (although she had a cough), that Monty was behaving (he was now confined to an invalid chair), and that the reception of *The Secret Adversary* was excellent. John Lane forwarded a set of reviews along with queries about Agatha's next book, which he hoped would be a mystery.

It was at this point in 1922 that Agatha Christie began to think of herself as an author. She was no longer the unknown housewife/mother with a writing contract for six books with The Bodley Head. She discovered in that moment that her publisher, who eagerly awaited her next novel, needed her.

To satisfy John Lane, she had begun work on a new mystery featuring Hercule Poirot, titled *Murder on the Links*, inspired by a newspaper article about a recent break-in and murder. And at the request of Bruce Ingram, editor of *The Sketch*, she had written twelve short stories featuring Hercule

Poirot for inclusion in issues of his magazine. On the trip, with
her small, newly purchased Corona typewriter, Agatha had
been able to continue to work, providing her with an escape
from the increasingly unpredictable temper of Major Belcher
and his anxious secretary.

Being able to keep up with her writing was especially
convenient on the long voyage aboard the SS *Aeneas*, the
onetime troop-transport ship now owned by the Blue Funnel
Line, carrying the group to the bottom of the earth on their way
to their next destination: Australia.

Due to the reversal of seasons down under, it was mid-
autumn and on the cool side when the British Exhibition
Mission reached their first stop in Tasmania. Belcher, who had
a touch of gout, was more belligerent than ever. "Wild Man
worse than ever this morning. He is in his room darkened like
a primeval cave," Agatha wrote in her diary.[viii] There were the
usual meetings and the selling of British products, described
as successful in letters home. Far more appealing to Agatha
were the trees and foliage of Melbourne and Sydney. In the
sun of the small town of Yanga, known for its views of the
adjacent Blue Mountains, with their blue-purple hue, one
could almost feel the fat in the eucalypt vegetation evaporate
in the heat.

By the time the foursome reached New Zealand, there
was no longer any pretense of friendship or camaraderie.
Belcher was "rude, overbearing, bullying, inconsiderate, and
mean," Agatha wrote.[ix] Despite his ability to occasionally
demonstrate the charm that had so endeared him to the
Christies over dinner in London, they were no longer fooled or
amused. When Belcher announced that he was taking a month
in New Zealand with Bates to handle personal business, he
gave Agatha and her husband permission to sail on by
themselves to Fiji and the Hawaiian Islands.

The aloha spirit of the Moana Hotel welcomed Agatha
and Archie to Honolulu with double plumeria leis that were
"scented by heaven and painted by God." It was the traditional
Hawaiian aloha blessing given to all guests, but to the
Christies, it felt personal. For the next four days, the pair surfed
and ate and danced under the stars in the Moana's banyan
courtyard until the reality of finances forced them into a nearby

cottage on the grounds of the Donna Hotel. If it was not exactly oceanfront, it was still adjacent to Waikiki, and for the next three weeks the pair explored paradise.

Archie's fair skin was ill equipped for the intensity of the sun and "blistered up and peeled...back and shoulder near rare again,"[x] Agatha wrote to her mother, without mentioning that Archie, much to the amusement of the locals, had taken to swimming in the ocean in his pajamas to protect himself from the burning rays. They marveled at the paved roads, the automobiles, the pineapples and bananas thick and ripe, "growing along side the road like weeds free for picking." When it was finally time to rejoin Belcher and Bates to head to their final stop in Canada, Agatha and Archie took one last look at the lovely Pacific and yearned to be able to stay forever.

With Archie's £1,000 fee nearly exhausted and four more weeks in Canada remaining on the Expedition journey, it became obvious even to Agatha that they hadn't enough money for her to be able to stay with her husband until the end of the tour. The most she could hope for was two additional weeks, and only then if she did not consume much in the way of hotel food. Cruising across the Pacific, of course, was no problem, but upon arriving in Victoria, British Columbia, the first restaurant they visited reinforced the challenge they faced.

Belcher's mood had not improved with his month in New Zealand, and his demands resumed almost immediately upon stepping foot in Canada. He argued with the concierge at the hotel in Victoria, the mayor in Calgary, and a restaurant chef in Edmonton, whom he accused of trying to poison him with some cured pork. Nothing, however, equaled his ire when Archie's sinuses flared up after a visit to a grain elevator in Winnipeg. When doctors ordered Archie to bed, Belcher, based on his limited knowledge of lung conditions, protested this interruption of business. Eventually Belcher moved on, leaving Agatha with Archie. She was frightened, alone in a foreign country, and caring for her infirm husband based on instinct and little else.

"His temperature was up to 104 for days," Agatha wrote her mother, "and finally a terrible bout of nettle rash came out."[xi] While this was hardly the finale to their glamorous around-the-world tour that she had expected, at least it provided her with a reason to stay by her husband's side a few days longer.

Archie, of course, eventually healed and, when he did, Agatha made arrangements to visit her Aunt Cassie in New York, staying at her apartment on Riverside Drive. Once there, Agatha turned this into a time for souvenirs, both given and accepted, with Aunt Cassie sharing her memories of Agatha's father, and a visit together to Nathaniel Miller's gravesite at Greenwood Cemetery in Brooklyn.

Looking back on her visit to America, Agatha would remember her final day alone with Cassie as her most exciting. On that day, the nearly ninety-year-old woman acceded to Agatha's request and took her to eat in the Horn & Hardart Automat on Broadway. Agatha dressed up as if going to the finest restaurant. She had heard of this cafeteria concept in England, where they were nonexistent. At the Automat she plucked her selections from behind glass doors and slid her tray along the counter, hailing the entire event as "most amusing."

If Agatha needed any reminder of their dire finances, it became quickly apparent after Archie joined her for their Atlantic crossing to England aboard the RMS *Majestic.* The Christies left New York on November 25, 1922, two days after Agatha celebrated her first American Thanksgiving. They had but £700 remaining in a savings account, *Murder on the Links* would not be published for months, and Archie not only had no job, he had no leads on finding one.

Making matters even worse, when they returned to Madge's home in Cheadle to pick up Rosalind, the three-year-old treated her parents as strangers, demanding to remain with her Aunt "Punkie." Agatha's pain accelerated when Archie, discomforted over his lack of employment, lashed out at Agatha, haranguing her with arguments.

In the days and weeks after their return to their flat in London, Archie became increasingly disagreeable, ultimately asking Agatha to take Rosalind and leave. "I'm not good, remember, if things go wrong," he told her. "I'm not much good in illness, and I can't bear people to be unhappy or upset."[xii] Well, things *had* gone wrong. He was not able to support his family, and the more Agatha attempted to help in her sweet, compliant manner, the more he disliked what he interpreted to be patronizing behavior.

Agatha refused to leave their home, even for a day, defying her husband. She could not allow him to deal with the situation on his own. They were no longer able to afford a maid, so Agatha insisted that she could at least keep the house clean. Rosalind still had a nurse, though she was new and nicknamed "Cuckoo" due to her habit of talking to herself.

Addison Mansions was no longer their loving home with shiny pink walls and black ceiling. There was now a harshness about the place, the air seemingly full of extra ions ready to discharge at any moment. Archie felt that he had lost control of his life and his wife, and grew increasingly desperate to find solitude. He turned inward, refusing to talk, or worse still, mocking his wife when he did.

Agatha, feeling her husband's burden but unable to help, attempted to lose herself in her writing, constructing the plot for a new book called *The Mystery of the Mill House*, a title suggested by Major Belcher during the Empire tour. Now feeling quite secure in her ability to create interesting and varied tales, Agatha's self-confidence gave her a new authority when dealing with The Bodley Head, including a rather heated exchange over the cover art for *Murder on the Links*.

"Apart from being in ugly colors," Agatha wrote in her autobiography, "it was badly drawn and represented as far as I could make out, a man in pajamas on a golf links, dying of an epileptic fit. Since the man who had been murdered had been fully dressed and stabbed with a dagger, I objected." [xiii]

Eventually, Archie found a job in early 1923, easing their financial concerns but not the tension in the household. The new job did not hold the prestige of his last. Worse still, the firm was thought to be rather disreputable, and its activities needed to be watched. Still, it was a job. That, it seemed, was the important part.

Archie's employment was followed by the release in March of the American version of *Murder on the Links*, published by Dodd, Mead & Company, with The Bodley Head issuing the British edition in May. The book was dedicated "To my husband, a fellow enthusiast of detective stories, and to whom I am indebted for much helpful advice and criticism."

Once again the reviews were nearly all positive. The *Literary Review* wrote: "The plot is really clever; its suspense is well kept up and the solution is fair enough. What more need one ask of a detective yarn?"[xiv]

The *New York Times* thought it a "remarkably good detective story, which can be warmly recommended to those who like that kind of fiction."[xv]

It was as if Mrs. Agatha Christie was suddenly *someone*. This creative, exciting spinner of yarns had a pool of imagination deep and varied. To her readers, she was a curiosity—a married woman with a career. This point was not lost on her husband, who, while appreciating the income that her writing produced, was beginning to feel uneasy about this woman author flowering within his home.

As 1924 began, Archie Christie experienced life with a woman who was not only generating her own income, but spending it as well. She was becoming a shrewd negotiator, demanding more control over how her books appeared in print, including their covers, titles, and various ancillary rights. She arranged for her Hercule Poirot stories—previously published in *The Sketch*—to be released by The Bodley House as a compilation book titled *Poirot Investigates*. This clever move earned her income without actually writing new material and counted as one of the six books covered under her original contract.

Agatha then decided on her own to pay publisher Geoffrey Bles to print a book of her poetry titled *Road to Dreams*. She also spent £400 of her personal capital to join her sister in paying for a cottage in Dartmoor to house their increasingly erratic brother. And she took the £500 advance she received from the *Evening News* for the serialization rights to her next book, *The Man in the Brown Suit* (the retitled *Mystery of the Mill House*), and spent it to buy an automobile—a 1924 Morris Cowley.

As if her behavior wasn't startling enough to her husband, she began an exchange of letters with John Lane's colleague, Basil Willett, criticizing the planned cover art of *The Man in the Brown Suit* as looking like a "highway robbery and murder in medieval times." This was, she pointed out, a strange choice, given that the plot centered on the death of a man in a London underground station witnessed by a stylish and modern young woman.

Chief among the characters in *The Man in the Brown Suit* is Sir Eustace Pedler, a bombastic eccentric with a striking similarity to Major E. A. Belcher, to whom the book was dedicated. "To E.A.B.—in memory of a journey, some lion stories, and the request that I should some day write 'The Mystery of the Mill House!'"

J. Franklin reviewing for *New Statesman* suggested that "*The Man in the Brown Suit* is the best of its kind I have met for a long time."[xvi] *The Saturday Review of Literature* felt that the book "maintains a swiftness of pace we have never seen surpassed."[xvii]

Unrivaled reviews from critics, coupled with the gradual increase in her popularity as demonstrated by rising sales, reinforced Agatha's confidence. As she continued to deal with Basil Willett through a series of letters and telephone conversations, he became increasingly aware that The Bodley Head's author—who was so willing to sign away her rights several years earlier—was becoming expert in demanding them now.

Much of that credit might rightly go to the Hughes Massie Agency, a firm of author representatives, which Agatha had once again approached as her contract with The Bodley Head was nearing its end. While Massie himself had since died, Agatha was introduced to his protégé, a young agent in his twenties named Edmund Cork, who immediately endeared himself to the writer through his sincerity, knowledge, and respect.

There was little Cork could do about her existing contract other than shake his head in amazement at its horrible terms. As he agreed to represent the author in future negotiations, he pledged to protect her rights and promised to always include her in any discussions about future work.

Despite his youth, Cork was a tall, elegant Englishman who was not only expert in the ways of publishing; he was also savvy about human nature. His slight stammer worked in his favor as he courted Agatha. She immediately felt protective of this man who promised to shield her from any and all who would seek to exploit her talents.

Agatha now turned to Edmund Cork rather than to her husband for advice, further reducing Archie's sense of self-respect. He was still courteous in conversation with his wife, though he no longer used nicknames like Angel. Not even a new and more prestigious position at a new company changed his feelings. If anything, after joining the financial firm of a friend, Clive Bailleau, he began to spend longer hours at work, eating more dinners at his club in London, and leaving Agatha alone with her talent.

Madge had been spending nearly every weekend with them in London, which pleased Agatha greatly. The woman who was now known as "the sister of Mrs. Agatha Christie, the novelist" had been writing again herself. Madge had scripted a play called *The Claimant* and had succeeded in getting it scheduled at the St. Martin Theatre in the West End to be produced by Basil Dean.

During much of 1924, the play was in rewrites and rehearsal, and Agatha was introduced to the backstage excitement of theatrical production before its premiere in September. That the play was only a moderate hit delighted Agatha's sense that she was, after all, *the preeminent* writer in the family, lest anyone forget that fact.

Through Edmund Cork at Hughes Massie she signed a new three-book deal with Geoffrey Collins of Williams Collins Publishing, guaranteeing her a £200 advance per book, plus extensive ancillary rights and royalties. She had one last book to hand in to fulfill her final obligation under her deal with The Bodley Head. Her contract allowed Agatha to feel secure enough financially to suggest to Archie that they move out of the city and into a larger place in the country where Rosalind could play away from city traffic and noise, and where her husband could enjoy his newfound love for playing the gentlemen's sport of golf.

While they initially looked at houses with grounds, the Christies ultimately selected a flat inside a home known as Scotswood in the London suburb of Sunningdale, where Archie had previously secured a membership in the local golf club. The house was a grand Victorian occupied by two families of tenants on the first floor. The Christies' flat had been converted to a comfortable two-story apartment on the second and third floors.

The role of decorator once again fell to Agatha, but there was to be none of the garish experimentation from

Addison Mansions. The taste and sophistication of the upper class golfing community would tolerate none of that. For Scotswood, Agatha chose lilac-colored cretonne curtains for the sitting room, a small tulip pattern on white curtains for the dining room, and buttercup and daisy fabric for Rosalind's nursery. Upstairs, Agatha selected scarlet poppies and blue cornflower drapes to highlight Archie's dressing room, while their bedroom curtains featured the variety of bluebells that covered the ground in local forests.

It was at Scotswood that Agatha hired a new nanny for Rosalind named Charlotte Fisher. There had been a string of nannies following Cuckoo, but none really seemed to possess the skill to handle the training and entertaining of Rosalind, who, even on her best days, was becoming a handful of undisciplined energy.

"I liked Miss Fisher as soon as I saw her," Agatha wrote. "She was tall, brown-haired, about twenty-three; had had experience with children, looked extremely capable, and had a nice-looking twinkle behind her general decorum."[xviii] Rosalind, now five, spent much of her day in school, allowing Charlotte to act as Agatha's secretary in her free time. At least, that was the original concept. In reality, Agatha was nervous dictating her books, and Charlotte, who became known as Carlo, was erratic in transcribing them. Eventually, the nanny became less secretary and more companion, handling a variety of duties and errands.

Agatha wrote her final book for The Bodley Head while moving from Addison Mansions to Scotswood. Titled *The Secret of Chimneys,* it was set on a rambling Berkshire estate, and introduced the square-faced Superintendent Battle of Scotland Yard. The story followed a murdered monarch and a missing tell-all biography. It was the type of book, the "light-hearted thriller type," that Agatha said she loved to write.

Released in October 1925 in Britain and a month earlier in America, *The Secret of Chimneys* was dedicated "To my nephew in memory of an inscription at Compton Castle[6] and a day at the zoo"—the nephew, of course, being Madge's son, Jack Watts, then in his early twenties.

Agatha should have been extremely pleased by the reception of what she labeled "my little book," but was distracted

---

[6] Compton Castle was a 14th century manor house located some five miles west of Torquay, and a favorite picnic spot for Agatha and Jack.

by the failing health of her mother. Agatha persuaded Clara to move into the empty flat next to hers in Scotswood, and, once installed, Clara seemed to lose all interest in life, becoming lethargic and forgetful. With her friends now gone and the familiar sights of Torquay only memories, there was precious little to call her own. Agatha credited it to the lack of spontaneity in Sunningdale, where most of the activity took place on the various golf courses. "Sunningdale society was mainly of two kinds," she wrote. "The middle-aged, who were passionately fond of gardens and talked of practically nothing else; or the gay, sporting rich, who drank a good deal, had cocktail parties, and were not really my type, or indeed, for that matter, Archie's."[xix]

Agatha had effectively become a golf widow, for when Archie was not working in London, he was playing on a nearby course with friends. Agatha had attempted to join him at the sport but found it tedious, reverting instead to her writing. Clara, now seventy-one, eventually moved into a friend's home in London where she had her own room and could get out easily to entertain herself with shops and city doings.

Occasionally Agatha drove herself to London, finding the freedom exhilarating. Yet, without Archie, it felt like forced laughter, a weak imitation when you've known the real thing.

She had Rosalind, of course. Her daughter was so unlike her, however, it was difficult for Agatha to understand where they could find common ground. Where Agatha saw elephants in the clouds, Rosalind saw, well, clouds—that is, if she bothered to look up at all. Rosalind was her father's daughter—seeing life in black and white. In their world fairy tales served little purpose other than to divert attention from essential things. All rather irresponsible to consider.

Agatha looked at children, including her own, as a mystery to be discovered as it unfolded. She said of babies, "it is like this strange plant which you have brought home, planted, and can hardly wait to see how it will turn out."[xx] She was connected, yet detached, in a way that even she was never quite able to completely explain.

Then there was her writing. There was always the writing: the place she felt safest and free to flow and dream and travel on airless wings. And so it was that in the fall of

1925, she submerged herself into writing *The Murder of Roger Ackroyd,* Agatha's first book under her new contract with Williams Collins. The story would prove to be her most controversial and used a device suggested to her by her brother-in-law, James Watts.

The publication of the book resulted in a critical controversy that served to imprint the name Agatha Christie as a writer at the top of her craft in this story labeled "the most brilliant of deceptions." Yet as she sat writing the book, she had no idea that it was special or particularly different from any of her others. When she did allow her mind to drift, it always went to one place only: Archie Christie.

Agatha was first and foremost a romantic, her husband's wife, and a woman who longed to please. She asked for little and demanded only attention—the one thing that her husband seemed determined to withhold. He credited all the time he was spending away from home as his dedication to his job. Keeping ahead of the fluctuating financial market was certainly time consuming, Agatha realized, but even when Archie found bits of time to spend with her, his demeanor was chilly and aloof, devoid of passion.

Perhaps that is why she agreed to another move—the very fact that they would be house-hunting threw them together if for no other reason than economics. And while it was certainly true that Scotswood was less than ideal, they could have easily remained there, very happily—if they had only *been* happy.

When Archie announced he wanted to own a home rather than rent, it made sense to the extent that a suitable and affordable property could be found. His first thought was to build on the new golf course being constructed. When the cost proved to be prohibitive, he next settled on a house that Agatha described as "a sort of millionaire-style Savoy suite transferred to the country and decorated without regard to expense."[xxi] He named it Styles after Agatha's first book, and despite the home's history of unhappiness—apparently tragedy lurked within its walls—the couple moved in during the first weeks of January 1926.

It was not a particularly smart time to take a vacation, but having just finished *The Murder of Roger Ackroyd* and settled into Styles, an exhausted Agatha attempted to convince her husband that a vacation was *exactly* what she needed. A trip to Corsica with its beautiful bay of Calvi was planned, and when Archie stubbornly refused to go, Agatha took Madge in his place, determined to prove that she was independent of his control. And then, of course, the entire time she was gone, she thought only of him, longingly.

Upon returning from Corsica, Agatha headed to Torquay, where Clara was back in residence and now ill with bronchitis. Her mother looked tiny lying in her large bed, shrunken into place between a down pillow and a green silk comforter. Most of Ashfield was closed off now, decaying just like the unkempt garden outside. It had been too long since Agatha had visited, she realized, and she did what she could during her weeklong stay to bring some life back to the place.

Relieved from watching over Clara by Madge, Agatha returned to Styles, hoping that Archie would be waiting, not knowing that he had traveled to Spain on business. The disappointment she felt upon entering the empty bedroom was a slow ache rather than a sharp pain, but it was real enough to still be there the next morning when she awoke. When Madge telegraphed to say she had taken their mother up to her home, Abney Hall, in order to provide better care, it raised no alarms. The Abney staff *was* excellent, and Clara loved being there. It was only after the next telegram, the one that said, "Come at once," that Agatha panicked.

On the impossibly slow train ride to Manchester, she knew she was too late. Her mother was dead. And with her death, the world as Agatha knew it ceased to exist. She remained unnaturally numb during the funeral, which Archie did not attend. He was no better at coping with death than he was with illness. She understood that and hadn't expected him to come.

And when she traveled to Ashfield to close up the house, she knew he wouldn't come there, either, although she tried and tried to get him to at least visit her. There was always something; each reason on its own sounding real enough, but taken together, obvious lies.

Agatha wallowed in her suffering, stalled like a storm front. She had only meant to be gone for weeks, not months, and certainly not half a year. But there it was. And when he did finally show up at Ashfield and demand a divorce, she wondered if this was the way death felt, a slow ripping at the heart that stopped beating because it could not stand to experience the pain.

The publicity that surrounded the release of *The Murder of Roger Ackroyd* was extraordinary, but Agatha neither read the reviews nor agreed to be interviewed. "There are doubtless many detective stories more exciting and blood curdling than *The Murder of Roger Ackroyd*," the *New York Times* critiqued. "But this reviewer has recently read very few that provide greater analytical stimulation."[xxii] "Uncommonly original," said the *New York Herald Tribune*.[xxiii] Yet none of it mattered. Not anymore.

The morning of Friday, December the third began the same as any other day in Sunningdale. Cook had served eggs, beans, sausage, and tomatoes—a proper English breakfast. And then Archie announced he was leaving her. He said he wanted a divorce. She heard him push the chair back from the table, her eyes covered by her hands as if hands alone could stop her life from ending.

Later that night, Agatha drew aside the thick velvet drapery and peered expectantly through the bedroom window. The fog, so typical of Sunningdale in December, had moved across the road and now threatened to block her view of the front drive completely. She hated fog; hated the way it leaned into familiar shapes, turning them sinister and threatening. As her body shivered, she pulled closed the drape, blocking the cold draft that found its way through the window at night, turning the room damp. It was a little after nine p.m. and she knew her husband wasn't ever coming home again.

FIVE

My Name Is Neele

Love passes out into the silent night,
We may not hold him who has served our will
And, for a while, made magic common things...

Agatha Christie
Love Passes

JUNE 13, 1925. THE PURLEY DOWNS GOLF CLUB SITS ON the site of a former sheep ranch in South Croydon on the edge of the London suburbs, its mature trees and contoured terrain retaining much of the charm and rugged appeal that originally drew golfers there in the late 1800s. When Agatha Christie first brought her husband to Purley Downs in 1923 and introduced him to the sport, it had less to do with the game than it did with spending time together. The weekend was *theirs*. She made a point of storing her typewriter and notebooks away to devote herself to the man she loved.

There would be many trips to Purley Downs for the Christies; many more when Archie went there on his own. Agatha had never been particularly fond of golf, although she tried her best and even won some small tournaments. The truth, Archie knew, was that she simply wasn't cut out for sports. She had the wrong shape to begin with. Her height would have been a natural advantage had she not grown rather thick through the middle since their return from the yearlong Empire Expedition Mission tour. Her widened hips redirected her natural swing, making for an awkward stance and unpredictable shots.

Archie, on the other hand, loved the game and played it well. As the weekend approached, he thought of little other than heading to any of the various courses in the area south of

Kensington. Since the Christie's recent move to Sunningdale, with its multiple courses, golfing became even more convenient, ensuring that he spent every weekend playing eighteen holes. He hadn't played particularly well on Saturday, June 13, suffering through double bogeys on the last two holes, and was nursing his bruised ego over tea and scones in the clubhouse when he noticed a familiar, striking brunette heading in his direction, along with Larkin Pierce, a colleague from his London office.

Rising, he extended his hand first to Larkin and then to the woman standing next to him. "Hello, Nancy," he said, before shaking her hand as well, allowing it to linger just a second too long for propriety.

Nancy Neele was a twenty-five-year-old secretary at the Imperial Continental Gas Association in London, having joined the company two years earlier upon graduation from Miss Jenkins Typing and Secretarial School. Imperial Continental Gas was one of the earliest companies to produce gas on an international level, and Nancy was one of only two women who worked at the firm—the other being her girlfriend who had introduced her to Archie Christie.

Nancy was bright and charismatic and had a special way of staring at a man that made him feel as if he were the only person in the room. At least, that's how she made Archie feel every time she looked at him with that half smile on her face that she knew drove him crazy.

They had known each other now for a little over a year. Agatha also met Nancy at the time. It was all very proper and innocent, as things tended to be in the mid-twenties—at least at first. The three had gone to a dance together, Agatha acting as Nancy's chaperone so that this nice young woman could go out in society. Archie, of course, was happily married and certainly not seeking to break his vows. Yes, innocent and completely platonic—until suddenly one day it wasn't.

It was unexpected when it happened, the first flush of love presenting itself during an unplanned meeting on the golf course. Nancy was a superb golfer. Almost better than Archie himself. And spending time with her was unlike anything he had ever experienced. She did not fret or cling as his own wife did. There was none of that eternal *brooding*, or whatever it was that caused his wife to go into one of her funks.

Still, Agatha was his wife, and though he no longer considered her to be the "Angel" she once had been, he knew that he had little choice but to respect his vows and stop this flirtation, for that's what it was—nothing more—with a younger woman. He told her as much as they strolled across the edge of the green next to the seventeenth hole. Onlookers saw only two friends in conversation, with not a hint that their friendship was ending.

Nancy responded as Nancy typically did, with genuine understanding of the situation and respect for the parties involved. She had never had any intention of being "the other woman," and was not about to argue now that it was apparent that Archie had decided to rededicate himself to his marriage.

Since Agatha knew nothing of his feeling for Nancy Neele, Archie did not mention the meeting to his wife that day in June and returned home to Scotswood to find her studying travel brochures on the Pyrenees mountain region. She was planning a rather extensive vacation there, in an effort to revive some of her joy from the past. She wanted to share with Archie the same places that had made her own parents so happy and in love when the family had traveled there together in her childhood.

Pictures taken during the trip show a rather withdrawn Archie, more often than not covering his face as if trying to remove himself from the scene completely. Agatha, by contrast, is beaming, completely impervious to the emotional drama percolating under the surface. There, surrounded by the Pyrenees and later in San Sebastian, Archie looked past the mountains, beyond the beaches, and saw his future. And no matter how he tried to make excuses, his future included Miss Nancy Neele. It was neither nice nor kind, but it was true.

Returning to Sunningdale and his golf, he pushed through his days with predictable regularity. His life was constructed around a timetable that preferred consistency over spontaneity, and every time his wife suggested any deviation from his norm, he fought the change and refused to budge from his position.

He had tolerated the move to Styles for the prestige it brought him in business and the community. He purchased a used Delage automobile for the same reason. He could not easily afford either one, but bought them as a statement of the very stability he needed to project in business.

And stable was exactly what his wife was not. After the death of her mother in April 1926, Agatha entered a depressed state of imagined slights, sleepless nights, endless tears, and no communication. Not that she didn't want to talk. She frantically, desperately needed her husband to listen at the very time he felt least available to hear. He was too guilt-ridden to make room for reason, and making matters worse, he no longer cared to try.

When Archie confessed his love for Nancy in August 1926, he announced it to Agatha with the same emotionless efficiency that had hardened his core personality—a personality with no tolerance for vulnerability, let alone the self-pity his wife could not resist. Just at the moment that she was emerging on the world stage as a writer of major talent, she found herself unable to write a single word. All work on her next book, *The Mystery of the Blue Train,* ceased, her creativity blocked by the insecurity of abandonment.

Desperate now for a second chance at love, she clung to the hope that her husband might change his mind, realize his mistake. She was ready to forgive him anything, waiting only for the apology that did not come. In its place, on a December morning in 1926, he demanded a divorce with the cold precision of a surgeon cutting a tumor from a rotting organ.

He made no attempt to soften the blow or ease her pain. In fact, he wanted her to understand his determination and feel its intensity without compassion. He left the house without a touch or backward glance. No time for weakness or for love.

She instinctively pulled her hair back from her face, the way she did when she was nervous, rolling the curls around her index finger, and staring into space, as if concentration alone could change the future. For the next twelve hours she moved through her day as if still fully alive, though the part of her that died knew differently. The heart beats, the lungs breathe, but the brain cannot command itself so easily.

She devised a plan, if one could call it that, and began to pack a valise with several dresses, a new nightgown, two

silk scarves, and two pairs of shoes. She had written several
letters and now placed them on the inlaid table in the dark
foyer where she knew they would not be overlooked.

Donning her favorite muskrat fur coat, velvet hat, and
leather gloves, she stopped only long enough to briefly glance
at herself in the hall mirror and button up her dignity. Hugging
her dog one last time for luck, she bid him good-bye, picked up
her valise, and left the security of the house, and the world she
knew, without looking back.

The night sky was crisp black, oil painted against a
watercolor still life. The air felt cold against her skin, which
flushed as she struggled with the weight of the valise, her
steamy breath leaving a vapor trail for her passion to follow.
The gravel under her feet sounded like a knife scraping burnt
toast as she walked slowly to her car. *This is it then,* she
thought, fear and determination pressing her foot on the
accelerator. A moment later, she was gone, disappearing into
the darkness.

Although Agatha's exact destination that evening has
never been determined with certainty, it is highly likely that,
given her state of mind, she would have gone to Hurtmore, the
small country village near Godalming, where Archie was
spending the weekend with friends Sam and Madge James—
and Nancy Neele. Hurtmore is some seventeen miles southeast
of Sunningdale and a half-hour away by car. If her purpose was
to confront them both, Agatha decided against that approach,
and by six thirty a.m. the following morning had deserted her
Morris Cowley near the desolate chalk pits of Newlands
Corner, six miles away from Godalming.

More important than how she spent the night was the
way her car was staged when she left it. There was no attempt
made to conceal her identity—her vehicle tags remained on
the automobile, her expired driver's license was left on the
passenger seat, and her clothes, including her fur coat, were
strewn in plain sight when gypsy Jack Best first found the car.

By that point, Agatha had made her way to the railway
station at Guildford, three and a half miles away, preparing to
catch a train to Waterloo, a forty-five-minute ride. How she
traveled to the train remains a point of speculation, since no
verifiable witness has ever come forward. It was near freezing

and the image of her walking along the pre-dawn downs is less likely a scenario than her hopping on the local bus that ran along the route. What is certain is that on the morning of Saturday, December 4, 1926, Agatha Christie was alive and well and having tea in London by eight a.m., just as a crowd was beginning to gather around her abandoned car in Newlands Corner.

As Agatha sat sipping her tea, she was calmer. The pain was certainly still there; she suspected that would never go away—or the feeling of betrayal. It had been a day since her husband had left her, and what had disappeared between then and now was the vitriol. The need to retaliate had dissipated, replaced with the forgiveness that comes between two lovers when an argument's initial anger subsides. Her plan had allowed for that, and her plan was going well.

Refreshing her cup with Darjeeling, she reread a note she had written to her brother-in-law Campbell Christie, before addressing it to him at the school where he taught—the Royal Military Academy in Woolrich. This was perhaps her best touch. The note that explained her absence was a letter that she knew Archie would read—but only after its receipt was delayed for the weekend, giving him time to think about the ramifications of his behavior. Yes, a nice touch, meant to frustrate but just enough.

She had gone to a resort in Yorkshire, she wrote, to rest from recent events. No need to be specific; Archie would know and Campbell didn't need to. This is where she had the advantage, writing the story as *she* intended it to play. Though she may not have controlled the beginning, she had now taken over the plot.

She realized it was exactly like writing a play, each piece in place without being obvious, or forecasting the conclusion before the last act. And of all the players, Campbell Christie was the one she was certain would remain completely neutral, performing his part predictably and without hysterics. *She* had already provided enough of that. Now clearer heads had to prevail to bring Archie back home to her. It was with no uncertain relief that she dropped the letter in a nearby postbox and continued on her way.

Her next stop was Whiteleys, London's first department store, and still one of its best. There she could find an inexpensive cloth coat, for the chill of December had settled on London in the past few days, and the predictions were for cooler nights ahead. She also bought a small travel case and filled it with essential toiletries, stopping to dab a touch of scent behind each ear before paying for the articles and continuing on her way.

Entering Harrods next, Agatha paused at the spectacle of the department store's Christmas display. The magic of it all. The trees and baubles and animated figurines glittered in syncopated splendor above the sales floor. When she first visited Harrods as a little girl, she actually thought she could live inside the store and never leave, it was *that* exciting. The same thought occurred to her now, but she had little time for fantasy. *The plan, the plan,* she reminded herself.

She moved quickly through the fine jewelry department until she found the service desk where Mr. L. Fien accepted a diamond ring for repair—a loose setting was a simple fix, he assured her, and took down her name and address to mail the item when it was repaired. "Mrs. Teresa Neele, Harrogate Hydro, Harrogate, HG1." And with that she was off to catch a train to the resort spas of North Yorkshire, just as her letter had said.

The staff of the Harrogate Hydro, the town's most elegant resort, was busily decorating the luxurious lobby with the final touches of Christmas, when a tall woman stepped out of a taxi and entered the hotel. It was just after seven p.m., and news of the missing novelist had yet to be broadcast on the radio or headlined in newspapers around the country.

The sigh that left her lips had less to do with the exquisite décor than with the relief of a tired woman reaching her final stop of the day. The trip had been pleasant enough as she followed the British countryside north, passing through Grantham, Retford, Doncaster, Headingsley, Wheaton, and Hornbeam Park before arriving in Harrogate, where the golden wash of sunset gleamed in the windows of the elegant resort town.

Harrogate is a place where large manor homes predominate, set far back from the highway, their brick walls covered in creeping fig and oleander. Vast lawns are carefully groomed to reflect the pride that locals take in this historic community. The hotel itself lay long and regal at the end of Swan Road, the gray stone façade offering its solid strength, silently waiting to heal the weary and infirm. For hundreds of years this area has been known for its sulfur- and iron-abundant water, heated and swirled with therapeutic results.

Agatha signed the register "Teresa Neele, Cape Town, S.A." and was given room 105 on the first floor, renting for five and a half guineas per week. A smallish room overlooking the garden, it featured a twin bed with springs that squeaked in complaint with every move. Yet she slept, this woman Teresa Neele from Cape Town. And when she woke, her chambermaid Rosie Asher made a fresh coal fire that brought glorious heat to the room, followed soon by a full English breakfast. She greedily consumed every morsel as if to say, "It has been so long since I've eaten a proper meal." And it was true.

Her lack of luggage made Rosie curious, but in her three years of working at the Hydro, she knew better than to ask questions about the guests. They were always rich, usually famous, and occasionally infamous. It was best to close your eyes to unusual behavior, particularly since she needed the work and jobs were scarce.

It was well into afternoon before Mrs. Neele left her room that first day, and then only to drift into the small hotel library looking for books. Instead she picked up a copy of the *Times* left by a guest next to a now vacant chair, his cigar still burning in the amber ashtray. Entering the large dining room for dinner, she took the table furthest from the door, in a corner next to an ornamental palm that threatened to consume her completely. She applied herself to the newspaper's crossword puzzle, while straining to hear nearby conversation, whispered in the hushed tones inspired by fine dining.

The coffee they served had an unfamiliar flavor—hickory, perhaps. It was delicious, and she ordered more when she slipped quietly into the Winter Garden Ballroom to watch as some of the guests danced to the music of the Harry Codd Band. She was attired in the same outfit she wore when she had left Sunningdale, all the stores in Harrogate being closed on Sunday. As her eyes followed the gossamer silks of the women's gowns, she felt the two days' travel on her green jumper. This shook her self-confidence in a way she had not experienced since Miss Florence Eva Hickey's dance classes at the Athenaeum Room.

On Monday, December 6, this woman known as Teresa Neele emerged from her room soon after breakfast, came down the hotel's staircase, and paused halfway across the lobby. It was hard to pass by Mrs. Carlton Potts, with her gray-blue hair piled in loose curls and lips the color of raspberries, and not pause. She looked up to nod at Teresa just long enough to smile and then continued reading the story on page nine of the *Daily Mail* about the missing writer named Mrs. Agatha Christie.

Mrs. Potts pointed to the picture under the headline "A Woman Novelist Vanishes" before announcing to the guests seated in the lobby that she had, in fact, read *all* of Miss Christie's books and found her very, very enjoyable. Some other guests, whom Teresa had not met, agreed that the missing woman was indeed talented and were still discussing the disappearance as Teresa fled the room and headed down Swan Road to buy some essentials. This was, after all, going to be a big day. She was certain that by this afternoon, Campbell Christie would have his brother on a train to Harrogate, hat in hand.

There was a dress to buy and a new hat, matching shoes, and purse—one with a zipper that was all the rage in Paris. That accomplished, there were further stops for a hairbrush at Courtmans, books and stationery from W. H. Smith, a vial of perfume from Bentalls, and a hot water bottle from the chemists.

It was a little after one when the purchases and their owner made it back to the hotel. She spoke with the hotel's manager, Mrs. Taylor, about her luggage—stored in Torquay with friends, the story went—and was handed a parcel from Harrods. The diamond ring had been delivered. The plan was working perfectly. All that was missing now was Archie.

At dinnertime, Teresa debuted her new outfit—a peach georgette gown and wrap—and even danced with a hotel guest named Laurence while a singer, Miss Corbett, offered her rendition of the Al Jolson hit "I'm Sitting on Top of the World." *If only it were true,* Agatha thought, while Teresa sang along at the chorus.

By Tuesday, Agatha's picture was on the front page of the *Westminster Gazette* with the headline "The Mystery of Mrs. Christie." Her face was also featured in the *Daily Express*, the *Daily Mail*, the *Daily Chronicle*, and the *Daily News*, which offered a £100 reward for "information leading to the discovery of her whereabouts."[i]

"I'm here, I'm here," Agatha wanted to shout, but didn't. She knew if she only waited, her husband would come to rescue her, driven by a deep-seated love that went beyond flirtations or girlfriends, an attachment forged by the very bond of marriage.

At the front desk of the hotel, extra copies of the newspapers had been ordered. The Agatha Christie story was big news and, as each paper attempted to out-scoop the others, the reporters seemed to add their own spin to fragments of the truth, creating their own new truth in the process.

From the *Daily Express*, Agatha learned her car was unscathed by its push down the hill toward the chalk pits. "The side doors were shut and the side screens were up in their places. The spare tin of petrol carried on the side step was knocked off by the collision with the bush and was lying on the grass," according to the newspaper's special correspondent at the scene. The paper quoted a Mr. Luford, who, it suggested, ran the tea shop at the top of the hill, only to later update his name correctly to Alfred Luland. "The car was not damaged," he said, "for when, under the direction of the police, we pulled it to the road, it started up easily and pulled away under its own power."[ii]

The *Westminster Gazette* ran one of Agatha's favorite photos, picturing her smiling at her desk, wearing a dress she had purchased on the Expedition tour. According to the *Gazette*, Archie was totally unable to explain his wife's actions, offering only the possibility that she "had a nervous breakdown and [was] suffering from loss of memory."[iii] *Nice touch*, she thought, and made a mental note to remember that.

On the photo page of the *Daily News* was a rather large picture of Agatha standing in front of the mantelpiece at Styles that showcased her collection of African art brought back from her trip to Cape Town.[iv] She had liked that photo as well. Carlo had seen to it that her favorite photos were included.

The *Daily Mail* had interviewed Edmund Cork. Efficient, calm Mr. Cork. He had reassured the press that there was nothing unusual about Agatha's behavior when they last met, the day before she disappeared. "Mrs. Christie seemed very cheerful when we saw her on Thursday," Cork said. "There was nothing peculiar in her manner or in the nature of her visit. She was engaged in writing a new novel entitled *The Mystery of the Blue Train,* which was about half completed."[v]

"Good morning, Mrs. Neele," Mrs. Taylor called out from behind the front desk as she caught herself staring at the newspapers. *Must be careful,* Agatha reminded herself, and smiled at the hotel manager before nodding and continuing out the door.

She liked being Mrs. Teresa Neele, she decided. Liked how carefree the woman was. She was pretty, too, wearing all the colors that Agatha would never have dared to try. It was for that very reason that Teresa selected a scarlet shawl, embroidered in deep blue and mauve. A perfect touch for dinner, she decided, thinking that perhaps tonight Archie would arrive. She would be ready for her husband.

But once again, Archie Christie did not arrive, and in the evening papers there was still no mention of the letter she had written to his brother, Campbell. This was *not* the way her story had been plotted, she reminded herself, catching her lips wondering out loud, "What had happened to the missing note?"

The mystery of her letter to Campbell was solved the following morning when the same array of newspapers plus the addition of *News of the World* heralded the discovery of a new letter from the "Missing Novelist." The *Daily News* labeled the find "dramatic," explaining that Agatha's brother-in-law had received the letter from her days before, on Sunday, but thought nothing of it since he had not heard that she was missing until reading about it in the newspapers on Tuesday.

Apparently Woolrich was the one spot in all of England not buzzing with the story, Agatha thought, irritated that Archie had not been in touch with his brother. At least, she reasoned, the contents of the note were partially revealed. The essential fact that she had gone to Yorkshire was stated specifically enough. Surely *now* they would discover her, Agatha thought, and prepared yet again for dinner and an evening of the Happy Hydro Boys of the Harry Codd Dance Band.

It was only as she was preparing for dinner that Agatha stopped to read the *Times*. The Surrey police had reported that, after contacting "certain centres" in Yorkshire, they were satisfied that Mrs. Christie was nowhere in the county and were preparing to dredge the Silent Pool for her missing body. *This is* not *going well*, Agatha thought, questioning how *any* crime ever got solved these days.

This time, not even the reporters were digging deep enough. According to the *Daily Chronicle*, "There was a suggestion that the place in Yorkshire that Mrs. Christie would most likely visit was Harrogate, but a *Daily Chronicle* representative visited all the big hotels there late last night without any trace of the missing woman."[vi] *I'm completely invisible*, Agatha thought, and, as she wrapped the scarlet shawl around her shoulders, made it a point to change that perception immediately.

That night at dinner, Teresa Neele made what was something of a grand entrance into the dining room, her red shawl turning appreciative heads among the men. Almost immediately, Mr. Alexander Pettelson arrived at her table and asked if she would join him in a waltz. Mr. Pettelson was already somewhat familiar to Teresa from his performance the previous evening at dinner, where he had sung a bit of Gilbert and Sullivan—quite well, actually.

Rising from her seat, she extended her hand in acceptance and felt the eyes of diners around the room following them as they glided effortlessly across the dance floor. Pettelson was Russian, he said, by way of introduction, and had always wanted to be a performer. She told him that he was an excellent dancer, and he smiled his acknowledgment without any sign of conceit. He had heard it before and knew it was true. Unlike Archie, the way he held her—secure and in charge—made her into a better dancer as well. There was light applause when they finished their dance, and Teresa found herself blushing despite knowing full well that they weren't clapping for her.

By Thursday, the newspapers had enlarged their scope of reporting on her case, much to Agatha's continued embarrassment. Instead of sending Archie to her side, there was now speculation in the *Daily Mail* that she was carrying a revolver, presumably to kill herself. Deputy Chief Constable William Kenward, in charge of the investigation, proposed a new and elaborate theory of her disappearance that included her wandering the downs in a daze, despite the reality of the freezing weather during the six days she had been missing.[vii]

Ignoring Agatha's instructions in her letter to Campbell, Kenward recruited three hundred additional police to do a "mass search of the Newlands Corner and Albury Downs area" where he insisted she would still be found.[viii] From the bathroom where she was cleaning the floor, Agatha's chambermaid Rosie heard her exclaim, "Yorkshire, you idiot!" without explanation.

In the *Daily Mail* there was a picture of Rosalind being walked to school by a smiling Carlo Fisher.[ix] They looked happy in a natural way; not those forced grins frozen in time by people who were trying too hard to show their lack of concern. She missed Rosalind, and oh, how she missed Carlo; but most of all, she missed Archie.

Teresa had made friends with a guest named Mrs. Robson, a ravenous reader, and together they went shopping for books, strolling into the W. H. Smith store just as it received its weekly shipment of new novels. Teresa had finished reading Douglas Timins's *The Phantom Train* and had a list of other mysteries she hoped to find. Mrs. Robson suggested an Agatha Christie, from a newly created window display featuring a large photograph of the missing novelist.

From the other side of the store, Teresa watched as shoppers picked up her books. She longed to return to London, to step back into her life, sit back down at her portable Corona and return to writing. It had been months since she had written a full sentence that was worth keeping. In another second, the daydream ended as suddenly as it had started, and Teresa headed back onto the street, clutching a copy of Patrick Wynnton's *Way of Escape* to her side.

Before returning to the Harrogate Hydro, Teresa went to the post office to place an advertisement in the *Times*. It was a cryptic four-liner: *Friends and Relatives of Teresa Neele, late of South Africa, please communicate. Write Box R 702, The Times. EC 4.* She asked that the ad run on Saturday.

That night at dinner, she made herself as visible as possible. Defying any suggestion that she was shy about performing in front of strangers, Teresa Neele played the piano with the Harry Codd Dance Band and accompanied Miss Corbett, who did a poignant rendition of "It Had to Be You." As Teresa left the ballroom, she realized that she was crying.

When Agatha Christie awoke on Friday morning from what even she had to admit was a deep, relaxing sleep, she walked to the window of her room and looked out upon the long curving drive of the Harrogate Hydro. It was winter now, but she imagined the gardens in spring, with wild roses and heather, some forsythia perhaps. As she wiped condensation from the window with her finger, she found herself smiling. It had been a long while since a smile moved from mind to lips instinctively, but there it was. More amazing, perhaps, was that it did not leave, for Agatha Christie realized in that moment that she was alone and she was fine.

The man around whom she had built her world had not come to rescue her. Her hero and flyer and husband and father was shut up in their home in Sunningdale, uncertain and afraid. The newspaper reports were replete with his statements questioning her sanity and suggesting that his own distress was caused chiefly by the intrusion of the press.

The news this day reported the first gossip: The Christies may have had a quarrel. The hints were becoming stronger that there was another woman. The *Westminster Gazette* headlined: "Mrs. Christie's Fate: Police No Longer Expect to Find Her Alive."[x] Perhaps, it was suggested, Archie knew more than he was saying. It was just speculation now, but how long before the reporters discovered it was true?

"It is absolutely untrue to suggest there was anything in the nature of a row or tiff between my wife and myself on Friday morning," Archie lied during an interview with the *Daily Mail*. "She knew I was going away for the weekend; she knew who were going to be the members of the little party at the house at which I was going to stay. And neither then nor at any time did she raise the slightest objection. I strongly deprecate introducing any tittle-tattle into this matter," he said.[xi] *I'm sure you do, Archie*, Agatha thought. *I'm sure you do.*

If it were Archie who was missing, Agatha could not imagine sitting inside a house doing little more than waiting for police updates. Agatha, for all her shyness and fear of confrontation, would have been leading the hunt. She certainly would have been up in Yorkshire, banging on doors, searching hotels, stopping at nothing to uncover the truth. It was difficult to watch her husband do nothing now but deflect suspicion away from himself. Fortunately, it also shone the spotlight on exactly who he was.

There was madness going on in Newlands Corner, and it *was* madness, nothing less. But while the police were doing their rattled best to make sense of her disappearance, her husband was playing cover-up to protect Miss Nancy Neele. Agatha knew that now, and it made her stronger.

It was therefore a different Teresa Neele who strode into the lobby of the Harrogate Hydropathic Hotel that day. Mrs. Taylor looked up from behind the front desk and commented on it immediately, suggesting it was the hotel's therapeutics that had caused such a miraculous lift in Teresa's step.

She left the hotel that day and took the train to Leeds. It was her first trip outside of Harrogate, and she loved the freedom she felt. No one staring, no one suspecting, just a lone woman having a free day window-shopping in a new town. She particularly liked the Victoria Quarter with its dramatic architecture: vaulted arched ceilings, lavish use of marble and skylights, and ornate moldings and carved balustrades.

Still, it was nice to return to Harrogate, the familiar lobby, the smiling faces, even though more and more guests were leaving as the Christmas holiday approached. She did not come down for dinner that evening, but on the following night joined Mr. Pettelson onstage, where she accompanied him on the piano as he sang in a voice that continued to surprise her with his professional tone and enchanting phrasing.

The air had warmed up considerably on Sunday morning, and Agatha spent much of it outside, walking the streets of Harrogate, studying the buildings and trying to avoid the newspapers. The front pages were filled with pictures of the thousands of people who had responded to Deputy Chief Constable Kenward's call to form a volunteer search party to comb every inch of the downs. Linked hand in hand, they crossed the fields and trod the brush, searching for any clue that might lead them to the missing mystery writer.

Sunday night the band was off, but a pianist was performing and the gentle arpeggios of the evening fit well with Agatha's relaxed mood. She triumphed over the *Times* crossword puzzle, accepted Mr. Pettelson's invitation for coffee and a game of billiards, and went to bed at about eleven thirty, totally unaware that her holiday was nearly over and that the all-too-real world of Agatha Christie was about to reemerge.

Robert Leeming, Bob to his friends, knew a few things about human nature. As a part-time saxophonist with the Happy Hydro Boys, he had watched guests arrive and depart over the years, most receiving benefit from the resort's legendary healing waters. But few were as transformed as Teresa Neele. He noticed her the first night as she sat half-hidden in a corner of the ballroom, pressed so far into a palm as to be part of the foliage. Her stockings were muddied, her hair matted, and her dress wore the wrinkles that travel brings.

Over the past week that she had been in residence at the Harrogate Hydropathic, he observed a caterpillar morph into a butterfly, as this attractive middle-aged woman shed years from her looks, along with the pain of unspoken hardship. Her silence was slowly replaced with animated conversation as her shyness gave way to socializing. Unlike all the other hotel habitués, Bob Leeming noticed one other thing as well: Teresa Neele bore an uncanny resemblance to the missing novelist, Mrs. Agatha Christie.

He talked this over with Rosie Asher, the chambermaid in room 105, who had come to the same conclusion but refused to speak out about her suspicions for fear that it might cost her her job. Harrogate was, after all, an exclusive resort whose famous guests were assured of their privacy. "It was more than my job was worth to get involved," Rosie said years later, after her retirement.[xii] Leeming, who was employed by Harry Codd, not the hotel, had no such fear and shared his observation with part-time drummer Bob Tappin, who agreed that the likeness was extraordinary. And there was the £100 reward offered by the *Daily Mail* to consider. Perhaps they would have a claim on it, Tappin suggested.

Over Sunday supper, the two Bobs and their wives, Nora and Barbara, discussed taking their suspicions to the police, with Nora threatening to go herself if the men failed to act. Their husbands, thus encouraged, went to speak with the West Riding Police, who assured the pair that they would discreetly verify the bandsmen's suspicions the following day.

The sergeant sent to the Hydro to investigate had little trouble locating Teresa Neele, for when he arrived at the hotel, she was in the lobby saying good-bye to several guests who were departing to spend Christmas with relatives in Sussex. Armed with a picture from her missing person's report rather than grainy newspaper photos, he made what he considered to be positive identification of the subject and reported back to his superior, Superintendent Gilbert McDowall from the Claro Division.

McDowall immediately contacted Deputy Chief Constable William Kenward in Surrey, who dismissed his contention with barely disguised irritation, chalking up the coincidence to a look-alike. This was, Kenward felt, *his* case, and *he* would be the one to solve it when he located Agatha's body on the North Downs.

At that very moment, a very much alive Agatha was looking particularly fresh in a youthful, pale yellow ensemble that complimented her eyes. She had undergone an "electro therapy" session in the Hydro's spa and felt a renewed energy that she credited totally to her treatment. After lunch, she walked briskly on her now familiar route downtown, stopping to buy some stationery and a piece of sheet music, "Angels Guard Thee," which Mr. Pettelson had sung in the ballroom several evenings earlier. She knew it would make an appreciated gift and signed it on the cover "Teresa Neele."

According to Monday's *Daily News* headline "Mrs. Christie Hiding in Male Attire," she was supposed to be living in London disguised as a man. "Mr. Christie has made a prolonged investigation of his own wardrobe to ascertain if any garments are missing," the reporter suggested. [xiii] A disgusting thought to Agatha, who adored being feminine and could not imagine giving up her dresses and fashionable hats. And as if to prove the point, she dressed particularly alluringly that night at dinner, a detail not missed by Mr. Pettelson, who thanked her for his sheet music by kissing her hand.

On Tuesday morning, Superintendent Gilbert McDowall again called his Surrey counterpart, this time insisting that someone in the Christie household be informed about the discovery of the look-alike woman in Harrogate. With no small degree of hesitation, Deputy Chief Constable Kenward telephoned Carlo Fisher at Styles and asked if she might travel to Harrogate to provide positive identification of this woman. Carlo was unable to travel since she was still responsible for Rosalind's care and was scheduled to pick up the child from school that afternoon. Carlo, in turn, telephoned Archie, who agreed to make the trip on the train leaving King's Cross station at 1:40 that afternoon.

Tipped to Archie's arrival in Harrogate, the press converged on the city, determined to land an exclusive interview with Agatha. Activity at the Hydro was kept to a minimum to eliminate any possibility that Teresa Neele would be embarrassed should she prove to be an innocent victim.

As Agatha herself had done the previous Saturday, Archie arrived just after the sun had set, dusk bathing the large, formal gardens of the elegant Hydro in tones of winter blue and mauve. Met by Superintendent McDowall, Archie entered the hotel's stylish lobby and was taken into the manager's office, where he was advised of Mrs. Neele's activities. Upon hearing the name, Archie's mouth went dry as every nerve ending reacted in defense. Informed that the woman was upstairs changing for dinner, Archie was shown to a seat alone in a far corner, and used an open newspaper to partially hide his face.

There was the slightest rustle as a tall, spirited redhead descended the stairs from an upper floor. Dressed in a satin evening gown of pale salmon georgette, a delicate silk shawl covering exposed shoulders against the night air, the woman was neither camouflaged nor shy as she walked with the refined grace of a debutante. Looking as lovely as he had ever seen her, Agatha Christie glanced across the lobby and stared directly at her husband.

As he rose to greet her, Archie realized that while the face was that of his wife, this woman was not the Agatha he remembered. She was confident and self-assured in a way that startled him. He found his palms sweating as she slowly walked directly to him and introduced herself with a handshake.

"Hello," she said. "My name is Neele. Mrs. Teresa Neele."

Archie hardly had a chance to respond, for no sooner had they been seated than Mr. Pettelson rushed to greet Teresa. For his effort, Mr. Pettelson received a wave of dismissal and an apology that she could not speak. "My brother has arrived unexpectedly," she said.

Pettelson, surprised by the rebuff, looked back over his shoulder at the man sitting next to her. "It seemed at the time strange to me for a brother to be as despondent as he was."

In minutes, Agatha was moved from the lobby into the dining room, where she and Archie remained in quiet conversation, left alone for nearly two hours, at which point she returned to her room alone. Archie had booked his own accommodations in the hotel and, before going to his own suite, turned to face the press.

He looked like a man defeated. Gone was the happy expression that the reporters or the police had expected. "There is no doubt at all that she is my wife. It appears to me to be a clear case of loss of memory and loss of identification.

"I hope to be able to take her away at once," he continued, "to London tomorrow so that I may have the best advice as to her condition. It is, of course, a very sad business for me. I am glad to have found her, even though she does not know me. It has at least set at rest the horrible doubts of the last few days." Archie could not have been more wrong.

The following morning while press, police, and curiosity seekers surrounded the normally staid grounds of the Harrogate Hydropathic Hotel, Agatha's sister, Madge, arrived on the arm of her husband, Jimmy. They immediately disappeared upstairs, Madge into Agatha's room, Jimmy into Archie's.

At 9:15 a.m., two hotel employees dressed to resemble the Christies, collars pulled high to hide their faces, rushed through the lobby of the Hydro and out into a waiting Daimler Laundelette, the press frantically following in pursuit. Only then did the Christies and the Wattses emerge down the stairs and proceed out a side door, jumping into a waiting cab. Only a single photo was taken of the departure by a photographer from the *Daily Mail* who had been left behind in the melee.

Inside the car, Agatha was poised and elegant, perfectly made-up and impeccable in a two-piece salmon suit with a full-cut coat trimmed at the collar, cuffs, and hem with mink. Her double strand of pearls and a matching black cloche hat completed an outfit that had obviously been coordinated for this photo opportunity. There would be no thought of Nancy Neele this day, not if Agatha Christie could prevent it.

When the quartet arrived at Harrogate station, there was pandemonium as reporters and onlookers alike jockeyed for a glimpse of the celebrated writer. The station platform had been officially closed to visitors, but was soon overrun in any case. Entering the platform from a delivery entrance, Agatha and Madge rushed onto the train and into a compartment marked "Mr. Parker's Party,"[7] while Jimmy and Archie stood at the outside door until the locomotive's whistle sounded.

The train was bound for King's Cross, which was the likely route into London. When the railroad cars reached Leeds station, however, the Christies and the Wattses made a sudden switch and boarded a train headed to Manchester. The chaos that resulted is captured in history by photographs taken of Agatha and Madge attempting to make their way through the press, their determined looks no match for the onslaught of this invasion of their privacy.

By the time the family reached Manchester's Victoria Station, the news of their destination had spread across England, and the police were ill-prepared to hold back the sudden influx of spectators and hastily commissioned local press. Just before the train pulled into the station, the Wattses' impeccable two-toned Wolseley limousine pulled to the side entrance and was waiting to escort the family back to Abney Hall.

Pictures taken of Agatha as she departed the station in Manchester show a remarkably happy woman. Enough time had apparently passed that the once press-shy writer had relaxed enough to enjoy the adulation and concern that was pouring in from across the country, and indeed from much of the world.

Once the family entered Abney Hall, the gates were chained and the curtains were drawn. Only the occasional glimpse of a curious Agatha glancing out was provided to the assembled throng of reporters. No one left the house that evening or the following day, although several visitors were admitted during the afternoon of December 16. Following that

[7] Mr. Parker was the stationmaster at Harrogate.

visit, an official statement was released and signed by two doctors: Ronald Core, credited with being a "mental specialist" and a lecturer in neurology at Manchester University, and Henry Wilson, M.R.C.S., the Wattses' family physician.

"After a careful examination of Mrs. Agatha Christie this afternoon, we have formed the opinion that she is suffering from an unquestionably genuine loss of memory, and that for her future welfare, she should be spared all anxiety and excitement." The doctors refused to answer any questions relating to their diagnosis.

Archie Christie, now seemingly recovered from his bout with nervous exhaustion, turned hostile to the press when asked if he intended to pay the costs of the extended police search for his wife. "Why should I?" he asked. "I have seen a statement that it is only a matter of a few teas for constables. In any case, I didn't ask them to make the search; and I pay rates and taxes, like everyone else, for the upkeep of the police.... I never wanted them to search for my wife on so big a scale. I had no doubt at all that she was suffering from loss of memory."[xiv]

The use of the name Neele had not escaped press scrutiny, and when questioned at her home, Rheola in Croxley Green, Nancy's mother was clearly distressed. "The fact is both I and my husband know Colonel Christie and his wife. I have known them for some time indeed," she said. "My daughter Nancy spent a recent weekend at Godalming with Mr. and Mrs. James. Colonel Christie was there, as he is also a friend of the James family.[xv]

"It is most unpleasant, both for my daughter and for all of us in the family, to have her name dragged through the mud; and, furthermore, it is quite unnecessary. My daughter has been a friend of both Colonel and Mrs. Christie for some time, but she has never been especially friendly with the Colonel. It was pure chance and misfortune that she should have been a member of Mrs. James' house party during the weekend Mrs. Christie disappeared. It might have been any other girl."[xvi] Shortly after this statement was made, Nancy Neele was sent off by her parents on an around-the-world cruise.

Archie Christie left Abney Hall on December 17 with his daughter, Rosalind, returning only on Christmas day and then for just a few hours. Carlo Fisher continued to act as Rosalind's nanny during the period that the house was listed for sale, while Rosalind continued to go to school in the area.

Eventually, Rosalind and Carlo moved with Agatha to a flat in Chelsea, while Archie remained alone in Styles, the "unlucky house's" reputation still intact. Agatha saw her husband only once in 1927, for a brief meeting. And while there has been speculation that she still carried a place in her heart for the brave flyer with the movie-star looks, it was more sentiment than fact, for she knew quite well who this man was and what he would never be capable of providing to her. She was forever a romantic; she was not, however, a fool.

Agatha filed for divorce from Archie Christie on April 20, 1928, without ever mentioning the name Nancy Neele. The court was offered a fictitious account of adultery that supposedly occurred at the Grosvenor Hotel. The divorce became final six months later. In another two weeks, Archie Christie married Nancy Neele. The two remained happily together for the remainder of their lives.

SIX

Finding Agatha

For it is not an open enemy that has
done me this dishonor....
But it was even thou, my companion: my guide,
and mine own familiar friend.

Psalm 55:12, 14

FEBRUARY 11, 1927. THE CANARY ISLANDS SIT OFF THE coast of Morocco, proud tropical ink blots in the Atlantic, where bananas and sunshine are the most publicized commodities, smiles from the locals ranking a close second. It was to this group of Spanish islands that Agatha Christie fled in early 1927 to find peace and regain her reason.

The previous month, *The Big Four* had been released as Agatha's eighth book, timed to capitalize on the publicity generated by the author's disappearance and subsequent discovery. Although presented as a new work, it was a piecemeal assembly of four short stories previously published in *The Sketch*, a pastiche suggested by Campbell Christie to provide his sister-in-law additional time to complete her next novel. Critics were not kind, lambasting the collection with scathing assessments like the one in the *Saturday Review*: "As a detective story, *The Big Four* is a failure."[i] Fortunately, fans of her previous books flocked to her newest one in record numbers, ignoring the reviewers' suggestion that it was substandard while continuing to discuss her erratic behavior and the rather feeble excuse she had suggested for it.

Leaving England had a rehabilitating effect on Agatha, who sat in a hotel garden in La Orotava on the edge of Tenerife. The location was idyllic, made more so by the company of Rosalind and Carlo. Once away from England, they were free of the pressures of publicity and prying eyes. Unfortunately, they were replaced by another kind of pressure—the contractual demand to create a new book, whether she was in the mood or not. "That was the moment I changed from an amateur to a professional," Agatha wrote in her autobiography. "I assumed the burden of a profession, which is to write even when you don't want to, don't much like what you are writing, and aren't writing particularly well."[ii]

When an author reaches that particular moment in the writing process where she *must* produce, *everything* becomes a distraction. In Agatha's case, that included her daughter, who was left to entertain herself while Agatha attempted to find the words to dictate to Carlo. "Rosalind's eye upon me had the effect of a Medusa," she remembered. "I faltered, stammered, hesitated and repeated myself. Really, how that wretched book came to be written I don't know."[iii] The "wretched book" in question was *Mystery on the Blue Train.*

Rosalind, not yet eight, was bored and impatient for attention, returning every ten minutes to reassert her presence. "Look here, Rosalind," Agatha told her, "You must *not* interrupt. I've got some work to do," she instructed, struggling to finish each and every sentence.[iv]

Considering that Agatha had begun working on the book before her mother's death, had attempted to continue during her depression, and endured what some considered to be a nervous breakdown only months before, it was hardly surprising that the process of creating a light, entertaining mystery novel was a difficult one. In the end, Agatha would label *Mystery of the Blue Train* as the one book she always "hated," presumably more out of memory of the events of her life at the time than the actual content.

When the book was published in March 1928, it received mild critical acclaim: often-harsh reviewer Will Cuppy, writing "Books" in the *New York Herald Tribune,* said, "Here is none of your fly-by-night dreadfuls, but a truly honorable thriller in the right classic tradition, warranted to restore the jaded reader's faith in clews."[v] Harkening to the dark period in her life during which Agatha found many of her friends to be fair-weather, she dedicated the book to "Two Distinguished Members of the O.F.D.—Carlotta and Peter."

The O.F.D. was her fictitious Order of the Faithful Dogs, membership in which was determined by the ability to remain loyal to Agatha during her bleakest hour. In this case, Carlotta referred to Carlo Fisher and Peter her wirehaired terrier. Those friends not in the O.F.D. were in the Order of the Rats, Third Class—a group that was considerably larger.

That year, 1928, was also the year that the first two films based on Agatha's works were produced, both silent movies. The first effort was the hour-long British film *The Passing of Mr. Quinn* [sic] (based on the short story "The Passing of Mr. Quin," published in *Grand Magazine* in 1924). The second film was the seventy-six-minute German film *Die Abenteurer G.m.b.H.* (based on "The Secret Adversary"). She ignored them both, her mind obviously on other things.

As the time approached to proceed to court with her divorce from Archie, Agatha created a smoke screen of activity that kept her mind occupied with writing. She did it in such a subtle way that no one could tell that anything was wrong, that her every subconscious thought was counting the days until she no longer could officially call herself Mrs. Agatha Christie. She had loved being married. Now, she would have to learn to love being single again.

For several months she devoted herself to the legitimate theater. *Alibi,* a play based on her book *The Mystery of Roger Ackroyd*, had been written by dramatist Michael Morton, and was in rehearsals for a May opening in London's West End at the Prince of Wales Theater. Charles Laughton was cast as Hercule Poirot, much to the horror of Agatha, who thought him a bit avoirdupois for the role of her dapper detective.

She was, however, attracted to the glamour of the stage and threw herself with enthusiasm into discussions with Morton about the adaptation of the play. At that point, Morton was attempting to chop years off Poirot's age, turning him into a young Casanova of sorts, while changing his nationality from Belgian to French.

Agatha attended many rehearsals of the play, sometimes sitting backstage with Laughton and sharing ice-cream sodas. It was over one such break that Laughton revealed the secret behind his colorfully difficult reputation. "It's a good thing to pretend to have a temperament, even if you haven't," he said. "I find it very helpful. People will say, 'Let's don't do anything to annoy *him*. You know how he throws temperaments.'"[vi]

At this same time, Agatha's agent Edmund Cork loaded her schedule with new writing projects, including a single book contract with Williams Collins & Sons. This deal launched a new nom de plume for Agatha: Mary Westmacott. Mary was an entirely new persona—a lovely, young woman writer of passionate and tragic romances. The first novel she completed was titled *Giant's Bread* and concerned love at first sight and a tragic miscommunication. Although the book would not be published until 1930, the writing of it occupied Agatha for much of 1928 and drew on feelings so personal that Agatha Christie could never have come close to writing those words.

Even as "Mary" was writing romance novels, Agatha continued to turn out mysteries—many of them as short stories for £60 a piece, to produce instant cash, which was in desperately short supply. Archie was supplying no alimony or child support for his daughter. In addition, she produced a sequel to her book *The Secret of Chimneys,* titled *The Seven Dials Mystery*—all this during an eight-month period. It was an incredible output of storytelling that Agatha would later pretend not to remember as anything unusual. What she would *never* forget, however, was her first trip on the Compagnie Internationale des Wagons-Lit's Orient Express near the end of the year. It was an event of such impact that it would change her career and her life forever.

Agatha said she had always had a love for trains, but in reality had taken very few trips on them before 1928, and most of those were local journeys—a far different creature from the sophisticated elegance of international travel. What was closer to the truth was that she had *seen* the trains, moving in and out of various stations, and fantasized about stepping aboard and chugging away to destinations unknown.

Having placed nine-year-old Rosalind in a private school in Bexhill-by-Sea known as Caledonia—one which the child had selected herself, since, as Agatha explained, "Rosalind was a person of the utmost good sense,"[vii] Agatha felt comfortable taking a vacation for a few months—until the

Christmas school break. Originally, she thought of following the sun to the West Indies and Jamaica and contacted the Thomas Cook Agency, who handled all her travel arrangements.

A few days prior to departure, however, she attended a dinner party and happened to be seated next to a naval officer named Howe and his wife. The Commodore had just returned from an extended trip to Baghdad, then considered one of the most exotic tourist destinations, and proceeded to regale Agatha with stories of how fabulous the region was.

"You must go to Mosul—Basra you must visit—and you certainly ought to go to Ur," the Commodore insisted.[viii] Basra was then known as the "Venice of the Middle East," and one of the loveliest of seaside ports, legendary home to Sinbad the Sailor, and a place Agatha had always dreamed of visiting. It took only the Commodore's mentioning of Basra along with the legendary train, the Orient Express that could provide direct transportation, and Agatha Christie was convinced. Had she been able to leave the table and call Thomas Cook at that moment, she would have. As it happened, she made the telephone call the next morning.

In less than ten minutes Agatha Christie, thirty-eight years old, newly divorced yet still incredibly naïve, made the decision to travel across the globe on her own. The courage such a move must have taken cannot be dismissed. It was as exciting as it was dangerous, but most of all, it was spontaneous. This was not the young woman who had been guided for fourteen years by her cautious husband, a woman who worried about money and suffered from acute shyness. This was a new person: an explorer intent on living *her* life and discovering who *she* was in the process.

Four days later, she bid good-bye to her sister and Carlo, took a forty-five-minute ferry ride from Dover to Calais, and set foot onto the marvel known as the Simplon Orient Express.

Agatha had booked herself in a second-class cabin, lush with inlaid wood and mother-of-pearl paneling, with drop-down sleeping berths for two. The woman sharing the space was a seasoned traveler who proceeded to insist on attempting to plan Agatha's itinerary, fortunately with little success, for this was an adventure, not a tour, and it was the untraveled road that Agatha now needed to explore. The train took her through Trieste, Yugoslavia, and the Balkans, and into a life that she hadn't known existed hours before. "Going through mountain gorges, watching ox carts and picturesque wagons, studying groups of people on the station platform, getting out occasionally at places like Nish and Belgrade and seeing the large engines changed and new monsters coming on with entirely different scripts and signs."[ix]

It was exciting and new and *wonderful,* made all the more special because, just as she thought it could get no better, Agatha realized that had Archie been along, she would have missed it all. He would have insisted on pulling the blinds closed, covered his nose against the smells, and been in bed every evening at ten thirty, as he was nearly every night during their marriage.

She traveled through Stamboul (the old name for Istanbul), stopping at the Tokatlian Hotel, where she was taken to dinner by a Dutch engineer she had met on the train. She then crossed the Bosphorus to arrive at Haidar Pasha Station with its chaotic customs hall, before continuing on from Europe into Asia, following the Sea of Marmara, where she imagined the Argonauts of Greek mythology struggling against the savage storms that drove them off course across Propontis, Marmara's former name.

As they moved into Asia, the food on the train changed from refined European cuisine to a more unpalatable mix: "fuller of hot, greasy, tasteless morsels as we went further east."[x] She stopped to view the Cilician Gates ("a moment of incredible beauty"), stayed in Damascus, Syria, for three days at the Orient Palace Hotel ("large marble glittering halls"), and eventually took a seat on a crowded bus to travel to Baghdad, only to encounter the very same woman with whom she shared her initial second-class cabin in Calais.

After a two-day trip across barren desert, she arrived at a camp in Ar Rutbah, a smugglers' town just across the border in Iraq, where they slept on primitive beds, five to a room. At dawn, they ate canned sausages cooked over a Primus stove and washed the meal down with strong black tea. It was *wonderful.* "This is what I longed for," she later wrote. "This was getting away from everything—with the pure invigorating morning air, the silence, the absence even of birds, the sand that ran through one's fingers, the rising sun, and the taste of sausages and tea."[xi]

Once in Baghdad, Agatha found touches of England everywhere. Here she had rediscovered civilization and luxury, but having savored adventure, she no longer found comfort in rooms and restaurants that reminded her of home. There were frontiers to conquer, and she did not intend to miss a single piece of it.

She requested and was granted access to Ur (now called Tell el-Mukayyar), several hundred miles south of Baghdad and the site of the temple of Nanna. It was at Ur that famed British archaeologist Dr. Leonard Woolley had been excavating for several years, unearthing treasures and transporting them back to the British Museum in London.

Known in the Bible as Ur of the Chaldees, the once great city existed 6,500 years ago, between the Tigris and Euphrates rivers, and is thought to be the home of Abraham. What Woolley uncovered under mounds of sand and rubble were treasures of gold, silver, bronze, and precious stones.

Guests at archaeological digs are irritations that are tolerated at best. When Agatha Christie arrived, however, she was welcomed like a celebrity, thanks to the eccentric Mrs. Katharine Woolley, who had recently enjoyed reading *The Murder of Roger Ackroyd.*

Agatha was given a personal tour of the dig by Dr. Woolley himself, a rare honor, and taken under the wing of Katharine, who would prove to be a good friend. But aside from VIP treatment, Agatha knew the real star here was the ancient kingdom of Ur itself. She was mesmerized by its ever-shifting beauty "in the evenings, the ziggurat standing up, faintly shadowed, and the wide sea of sand with its lovely pale colors of apricot, rose, blue and mauve."[xii] It was the first time she had encountered "true mystery." Not the sort she wrote about, but the type that had been created thousands of years earlier by people who had left reminders of their existence, waiting to be uncovered, one grain of sand at a time. The dust, the hot arid wind, the smell of camels and exotic foods, all blended into a potpourri of excitement and amazement. This made her wonder if she should have been an archaeologist herself, so intense was her attraction to this place and these people.

Agatha stayed a few extra days in Ur, settling in at a hotel on the river Tigris, watching the endless parade of junks and boats. There she met Maurice Vickers, a man who was only passing through her life, but who influenced her profoundly. Maurice, an Anglo-Indian student of life, introduced Agatha to a book by J. W. Dunne titled *Experiment in Time,* in which he offers the theory that the past, present, and future coexist together. As Agatha remembered it, the book provided a global shift in her perception of her own importance in the grand scheme of things. As a girl she felt cherished as the most important human on earth, but now she broke through to a wider view of life, seeing that she was a minuscule fragment of a larger plan.

"I did feel from that moment onwards a great sensation of comfort and a truer knowledge of serenity than I had ever obtained before," she said.[xiii]

Returning to England for the annual Christmas celebration at Abney Hall, Agatha entered 1929 well financed and flush with work completed: books to be published throughout the year, keeping her name constantly in front of the reading public. Edmund Cork had negotiated a new contract for Agatha at Williams Collins & Sons that guaranteed her £750 per book for her next six novels with a royalty of twenty percent on all sales for the first 8,000 copies. In America, she was now being paid $2,500, with royalties of fifteen percent on the first 25,000 copies, increasing to twenty percent thereafter.

With the publication of *The Seven Dials Mystery* in January 1929, Agatha found herself back in a favored position among the book critics, who were happy to see her returning to form and the familiar setting of the rambling Berkshire estate of Chimneys. The *Outlook* called *Seven Dials* "an amusing, exciting, well-written story,"[xiv] while the *New York Herald Tribune* said, "This is her gayest thriller and mustn't be missed."[xv]

Never one to pay particular attention to reviews, whether good or bad, Agatha was reassured by these, her first notices post-divorce. Soon after, she also used some of her cash to purchase a mews house at 22 Cresswell Place in Chelsea, and proceeded to decorate the place with her usual attention to detail. With the help of a contractor referred to her by friend Nan Kon (now on her second husband), Agatha knocked down walls and rearranged the downstairs rooms, incorporating an area that had previously housed a stable. Soon the horse stalls were replaced with a generous sitting room wallpapered with a large herbaceous border, giving the entire space the look of a country garden. The remainder of the lower level was transformed into a maid's room and a garage for her Morris Cowley. At the top of a steep narrow stairs were a bedroom, a bath with dolphins painted on the tiles, a dining room (and sometime second bedroom), and a minuscule kitchen.

It was at 22 Cresswell Place that Agatha received her first official guests as a single woman: Dr. and Mrs. Woolley stayed in the mews house in May for three weeks, filling the rooms with flowers and luxuriating in Agatha's hospitality. It was during this visit that the Woolleys invited Agatha to return to their dig the following year at the end of their season in March, after which the three planned to travel and tour Syria and Greece together. Agatha was thrilled by the offer and accepted immediately, the taste of adventure still fresh and the desire to escape into the unknown stronger than ever.

From that moment through the following February, Agatha scheduled her work around her anticipated holiday. A collection of stories featuring Tommy and Tuppence had been assembled in a unique compilation, each tale written as a parody of a famous detective of the day and released as *Partners in Crime*—her eleventh book. Published in America in August 1929 and in October in England, *Partners in Crime* "may be taken as hilarious burlesque or parodies of current detective fiction," said the *New York Times*. "Or they may be taken as serious attempts on the part of the author to write stories in the manner of some of the masters of the art. Taken either way, they are distinctly worthwhile."[xvi]

Unimpressed with the adaptation of her work by Michael Morton in *The Alibi*, Agatha also attempted to write her first stage play—an original Hercule Poirot mystery titled *Black Coffee* that would go into rehearsals in the fall of 1930 with Francis L. Sullivan as a six-foot-two-inch Poirot. The play ran for several months, though it was never a financial success.

Agatha's pleasure in writing was on display with each chapter that found its way into print, and not even the unexpected death of her brother, Monty, caused her to lose her passion for work. Monty had only recently moved out of his cottage in Dartmoor. His housekeeper, Mrs. Taylor, who provided his care, had fallen ill herself from bronchitis and nearly died as a result. Anticipating that a warmer climate might help them both, Agatha and Madge moved the pair to a small pension in Marseilles. Unfortunately, the trip was too much for Mrs. Taylor, who developed pneumonia and died shortly after reaching the south of France.

Monty reacted to her death with his usual histrionics and refused to take his medication. Madge raced to his bedside, by which time he was hospitalized in Marseilles. In keeping with his ability to still exude charm when necessary, his ward nurse offered to take care of him in her own cottage, a proposal to which he immediately acceded. Soon after, Monty died of a cerebral hemorrhage while sipping espresso at a seaside café during a discourse on the absurdities of life.

The annual Christmas celebration at Abney Hall was dedicated to his memory. Although Monty had never attended one of the events, he was, even there, a legend. Soon afterward, a friend of Rosalind exposed the entire household to the measles, a disease Rosalind predictably contracted some ten days later. It was, however, Agatha who ended up in a nursing home, the result of an infection caused by her own vaccination, which she requested to have injected into her thigh rather than the arm because "vaccination marks look so dreadful in evening dress."[xvii]

Her weeklong recuperation certainly was speeded by the anticipation of her pending vacation, which began as soon as Rosalind was well enough to be deposited back into boarding school and the appropriate tickets booked by the Thomas Cook Agency. For the return trip to Ur, there was to be no Orient Express, since a speedier route via the Lloyd Triestino Lines boat to Beirut was now required to keep on schedule. Upon arrival in Beirut, however, a brutal sandstorm kept everyone inside their cabins for five days—the appearance of sunshine on day six was universally praised as a gift from God.

The Woolleys were appropriately apologetic at Mother Nature's reception of the celebrated authoress, as was Dr. Woolley's assistant Max Mallowan, whom Agatha described as "a thin, dark young man and very quiet—he seldom spoke."[xviii]

Max Edgar Lucien Mallowan was a twenty-five-year-old Oxford graduate who had been absent during Agatha's first visit to Ur, the victim of an appendicitis attack. He had, of course, heard of Agatha and her previous visit, though had never read any of her fiction.

When introduced to the writer, he found her "immediately a most agreeable person," and when Katharine Woolley instructed him to show Agatha around the sacred city of Najaf and the mosque of Kerbala, he thought the prospect "pleasing."[xix] Agatha, on the other hand, found the suggestion mortifying, presuming that a young student of archaeology would find little of interest in "a strange woman, a good many years older than him,"[xx] and attempted to make excuses.

"He was a grave-looking young man, and I felt slightly nervous of him," she wrote. "I worried whether I should offer some apology. I did essay some stumbling phrase to the effect that I had not myself suggested the tour, but Max was calm about it all."[xxi]

Max was calm because Max had little other choice. The rule of Katharine Woolley at Ur was akin to that of Cleopatra in Egypt, and as one of the others at the dig observed, "If Katharine has made up her mind, then that's settled, you see."[xxii] Agatha apparently did see, for she acquiesced and agreed to serve as VIP on a private tour that took her first to Nippur, a sacred city one hundred miles southeast of Baghdad. They made a strange couple, this pair, formally dressed as if to lunch at the Savoy—Max in his suit, tie, and fedora; Agatha in a billowy long-sleeve dress, gloves, scarf, and large-brimmed hat. Even in a climate where protection from the blistering sun required covering every inch of exposed skin with fabric, Max and Agatha stood out as layered to excess.

After a five-hour trip, they spent another four walking the stony ground of the Nippur excavations before arriving in Al Diwaniyah, eighty miles south of Baghdad, around seven p.m. Heavily cultivated and abundant with birdlife, Diwaniyah

was an oasis in an otherwise desolate area, and as Agatha sat
in evening dress being entertained by their hosts at dinner and
seated across from stoically silent missionaries, the oddity of
her circumstance inspired her imagination with fresh mystery
plots and suspense.

By five a.m. the following day, the pair was back in
their car, traveling to Najaf, the holiest of Shi'ite cities and a
place even then of political turmoil and extremists. This was
followed by a visit to the grand mosque of Kerbala, where the
pair spent the night sleeping on mats on the floor of the local
police station. Agatha's amusement and lack of complaint at
such rudimentary accommodations was Max's first clue that his
VIP was hardly typical of her celebrity rank. That assessment
was reinforced the following day when, while taking a detour
to visit Ukhaidar, site of a well-preserved palace, they came
upon a lake—a crystal blue pond, refreshingly cool in the heat
of the desert.

Given her fondness for bathing, Agatha suggested
wading in. The idea was met with mild amusement by her
cultivated tour guide, who moved his car and driver a polite
distance from the lake while Agatha changed into an
impromptu bathing suit that she described as a pink silk vest
and a double pair of knickers. Upon seeing her frolicking in
the water, Max stripped down to his own vest and shorts and
plunged in after her. If the twenty-minute swim were not
enough to convince Max Mallowan that Agatha Christie was a
very special woman, he received his second reminder when,
emerging from the lake, they found that their car had become
mired in the sand, requiring hours of digging to extricate
the vehicle.

"It was still ragingly hot. I lay down in the shelter of
the car, or what shelter there was on one side of it, and went to
sleep," Agatha later remembered. "Max told me afterward,
whether truthfully or not, that it was at that moment he decided
that I would make an excellent wife for him."[xxiii] At that point,
they had known each other six days.

Their eventual arrival in Baghdad having been
delayed by a full twenty-four hours, Agatha and Max found a
highly irritated Katharine Woolley, upset over the delay in her
travel plans. After a verbal skirmish and the concomitant

Agatha Christie, circa 1925, early in her mystery-writing career. Agatha Christie never imagined she would become the best-selling author of all time with over two billion books sold around the world.

Photo © Getty Images

THE DAILY NEWS, SATURDAY, DECEMBER 11,

HE

ORTS
ED.

IGN
RS.

espondent.

Friday.
hat in the
ome illegal
country to
ngs in the
al proceed-
urt, in any
come under
f England,
ncerned—a
e first time.
hrough the
ok, at the
u., of the
gulation of
d its third

MRS. CHRISTIE DISGUISED.

Mrs. Agatha Christie as she was last seen (centre), and (on left and right) how she may have disguised herself by altering the style of her hairdressing and by wearing glasses Col. Christie says his wife had stated that she could disappear at will if she liked, and, in view of the fact that she was a writer of detective stories, it would be very natural for her to adopt some form of disguise to carry out that idea.

DISAR
GE

"NOT

BRITISH
HOLD

From Our

The agenda
League of
finished, and
hoped, will b
sions regardin
man armame
however, that
necessary.
The British,
and Belgian F
morning, and
outstanding di
That, howev
the Conferenc
Paris having
conscientiously
had fulfilled h
tions and Ger

HANKOW | THE PHILLIPPS

On December 11, 1926, the *Daily News* reported on how Agatha Christie may have disguised herself after her disappearance. Her mysterious eleven-day disappearance, which initiated a massive manhunt, has never been fully explained. Photo © Getty Images

Agatha Christie and her second husband Max Mallowan, a renowned archaeologist, posed for the camera on the grounds of Greenway House, their home in Devonshire. Photo © AFP/Getty Images

Agatha Christie and Max Mallowan walk the grounds of their summer home Greenway House. Recently restored and open to the public, Greenway House was donated by Agatha Christie's family to Great Britain's National Trust in 2000. Agatha Christie once described the property as "the loveliest place in the world."

In 1946, successful, prolific mystery writer Agatha Christie relaxes at home in Greenway House, one of several residences she enjoyed decorating and remodeling in her lifetime.
Photo © AFP/Getty Images

Agatha Christie stands in her library at Greenway House after World War II. Note the mural on the wall, which was painted by an American Coast Guard officer billeted there during the war when Greenway House was used by the British military to house American troops. Photo © Popperfoto/Getty Images

In 1950, Agatha Christie posed at the gate of Winterbrook House, her home in Wallingford, Oxfordshire. From 1971 until her death in 1976, Agatha Christie spent most of her time at Winterbrook and is buried in a local churchyard not far from her beloved home. Photo © Popperfoto/Getty Images

Agatha Christie posed with her grandson, Mathew Prichard, at an airport in 1955. Mathew's famous grandmother gifted him the copyright for her play, "The Mousetrap," as a birthday present when he turned nine. Photo © Getty Images

Agatha Christie cuts a huge cake commemorating the 10th anniversary of her long-running play, "The Mousetrap," on November 26, 1962. The play holds the record for the longest initial run of any play in the world, with nearly 25,000 performances in its 55-year run in London's West End. Photo © Getty Images apologies, their itinerary was reconstructed to place the quartet on the road to Delphi with intermediate stops along the way.

For Agatha, the more impromptu the plan was, the more exciting the adventure. This was in direct opposition to Max, who allowed every contingency to be calculated and alternative arrangements prepared "just in case." She marveled at his ability to stay calm during calamity; he found her excitement over the smallest fallen leaf or shard of glass to be enchanting. The Woolleys found the entire budding friendship to be borderline annoying and did their best to ignore it.

Traveling by train to Kirkuk, the group set out on a six-hour drive to Mosul that was capped by a ferry ride on a boat so primitive that Agatha said "one felt almost Biblical embarking upon it."[xxiv] After several hurried days in Mosul, two hundred fifty miles northwest of Baghdad, the troop rejoined their driver and reenergized themselves with a local narcotic brew made for them in Tal Afar, where the Woolleys had friends.

With rather spotted success, the group arrived and left hotels and campsites either late or early, depending on the day, and while not exactly as on schedule as Max would have liked, they maintained a bohemian spontaneity that to Agatha was pure bliss. When they eventually made it to Aleppo, one of the oldest cities on earth, Max took on the role of educator and used their tour of the north Syrian city to recite an abbreviated history of the world's religions. And if it was showing off just a bit for his female companion, it was not without good reason. Max Mallowan, it seems, had fallen in love.

A boat trip to Greece was to culminate the trip, with stops along the way to Delphi at various bathing beaches, where Agatha immediately disrobed and plunged into the Mediterranean. At the Turkish port of Mersin, Max romanced Agatha with a necklace made of wild marigolds picked from the beach, a man completely uncertain of his path yet directed by his emotions.

Upon arriving in Athens, Agatha was greeted at the hotel by a waiting stack of mail from her agent and a half-dozen telegrams, each alerting her that Rosalind had fallen seriously ill with pneumonia and was being cared for by

Madge and the staff at Abney Hall. Rosalind, now eleven years old, had not been thought about for weeks. Away in school, mature for her age, always able to cope and manage, Rosalind had never before presented a problem. Indeed she had been a child to be cherished—when convenient. Now, however, she was in need. In Agatha's guilt-stricken mind, her daughter could have been dying while she was swimming in the shadow of the Temple of Apollo.

She announced to her hosts that she must leave Greece immediately and return to England by the fastest method possible. Max took control of planning the trip and left to make arrangements, leaving Agatha to wander through the streets of Athens, worrying, suffering, blaming herself for her daughter's condition. In the course of her wandering, Agatha stepped into a hole being prepared for a tree and painfully twisted her ankle, the full weight of her body collapsing upon it.

Limping back to the hotel, she was rescued by Max—always calm and present-of-mind Max—who took charge of the situation, ordering up bandages to wrap her sprain. He announced that he would accompany her back to Devon via the Orient Express, departing the following day. He was, to Agatha, her knight—that sword-wielding prince who charged across the forest of childhood books to rescue the damsel in distress. He was her hero, nothing less, and she willingly collapsed into his protective arms without the slightest protest or thought about what people might say.

On the trip back to England, she spent nearly every waking moment with Max, who only weeks ago had been a complete stranger. He was not handsome—more bookish in appearance, with thinning hair and a black moustache that made him appear older than his years. No, there was not a bit of Archie in this hero, but, oh, how she listened to his every word, and equally surprising, how he listened to hers. He was smart and unflappable and most importantly did not run away at the first sign of illness or discomfort.

He spoke of his parents—his Austrian father with a stubborn streak and his French mother, who loved reading poetry and the classics, and whose own mother was the opera star Marthe Duvivier, winner of the *Prix de Consérvatoire*. He talked about attending the New College at Oxford, only finding his way into archaeology when there was an opening with Dr. Woolley. Now, he said, he thought of nothing else, but that was not true. Now he was thinking of Agatha Christie.

A mother's concern for her child is often frantic beyond reason and protective beyond endurance. It is little wonder that when Agatha limped into her London home, she immediately telephoned Madge for an update on her child. Madge was happy to report that Rosalind was feeling substantially better. Agatha was at her daughter's side in another six hours, despite her complete exhaustion from her trip. Agatha found Rosalind looking thin and frail, having obviously endured quite an illness.

Max had left Agatha when they passed through Paris, stopping to visit his mother. Agatha sent him a letter rife with the drama of the moment. "My Rosalind was so much worse than they told me—it wrung my heart to see her—skin and bones and pitifully weak. Oh Max!—everything has been beastly...."[xxv] Though weak, Rosalind still had her father's stubborn resolve, insisting, "Aunt Punkie has taken perfect care of me, mummy. You needn't have come. I certainly would not have wanted to *interrupt* your writing for anything."

Agatha had written to Max from Ashfield, where she had traveled with Rosalind, determined to heal her sprained ankle and her daughter by the sea. Agatha invited him for a weekend visit at Ashfield, which he readily accepted. There were, predictably, the usual domestic disasters during his stay. Her terrier Peter bit Freddie, the son of her housekeeper, in the face one day, and a picnic with Max concluded in a downpour. Yet, through it all, he remained good-natured and seemingly undisturbed by what must have been chaos and confusion.

The night before Max was set to return to London, he came to visit Agatha after she had gone to bed. She invited him into her bedroom. Max sat near the footboard and boldly proposed marriage. Agatha was stunned, and, after some polite conversation bordering on stammering, she refused his offer, citing the differences in their ages. What she did not mention was that she simply did not *want* to get married again.

It wasn't that she didn't like Max, for she thought he was the sweetest and most considerate man she had ever met. She thought of him as a friend, a *good* friend, for that is what he had become. And Agatha had very few people in whom she could confide and trust. After two hours of discussion, Max finally went back to his room, with Agatha convinced that the marriage issue was also put to bed.

Max, however, was not to be easily dissuaded. He began a letter-writing campaign from London that was both thoughtful and consistent. These missives were not the romantic ramblings of a poet, but the more logical sentiments of a scholar placing his case before a provost. For her part, Agatha was not easily convinced, less for the reasons she had given him than for the feelings she eventually revealed in a note: "I'm an awful coward and dreadfully afraid of being hurt."[xxvi]

By May, Agatha had softened the tone of her letters, reveling in their growing intimacy with charm and wit. When he wrote and asked her if she minded that his profession involved "digging up the dead,"[xxvii] she answered saying she *adored* "corpses and stiffs."[xxviii] And more than that, she *adored* him.

As the weeks progressed, her notes became more and more childlike, a teenage girl with a crush. After reading a note in which he declared his love, Agatha responded: "Dearest— Do I really mean what you say to you? I've just got your letter— oh! my dear. I would love to mean that to you."[xxix] By June, the pair had agreed to wed in September, an appropriate waiting time just "to be sure."

This woman who only a year earlier was suffering through a professional and emotional crisis had emerged not only confident but triumphant. She was in love, she owned three houses (having bought a second house in the Kensington area of London), she had fearlessly traveled the world, and she was famous—not for her odd disappearance, but for her writing about all those "corpses and stiffs."

Her publication schedule expanded to the point that in 1930 alone Collins & Son published three books. Among them was a compilation of stories previously published in *The Sketch,* all featuring one of Agatha's favorite characters, Mr. Harley Quin. To Agatha, these compilations were "free money," requiring no work except on the part of the publisher.

The Mysterious Mr. Quin, officially her twelfth book, was published in April 1930 in England. The *Saturday Review of Literature* said "this book will give you many problems to solve and a chuckle over Mrs. Christie's entertaining and subtle humor."[xxx] Not so subtle was what proved to be her first example of the anti-Semitism typical of her class and age, but no less offensive to those whose skin it pricked. Agatha was by no means deliberately cruel when, in "The Soul of the Croupier," she wrote about "men of Hebraic extraction, sallow men with hooked noses, wearing flamboyant jewelry." She was, quite simply, reflecting her upbringing, and that worldview was inherently bigoted, innocent but insulting.

Interestingly, anti-Semitism did not surface in her daily life, for this was a woman who took great effort to applaud those from an assortment of classes and races and levels of education, finding in each a talent and charm unique to them. It was a quality not lost on Max, who often found it tedious to relate to his workers, to whom he laid out duties with severe precision and expected perfection. Archaeology demanded nothing less.

His own reading habits tended toward reference books and scholarly nonfiction. Along with his affection for Agatha came a desire to know all about her and her life. This certainly included her writing, and Max set about committing himself to reading every book, including the latest, *The Murder at the Vicarage*. This was the first novel to showcase the elderly spinster Jane Marple, who had previously been a small character in a short story, "The Tuesday Night Club," published in *The Sketch* in 1928. With *Vicarage*, Agatha added the country village of St. Mary Mead to her repertoire of recognizable locations, the home of the eagle-eyed sleuth Miss Marple.

Agatha selected the Marple name after visiting her sister Madge and attending an estate sale at nearby Marple Hall, a grand English manor house that had fallen into disrepair after being vandalized. Agatha never forgot the graceful decay she saw at this once fine house and named Jane Marple in its honor.

In Miss Marple, Agatha found a kindred spirit whose observations she enjoyed creating. The character herself was a spin-off from Caroline Sheppard, a spinster in *The Murder of Roger Ackroyd*. With Miss Marple, that character was enlarged and her wisdom widened. Dedicated to her daughter, Rosalind, *The Murder at the Vicarage* was another Christie critical success, with *Saturday Review of Literature* saying, "she is hard to surpass."[xxxi]

Agatha was far more excited to see *Giant's Bread* appear in bookstores in August, walking past the stack of books with the name "Mary Westmacott" printed in large black letters across the bottom of the book jacket. It was a cover in chaos—orange, yellow, and black, the picture of clocks and musical instruments depicted in impressionistic style. Again, the reviews were positive, with the *New York Times*, aware the writer was using a pen name, stating, "Whoever is concealed beneath the pseudonym of Mary Westmacott may well feel proud of *Giant's Bread*."[xxxii]

By the time of *Giant's* release, Agatha had traveled with Rosalind, Peter, Carlo, and Carlo's sister Mary to Broadford on the Isle of Skye, to establish residence for several weeks during which the banns of marriage might be announced according to Scottish custom. On the marriage license, Agatha gave her age as thirty-seven, instead of forty; Max gave his age as thirty-one, rather than twenty-six. The age on Agatha's passport was also changed to agree with the document and remained incorrect for the rest of her life.

The ceremony took place in a beautiful gold-ladened chapel at St. Cuthbert's Church in the St. Giles district of Edinburgh. The date was September 11, 1930, with only Agatha's daughter and the Fisher sisters as witnesses.

In her autobiography and in many other biographies that followed, the church was listed as St. Columba's, a mistake of saintly proportions on Agatha's part that is corrected here. Adding color to the ceremony, the minister officiating at the wedding was the Reverend George MacLeon, known as the Rudolph Valentino of the pulpit for his dark good looks.

Madge and Jimmy Watts did not attend the ceremony, for they always looked upon Max as a potential gold-digger. This impression was not helped by the amount of money he contributed to the cost of the honeymoon—which was entirely paid for by Agatha. Several days after the ceremony they were in Venice, where Max wore a white dinner jacket custom-made for their romantic first nights as husband and wife. They thoroughly enjoyed the prerequisite gondolier rides with accordion complement. The honeymoon continued for five weeks as they traveled along the Dalmatian coast of what was then Yugoslavia.

In Dubrovnik, they bathed in the Adriatic Sea. (Always concerned about the press, Agatha wrote in her journal, "Did touch betray our guilty secret?"[xxxiii]) They then moved on to Split, where Agatha was stunned by the artistry of Ivan Mestrovic's statue of St. Gregory of Nin. They explored the countryside and Yugoslavian food and ventured to mountainous Montenegro before moving on to the port of Kotor, with its orange-tiled roofs.

From Kotor, the pair boarded a tiny boat called the *SRBN* that Agatha described as "the size of a cockle shell," holding only two cabins, four passengers, and so much delicious food that the pair wished they could spend a lifetime at the chef's table. They coasted, as if drifting on air, through small ports named after the saints—Anna, Maura, Quaranta— slipping onto land and leisurely strolling the vineyards and olive gardens, hand in hand, lovers of life.

There was no Agatha Christie here. This was Mary Westmacott's moment to hear every whisper of affection that her idolizing husband uttered. "It was a Garden of Eden. A Paradise on Earth!" she remembered.[xxxiv]

Once they reached Greece, their final destination, there was a fourteen-hour mule ride to Andrítsena (Max said the ride was only nine hours, but *felt* like fourteen) to reach the Temple of Apollo Epicurius that nearly ended their short marriage, so exhausting and painful was the journey. It took two days for forgiveness, but Agatha finally succumbed to the lyrically soothing words of her lover, who promised never to repeat the mistake of such an overly ambitious detour.

They continued on to Mycenae, Epidaurus, and Nauplia, before ending in Delphi, where at last Agatha got to see why the Woolleys found it so special. It was only after returning to Athens that the first hint of trouble in paradise came upon them. Agatha was gripped by Athens tummy, something akin to Montezuma's revenge. A doctor diagnosed the cause as ptomaine poisoning due to eating some ill-advised mullet, and while Agatha eventually recovered, it was *not* the way she had anticipated spending the last leg of her honeymoon.

As it was, Max had to leave her in Greece in order to rejoin the Woolleys and stay on schedule with the dig in Ur.

The Woolleys had made well known their views on the inappropriateness of newlyweds on an archaeological dig. Agatha was fine with this, fully prepared to spend the season away from Max, awaiting his arrival in London.

Returning to England on the Orient Express, Agatha settled back into her house on the mews, playing piano for leisure and reluctantly eyeing her typewriter. Time to begin working again. When she struck the first keys, she had an uncontrollable urge to smile. Not because she found something amusing or even because she was happy. As those first words appeared on the page, Agatha realized that she was *content*. For perhaps the first time in her entire life, she had found bliss. And she vowed then and there to never allow anyone or anything to take it away again.

She summed it up best to Allen Lane, the nephew of her first publisher and now a neighbor. "Oh Allen," she said. "1930 was a marvelous year!"

SEVEN

Mrs. Max Mallowan

We enjoyed things together...we seemed to be able to share things. And he didn't mind if I was myself. I mean I could say I was enjoying myself and be enthusiastic without him thinking me silly.

Agatha Christie
Unfinished Portrait

NOVEMBER 1930. KATHARINE WOOLLEY WAS NOT WELL. This is not to say that she was physically ill, although she did have recurrent headaches for much of her life. More precisely, she was perpetually irritated—the cause most likely being another woman. In the autumn of 1930, that other woman was Agatha Christie Mallowan.

Katharine, beautiful, spoiled, and controlling, had returned with her husband, Dr. Leonard Woolley, to Ur a week later than they had anticipated. This apparently was the fault of Katharine's inability to make up her mind regarding the amount and type of clothing that needed to be packed for five months in the barren desert. Max Mallowan, unaware of their delay, had left his honeymoon and a seriously ill wife to arrive in Mesopotamia on time, and when he discovered that his sacrifice went unnoticed, he took his fury and frustration out on the workers at Ur.

He was already irritated with Katharine, for she was the one who forbade his new wife from returning to the archaeological site with him. "It simply will not do," Katharine had said. Agatha, now a married woman rather than a single celebrity, was no longer welcome—just as no other wives were welcome in these remote, dusty locations. None, of course, except for Katharine herself.

Hers was a unique karma. Her first husband, Lieutenant Colonel Francis Keeling, shot himself at the base of the Great Pyramid in Egypt. She thought nothing of tying a string to her big toe and attaching the other end to Dr. Woolley's toe in the next room so that in the event she woke with a headache, she could alert him without rising from her bed. She directed that the workers, including Max on occasion, brush her hair nightly and found it perfectly appropriate for them to service her with massages after they had completed a long day at the dig site.

While Max had endured five years of Katharine's dramatics during his previous assignments at Ur, his post-marriage tolerance for this outrageous conduct had greatly decreased. Knowing that he could never continue under such conditions without Agatha by his side, he sought work elsewhere and was offered a position by famed archaeologist Dr. Reginald Campbell Thompson at Nineveh, beginning the next season. Katharine, who had come to rely on Max as her personal factotum, was not happy to see him go. Agatha, on the other hand, was thrilled.

Upon her return to England and the mews house, she wrote her new husband and confessed, "My dear—you have lifted so much from my shoulders—so much I didn't even know was there."[8] More than anything, Max Mallowan had given Agatha permission to once again dream like a child. In the years since her divorce from Archie, she had successfully taken control of every element of her life. Now, she was only too happy to relinquish it to a man. In what might be viewed as a step backward by modern feminists, Agatha loved having a husband on whom she could lean. Less a need than a comfort, this was a selection, and one made with total understanding of its ramifications.

Max had proven himself to be reliable, nonthreatening, and highly educated. More importantly, he was devoted to her and her interests. What he was not was sexual and was most certainly a virgin when he married Agatha, having come from the New College at Oxford straight to the desert of Mesopotamia, with no benefit of female companionship. At Oxford, he lived in Robinson Tower, where his closest friend was Esme Howard, the oldest son of the First Baron Howard of Penrith.

[8] The 5th Earl of Carnarvon financed the dig of Howard Carter that discovered the tomb of Tutankhamen in 1923.

Max thought at the time that the most important gift one could share was "congenial friends of one's own age," and with that in mind, Max gave of himself to Esme—emotionally, if not sexually. The two were inseparable, kindred souls. Before meeting Esme, Max had been afraid of revealing too much about himself, his interests. He had seen what bullies could do at his previous public school, Lancing College in West Sussex. Then along came Esme—smart, outspoken, and free, the son of a baron who did not fear bullies, or much of anything else, including public opinion.

In 1920s England, it was fashionable to play at being homosexual, particularly in academic circles. It was also illegal, which explains why the arts, literature, and homosexuality were debated and explored in private college clubs. Esme was a member of one such club. So too was Evelyn Waugh.

Evelyn, who had attended Lancing College at the same time Max was there, was renowned for his skills at sadistic bullying. And little would have changed on that front by the time he matriculated at Hertford College, Oxford, if Evelyn had not met Richard Pares. Evelyn described Pares in a letter to novelist Nancy Mitford as his "first homosexual love"[i]—and some consider that to have been the relationship that inspired him to write his celebrated novel Brideshead Revisited, heavy with its homosexual undercurrent supplied by the character Lord Sebastian Flyte.

The exact nature of the friendship between Esme and Max is less well known, since Esme died at the young age of twenty-five on November 27, 1926, the victim of leukemia. What is known is that Esme was tall, charming, and intelligent, "a lover of the arts with a sparking wit and humor," according to Max. Over fifty years after Esme's death, Max wrote that the "memory of his companionship still carries with it a warm glow."[ii]

Max had seen his friend for the last time the year before his death, visiting him for three days at Alta Chiara, Portofino, at the grand villa of Mary Herbert, the Dowager Lady Carnarvon. Esme's father, Lord Howard, at one time was the assistant private secretary of the Fourth Earl of Carnarvon, and after the Earl's death, Carnarvon's widow maintained the pinkish-white stone estate on the Ligurian coast of Italy, terraced on the side of a mountain, with its semi-wild pathways bordered by lavender, roses, and rosemary.

The memory of Esme Howard was still weighing heavy on Max when he met Agatha, and later he wrote, "My love for you is the perfect continuation of that friendship with Esme that I thought I should never recover."[iii]

Max's absence from Agatha's life so soon after marriage turned out to be a perfect arrangement. He was not underfoot to distract her from regaining her momentum with writing, yet he was only a letter away from providing her with the reassurance of his devotion and stability that she craved.

In preparation for Max's eventual return, she placed the mews house up for lease and moved into her larger home at 47-48 Campden Street, in the Campden Hill section of Kensington. It was close to the Notting Hill Gate underground station, allowing Max to get to the British Museum with ease. It also provided a new decorating diversion for Agatha in his absence.

Agatha wrote often to her new husband, usually prattling on about furniture and draperies. What cannot be hidden is the happiness she felt, as these notes positively bubble with childish touches. "I love you frightfully and I might fill up the page with kisses like children do—! Very sweet kisses...," she wrote in December.[v]

It would prove to be a very busy month. Her play Black Coffee was set to open in London on December 8, and Agatha attended the first night. The play was not very well received, with the Times suggesting, "Mrs. Christie steers her play with much dexterity; yet there are times when it is perilously near the doldrums."[vi]

Also in December, Agatha agreed to contribute one episode of a six-part mystery to be broadcast over the BBC the following month. Writer Dorothy L. Sayers had convinced Agatha that it was an honor to be asked by the BBC to participate in the project, which called for each of six different eminent mystery writers to compose an installment of a single story, later reading his or her chapter on the air. Sayers's half-hour began the story on January 10, with Agatha reading her material the following week.

The writers were selected from members of The Detection Club, founded the previous year. Meeting every few months in various restaurants, the club was a silly distraction for Agatha, who laughed at Sayers's formidable secret oath and rules, accompanied by a prop known as "Eric the Skull," with glowing battery-operated eyes. Still, it was a mark- of distinction to be asked to be a member, and there was nothing silly about Agatha's pride in wanting Max to listen to her on the radio. After much effort and a frantic horseback ride across the desert, he managed to hear the BBC on a wireless in the office of the political officer at Nasiriyeh, later writing Agatha that he only wished she could have included a cryptic message to him.

When she finally returned to Ur and reunited with her husband in March 1931, Agatha was nervous at the reception she would receive, both from Max and from Katharine. "It was as if we had met the day before,"[vii] she later wrote, relieved at seeing Max's crocodile grin when she first spied him. And Katharine, too, was pleasant and greeted her with gracious welcome, her hospitality having been well lubricated with a signed edition of The Murder at the Vicarage.

The Mallowans decided to return to England via Russia, a rather unpredictable itinerary, given the rapidly changing political climate of the region. They traveled from Baghdad to Persia, "a dark emerald jewel in a great desert of grays and browns," before driving into Isfahan ("never have I seen anything of its glorious colors, of rose, blue and gold—the flowers, birds, arabesques, lovely fairytale buildings, and everywhere beautiful colored tiles—yes, a fairytale city.")[viii]

Max and Agatha stopped briefly at an Iranian bank to exchange currency into local tomans before motoring along the Caspian Sea to Rasht, where they boarded a boat to take them to Baku, the largest port of Azerbaijan. From Baku it was a three-day train trip to Batumi, Russia, during which they existed on a diet of duck wings and pineapple marmalade, plus tea made from water retrieved from the engine's boiler.

By the time they arrived in Batumi in the middle of a downpour, Max had begun to doubt the wisdom of traveling by impulse rather than by the Thomas Cook Agency. But for her part, Agatha found the entire trip an adventure, including having to be hoisted up a rope ladder to reach their garret room in the Batumi hotel.

The following day, the pair caught their scheduled Messageries Maritimes boat sailing home on the Black Sea, where fellow passengers included goats and homing pigeons being transported as loose cargo. They arrived back in London just in time to see placards being pasted into frames at movie theaters advertising Austin Trevor's starring role as Hercule Poirot in *Alibi*. It was a film based on the Michael Morton adaptation of Agatha's *The Murder of Roger Ackroyd*, and over which she had no control. The pained look on Agatha's face was enough to prevent Max from even bringing up the subject.

In mid-1931, *The Sittaford Mystery*, Agatha's fourteenth book, was published, the first to have a different title in America, where it was released as *Murder at Hazelmoor* for a reason not readily apparent. The setting for *Sittaford/ Hazelmoor* was the isolated Dartmoor countryside, the silence of which Agatha had so cherished when finishing *The Murder of Roger Ackroyd* years earlier.

Critically, the novel universally impressed reviewers, with the *New York Times* hailing it an "excellent book to take away for a weekend reading."[ix] The *New York Herald Tribune* suggested, "You can't go wrong with this one, certainly the best of the always high-grade Christie items in quite some time."[x]

Perhaps most important, from Agatha's standpoint, was the dedication of the book to her new husband: "To M.E.M. with whom I discussed the plot of this book, to the alarm of those around us."

As Max and Agatha settled into home life, Agatha discovered happiness—the giddy happiness of love and childhood. Even Rosalind, who was away at school, shared in the joy, for she genuinely liked Max. He was, after all, a far more serious sort than her mother, and she thought it rather "fun" to have two sets of parents.

There were moments when Agatha would catch herself staring at her husband, working at his long desk in the new house on Campden Street, chain-smoking his cigarettes, concentrating. It was in those moments of unbridled bliss, caused by nothing in particular and meaning everything in particular, that she knew love. If not the romantic love of her attachment to Archie Christie, this was, in fact, something even better. This was dependable affection, a mutual caring without fear of criticism. Agatha felt a soaring happiness and did not hesitate to share her exuberant joy.

Max was content to provide the stability that his wife had always been denied in return for the comfort of beautiful homes, luxurious clothes, and the satisfaction of her companionship. For Max, this was the most he could give and the most he could expect. And it was enough.

Agatha spent the summer writing a new book, *Peril at End House,* and a compilation of previously published short stories, *The Thirteen Problems.* In each, the plots flow smoothly, without the restrictions of stress or deadlines, and the finished products benefited from it. By the autumn of 1931, Agatha began writing a third book, *Lord Edgeware Dies,* during a vacation trip she took alone to Rhodes. Max had traveled to Iraq to begin his new job with Campbell Thompson, known as C.T., giving Agatha a few weeks to relax before joining him on the dig in Nineveh.

She wrote to her husband each day, often combining letters and sending them as a group several times a week. These were not missives aimed at sharing news as much as notes of nonsense to say hello. "Lord Edgeware is getting on nicely. He is dead," she wrote. "Carlotta Adams (Ruth Draper) is dead—and the nephew who succeeds to the property is just talking to Poirot about his wonderful alibi!" [xi] These were the chatty letters of friends, sharing thoughts about their work, rather than passionate prose, but in these musings was emotion warmed through absence and edged by the anticipation of reuniting.

Leaving Rhodes and joining Max at Nineveh, Agatha's first task was to locate a sturdy secondhand table ("under which I could get my knees") on which to place her typewriter. Discovered at an Iraqi version of a garage sale, the table cost £3, which, given the simplicity of the accommodations, was a luxury.

In comparison to Ur, the dig at Nineveh was paradise. Max and Agatha lived in a house with a garden at Assyria on the upper Tigris River, a twenty-minute horse ride from Nineveh—a house that Agatha always remembered "with love and affection." There were turkeys that ran wild in the backyard, making food plentiful, and the easygoing nature of C.T. made work a pleasurable experience.

When in December 1931 Agatha left Nineveh to return to England to spend Christmas with Rosalind and the Watts family, she was looking forward to taking the Orient Express, luxuriating in its first-class splendor and fine dining. Such was not to be, however. The train began the journey during a violent rainstorm and sometime during the night became stalled due to a series of flooded tracks.

During the course of the next day, Agatha huddled with other passengers, attempting to conserve their body heat. "We spent the morning wrapped up in rugs and the conductor fetched my hot water bottle and said the last time they had stayed in that particular place three weeks!!" she wrote.[xii] Never one to waste good material, the story became the source of the future book *Murder on the Orient Express.*

Peril at End House was published in March 1932 and told the story of the occupants of a strange house built on the edge of a rocky cliff in St. Loo. It was an exciting, fun read, which managed to enchant the critics. "The actual solution is quite unusually ingenious and well up to the level of Mrs. Christie's best stories," according to the *Times Literary Supplement.*[xiii] Isaac Anderson, writing in the *New York Times,* said, "This person responsible for the dirty work at End House is diabolically clever, but not quite clever enough to fool the little Belgian detective all the time."[xiv]

Peril at End House was dedicated to Eden Phillpotts,[9] "to whom I shall always be grateful for his friendship and the encouragement he gave me so many years ago."

In June 1932, a collection of Miss Marple short stories was published under the title *The Thirteen Problems* in England and *The Tuesday Club Murders* in the United States several weeks later. Accepted as great fun by reviewers who had begun to see Agatha as an entertainer as well as a writer, they made mention of her humor, which had begun to creep into her writing as she became more comfortable with the art. (Perhaps the ultimate inside joke was the book's dedication: "To Leonard and Katharine Woolley.")

"The fact that these thirteen stories are extremely amusing in spots," wrote Will Cuppy in the *New York Herald*

[9] Eden Phillpotts was the Devon novelist who encouraged Agatha to write.

Tribune, "is nothing against them in our eyes, and we trust all good fans to rally round them and enjoy them. You'll be delighted with Miss Marple, the capped and mittened spinster in whose house at St. Mary Mead most of the yarns are told."[xv]

And while it seems that Agatha agreed with Cuppy that dear Miss Marple was a fun character with whom to spend some entertaining moments, she nevertheless chose to ignore her for the next ten years in favor of other efforts. The first of these was a deeply personal and thoroughly revealing second Mary Westmacott novel, titled *Unfinished Portrait.*

The central character in the book is a girl named Celia, a lightly disguised Agatha, and her Archibald Christie-like husband named Dermot. According to Max, who was with her during most of the writing of *Portrait,* "we see many intimate flashes from earliest childhood to the beginning of middle age…. Only the initiated can know how much actual history is contained therein, but in Celia we have more nearly than anywhere a portrait of Agatha."[xvi]

That Agatha should have become suddenly introspect at a time of exceeding happiness was most likely due to her unexpected pregnancy in 1932. She had made no secret of the fact that she would have adored to have a son in addition to her daughter and had continued to push for a baby during the latter years of her marriage to Archie. Because of Agatha's age, having children was never an issue after her wedding to Max, yet they took the news of the pregnancy with calm and organized anticipation.

In much the same fashion, they accepted the news of a miscarriage, which occurred while she was staying at Ashfield in the spring. While Agatha took the disappointment without much outward emotion, she went through a period of silent mourning that surfaced with the self-evaluation of *Unfinished Portrait.*

Much of *Unfinished Portrait* was written in Tell Arpachiyah, not far from modern Mosul in northern Iraq, where Max had been awarded the first excavation of his own. Funded by the British Museum and Sir Edgar Bonham Carter of the British School of Archaeology in Iraq for £2,000, the dig was a highly successful one, under Max's meticulous organization, augmented by notes taken by Agatha and mapping done by architect John Cruikshank Rose.

They lived for six months in a small house with a marble verandah and a garden. There was a houseboy and cook and a "large fierce dog to bark at the other dogs in the neighborhood."[xvii] It was rather fancy for the neighborhood, with rugs on dirt floors and a chamber pot instead of the prerequisite hole-in-the-ground as a toilet.

After weeks of digging, the excavation eventually uncovered a burned potter's shop, left untouched for several thousand years. Max raced back to Agatha, found her writing in their house, and pulled her up the hill to witness the discovery firsthand. "There were glorious dishes, vases, cups and plates, polychrome pottery, all shining in the sun—scarlet and black and orange—a magnificent sight."[xviii] The find made archaeological history and added an integral piece of knowledge to the puzzle that was Tell Arpachiyah.

Upon their return to England in triumph, Max went to work cataloging his find inside the British Museum, while Agatha watched as *Lord Edgeware Dies* was published in Britain (in America it was called *Thirteen at Dinner*). Agatha dedicated her thirteenth book to "Dr. and Mrs. Campbell Thompson." The plot was inspired by a chance performance of diseuse Ruth Draper, during which she gave several characterizations that were so startling in their variety that they started the Christie compass spinning toward intrigue.

Reviewers found the book a triumph of deception. The *New Statesman and Nation's* Ralph Partridge declared, "Mrs. Agatha Christie is quite beyond criticism, unless it be that she does not write enough novels. *Thirteen at Dinner* is the best detective novel published this year."[xix]

At that same moment, flush with capital and armed with time, Agatha went house hunting yet again, stopping to look at a location recommended by Carlo in Kensington, not far from their place on Campden Street. It was positioned on a beautiful block on Sheffield Terrace, the number 58 attached in brass numbers to the white wall surrounding the property.[10] It was a large, three-story stucco home with a carved lion and unicorn over the front entrance, and when Agatha first saw it, she was overcome with déjà vu and that special karma that sweeps away cobwebs and fills in cracks. "It was perfect," she wrote in her autobiography, and if it wasn't exactly true, she set about making certain it felt that way.

[10] In her autobiography, Agatha mistakenly gave the address as 48 Sheffield, an error that was duplicated in other biographies but corrected here.

The ground floor had a sitting room, dining room, and kitchen, with two large rooms on the second floor—a library for Max over the dining room and a master bedroom for the Mallowans over the sitting room—each with large bay windows overlooking the street. On the third floor were Rosalind's room, a guest bedroom, and a giant private study known as "Agatha's Room." It was equipped with a Steinway grand piano, a "large firm table, a comfortable sofa or divan, a hard upright chair for typing, one armchair to recline in, and there was to be *nothing* else"[xx]—especially a telephone. It was also a first. In spite of all her homes, Agatha never reserved a room marked "off-limits," just for herself and her writing. It now became her sanctuary.

While the Sheffield Terrace house was being remodeled—Max added a fireplace in his study and had new electrical outlets installed in the walls—Agatha insisted she smelled gas, especially in the vicinity of the master bedroom. Since there was no gas in the house and no gas meter either, her persistence with this absurd notion was endured with that special grace given to those who love one unconditionally. The gas men came; so too did contractors, electricians, and plumbers. They lay on their stomachs, joining her under the bed, detecting nothing. At best, they all suggested, what Agatha smelled was a dead mouse, and as they turned away, gave each other knowing smiles as they shook their heads.

"Gas," Agatha insisted, having the floorboards pulled up, the second floor bedroom nearly demolished in the process. "Finally, after I had driven everyone nearly insane," Agatha wrote, "I was vindicated. There was an obsolete gas pipe under the floor of my bedroom, and gas was continuing to escape from it."[xxi] *Her* satisfied smile was its own reward.

Through it all, business continued. Agatha's seventh book of short stories, and her eighteenth published book, reached the shelves in early 1933. *The Hound of Death and Other Stories* is unique in two ways. First, it dealt almost exclusively with the supernatural, a subject of increasing interest to Agatha; plus, it was her first book not published concurrently in America.[11] It was, however, to be well received, for buried within its pages was a story titled "Witness for the Prosecution," a few thousand words that were later to bring Agatha Christie increased fame and fortune.

[11] Several of the stories did eventually get published in America after 1948 as part of other anthologies.

For the moment, however, she was quite content with her annual travels to Max's archaeological digs, at which she was now becoming quite seasoned and an extremely valued assistant to her husband. With her eye for detail and her creative imagination, it was a complementary matchup that helped launch Max's career.

While mentally they were perfectly matched, physically they looked a bit on the eccentric side. Dressed in matronly suits and sensible shoes, Agatha was a bit large to be a natural complement to her smallish husband in his proper British tweeds and pipe. Yet, there was that look they shared that said, "We are a couple, and we are happy."

Agatha was supportive in other ways as well, purchasing yet another house, this one in the country, thirty-six miles from London in Wallingford, on the western side of the river Thames. The three-bedroom Queen Anne house sat close to the road, but had a large backyard that rolled to the river at its furthest boundary. In the center of the property stood a gracious old cedar, under which tea was served as a matter of style in the afternoons during warmer months.

Agatha chose to decorate this dwelling, called Winterbrook House, in mauve and white. It was quite the departure from her colorful splashes of scarlet and turquoise of the past. But this, above anything else, was to be Max's house, and Max was all about subtlety and refinement. His library was the most dominant space on the first floor, a double-sized room with a table on which he could spread out his shards of pottery and look out upon the Thames in the distance.

During the damp winter months, they continued to journey to archaeological sites. In late November 1934, Agatha and Max traveled to the Habur Valley of northeast Syria to scout sites for a future dig sponsored by the British School of Archaeology in Iraq. This was a largely unexplored area of Syria, then under French mandate, and as such was terra incognita, as Max loved to say. The prospects of discovery were unlimited, and Agatha joined him in thrilling at the unknown.[12]

Preparing for the trip required the usual buying of clothing and supplies—for Agatha, fountain pens and typewriter ribbons were essentials; for Max, several dozen rare (and heavy) books on archaeology. As with all trips, there was

---

[12] She was also delighted to escape the release of the film version of *Lord Edgeware Dies*, returning Austin Trevor to the role of Hercule Poirot, a horrible choice in Agatha's mind.

a rush at the very last moment, as things were squeezed into the last available bit of space. "At 9 a.m., I [was] called as the heavyweight to sit on Max's bulging suitcases," Agatha remembered. "If *you* can't make them shut," Max said rather cruelly, "nobody can!"[xxii]

Traveling to Syria involved several train rides, which always put Agatha in the correct adventuresome mood. She arrived at Victoria Station for the start of the long trip, "snuffing up the sulfurous smell ecstatically—so different from the faint, aloof, distantly oily smell of a boat, which always depresses my spirits with its prophecy of nauseous days to come. But a train—a big engine, sending up clouds of steam, and seeming to say impatiently: 'I've got to be off, I've got be off....'"[xxiii] The ride on the Orient Express was at once nostalgic and prophetic, for, other than Max, none of Agatha's fellow passengers were aware that she was the author of the popular mystery *Murder on the Orient Express*, published the previous January.

Agatha's nineteenth book, called *Murder in the Calais Coach* in America, was dedicated to the man by her side, "To M.E.L.M., Arpachiyah, 1933." The critics were breathless as they gushed with praise for the intricate planning of a murder so involved that some wondered how Agatha herself could keep the pieces straight.

"Although the murder plot and the solution verge on the impossible," commented Isaac Anderson in the *New York Times*, "Agatha Christie has contrived to make them appear quite convincing for the time being, and what more than that can the mystery addict desire?"[xxiv]

In London, the *Times Literary Supplement* said, "Need it be said—the little gray cells solve once more the seemingly insoluble. Mrs. Christie makes an improbable tale very real, and keeps her readers enthralled until the very end."[xxv]

Arriving in Syria by way of the Grand Hotel Bassoul in Beirut, Agatha, at age forty-four, crawled into a tent erected in a large courtyard at Meyadin, wiggled with some considerable effort into a sleeping bag, and proceeded to fall asleep, as content as any time in her life. The next morning, she was up before the sun to roam between ancient mounds of dirt, hiding secrets unseen for thousands of years. Two chauffeurs, Abdullah and Aristide, were in charge of transportation for the group that also included their guide Hamoudi and a strangely quiet architect named Mac. It was with these four men as well as several male diggers that Agatha would spend the next two months or so, her nails as dirty with earth as theirs, sharing their meals, and their lives. Her complaints were rare, and she saved those for the horseflies that attacked her thighs or the giant black rats that seemed to enjoy the protection of her sleeping bag as much as she.

In her absence back in England, the publishing phenomenon that was Agatha Christie added more new product to bookshelves across the continent. Agatha allowed Collins to compile more short stories for *The Listerdale Mystery*, a slick assortment of a dozen tales, of which the London *Times* said, "After a heavy meal of full-course detective stories, these *friandises* melt sweetly—perhaps a shade too sweetly—on the tongue."[xxvi]

After dessert, she brought the three-dish main course. Agatha's twenty-first book, *Why Didn't They Ask Evans?* (titled *The Boomerang Clue* in America), was released in September 1934; a book of short stories called *Parker Pyne Investigates* (*Mr. Parker Pyne Detective* in America) came out the same month; and Mary Westmacott's *Unfinished Portrait* was published as well. It was, as they say, a very good year.

Max Mallowan moved into his new office at Winterbrook House, quite smug in his fresh surroundings. He had just finished an incredibly successful survey of the Syrian Habur and Jaghjaghav valleys, and began to work on the serious details of the actual dig the following year at Chagar Bazar on the River Dara. As long as Max was happy, Agatha was happy—*deliriously* happy. And as if to prove it, she set about finalizing her next wash of books being marketed by Collins & Sons with the backing of a huge advertising budget. Clearly they anticipated that these would be best-sellers. They did not have long to wait.

Three Act Tragedy,[13] published in 1935, sold ten thousand copies in its first year—a best-seller by any definition. While the critics found fault—the *Saturday Review of Literature* deemed it "Not so good,"[xxvii] her fans spread the word to the contrary. For her part, Agatha remained cloistered, unreachable, even to her agents, who resorted to corresponding

---

[13] Titled *Murder in Three Acts* in America.

by letter and were often ignored. The writer, it seemed, was writing again and could not be disturbed.

Her twenty-fourth book, *Death in the Clouds*,[14] followed several months later in July and was an immediate hit in the summertime book market. "A crime puzzle of the first quality, and a mighty entertaining story besides,"[xxviii] wrote Isaac Anderson in the *New York Times*. Next up, *The ABC Murders*, written atop a stack of wooden boxes on a dig at Chagar Bazar, where Max continued to "make love" to the sand dunes that loved him right back, opening up to him and releasing their treasures of clay pottery and tablets.

It was also at Chagar Bazar that Agatha wrote the 1936 *Murder in Mesopotamia*, dedicating it to "My many archaeological friends in Iraq and Syria." Among them, of course, were the Woolleys. The murder victim—one Mrs. Leidner—was the wife of the lead archaeologist in the fictional dig of the novel. She bore no small likeness to Katharine Woolley, who somehow remained none the wiser that her imperiousness was the inspiration for the character. "This latest Christie opus is a smooth, highly original and completely absorbing tale," reported the *New York Times*.[xxix]

It was rare for Agatha to use a real person as inspiration for a character, as she had done with Katharine Woolley's Mrs. Leidner, but in creating the character of mystery writer Ariadne Oliver in her twenty-seventh book, *Cards on the Table*, Agatha wrote herself into the fiction. Mrs. Oliver, with her gray hair, love of apples, and dislike of crowds, was Agatha Christie wrapped in the gauze of a feminist. Originally the character had been introduced in two short stories within *Parker Pyne Investigates*, but with *Cards on the Table*, Ariadne was added to the growing list of Agatha's recognizable star sleuths, each with a growing fan base.

There was now a certain predictability to her annual schedule—winters in Syria, living in the most remote outposts of civilization, followed by spring in London, refining the stories written in the desert. Summers were spent at Ashfield, relaxing by the sea, bathing and picnicking, playing croquet, before returning to London and preparing for another archaeological expedition. The constants were always Max, Rosalind, Carlo, and Peter—but mainly Max, since the others rarely traveled abroad.

[14] Titled *Death in the Air* in America.

There were occasional social outings, of course. Agatha's short story "Philomel Cottage" was adapted as a play by dramatist/actor Frank Vosper under the title *Love from a Stranger* in 1936, and she attended a performance without taking much pleasure in it. The following year, when the short story was turned into a film starring Ann Harding and Basil Rathbone, she avoided the movie completely. Never much for movies, she enjoyed them even less when she witnessed the way they took uncontrolled, and contractually allowed, liberties with her characters.

Though Agatha's books were supplying most of the funds for their luxurious lifestyle, Max was the absolute head of the house. Agatha saw to it that he was not only perceived that way, but was, in fact, in charge. Rosalind respected his place in her life, and respected him, for he was, like her, an observer of fact. Her mother, by comparison, was all about fiction and was producing it in record numbers.

Agatha published three books in 1937: *Murder in the Mews* [15], a collection of four novellas showcasing the talents of Hercule Poirot; *Dumb Witness* [16], the witness of the title being a wirehaired terrier on the cover who looked an awful lot like Peter; and her thirtieth book, *Death on the Nile*. Of *Nile*, the *New York Times* said, "Poirot is traveling for pleasure, but the moment you see his name on the passenger list, you know there is going to be a murder or two or three, and that the little gray cells of the great Poirot are going to solve the mystery." [xxx] They, of course, do, in their own precise way.

In September 1937, Agatha spent her birthday with Max at the site of their newest dig—Tell Brak, the old Syrian town of Nagar not far from Chagar Bazar—celebrating with a cup of hot tea. Max had attempted to get her interested in both of his vices—drinking and smoking—but she would have none of it. It was not so much the unhealthy aspects of vice that deterred her, but rather the taste. Her palate skewed more toward Devon cream and milk; his to scotch and strong tobacco.

Rosalind joined her mother and stepfather at Tell Brak to handle the duties of sketch artist—never one of Agatha's better talents. It was her first opportunity to see the rigors of archaeology in action and appreciate the primitive living conditions in Syria, the place her parents called home for

[15] Published in America as *Dead Man's Mirror*.
[16] Published in America as *Poirot Loses a Client*.

months of the year. Now graduated from high school, Rosalind's time in the desert added maturity and provided somewhat of a further education to Agatha's only child, who followed her duties on the dig with an official debut to society in London. This was not coordinated by Agatha, who knew little of such things and as a divorcee could not present her daughter at court, in any case. Rather, this task fell to Mr. & Mrs. Ernest Mackintosh—Mr. Mackintosh being the head of the Science Museum in London and a onetime friend of Monty Miller.

Rosalind went with her friend and fellow debutante Susan North to the various balls, after which the girls took a cruise to South Africa, chaperoned by Mrs. Dorothy North and far removed from her mother's reach. It was during this period that Agatha published *Appointment with Death*, set in the city of Petra in the area now known as Jordan.

A complicated plot, the book garnered typically kind reviews, although many, like that in the *Saturday Review of Literature*, pointed to a disappointing denouement. "Starts well and progresses beautifully against a rich background and interesting characters—but then the durned thing blows up in your face. Disappointing."[xxxi]

When Agatha and Max returned to England in the spring of 1938, she had finished *Hercule Poirot's Christmas*,[17] her thirty-second book. It was dedicated to her brother-in-law James Watts, in the form of a letter:

> *My Dear James*
>
> *You have always been one of the most faithful and kindly of my readers, and I was therefore seriously perturbed when I received from you a word of criticism.*
> *You complained that my murders were getting too refined—anemic, in fact. You yearned for a 'good violent murder with lots of blood.' A murder where there was no doubt about its being murder!*
> *So this is your special story—written for you. I hope it may please.*
>
> *Your affectionate sister-in-law,*
>
> *Agatha*

[17] Released in America with the title *Murder for Christmas* and in subsequent paperback edition as *A Holiday for Murder*.

So there it was. Agatha had given in. She had created a mystery in which murder was committed, not by poison or the single neat shot, but by a slit throat. A messier crime is hard to imagine. "In the middle of the hearthrug in front of the blazing fire lay Simeon Lee in a great pool of blood."[xxxii] This was, it seemed, as close to gore as Agatha Christie could bring herself to write.

The critics, for their part, did not seem to notice, seeing only a finely tuned mystery plot that did not disappoint. "Poirot has solved some puzzling mysteries in his time", Isaac Anderson wrote in the *New York Times*, "but never has his mighty brain functioned more brilliantly than in *Murder for Christmas*."[xxxiii]

Yet this was not business as usual. Change was afoot. When the Mallowans left Syria, they did so with a great sense of foreboding and apprehension. Adolf Hitler had begun to remilitarize the Rhineland in direct violation of the Versailles Treaty, and there was talk of the possibility of war. The expedition left Syria with the knowledge that it would likely be a substantial amount of years before they would be allowed to return.

Somehow, that uneasiness made it simpler for Agatha to decide to sell Ashfield. The world had changed, and, much to Agatha's horror, Torquay had changed with it. No longer the resort for the rich and royal, it was now just another beach town on the British Riviera that had been overbuilt without an organization plan. The acres around Ashfield had been sold, and now buildings blocked what once was an unobstructed view of the sea. The house itself was in drastic need of repair, and the home seemed to have lost its heart. "It was as though Ashfield had become a parody of itself," Agatha thought,[xxxiv] when she dared to remember the old days of joy, with her rolling hoop providing endless hours of imagined fascination.

The decision to sell was eased when Greenway, a great white house that had sat for nearly two hundred years overlooking the River Dart in Devon, not far from Torquay, came on the market, listed for a remarkably low £6,000. It sat on just over thirty-three acres of land, reaching to the river, and Agatha had fantasized about owning the home as far back as childhood, when her mother first pointed it out from the water.

Encouraged by Max, who loved the property and the
wealth it represented, Agatha made a full-price offer through
her Torquay attorney and had it accepted immediately. The
sale of Ashfield took longer, but eventually it, too, was bought,
by a family that was interested in renovating the house.

Australian architect Guilford Bell (who had been with
the Mallowans at the dig at Tell Brek and was visiting Ashfield
at the time) suggested that Greenway's newer Victorian
additions be removed. This essentially reduced the size of the
house by one-third, but returned it to its original, delightful
Georgian design. It was a concept that Agatha embraced
immediately and, placing Guilford in charge, set about
beginning the largest remodeling project of her life.

It was not to be as simple as knocking down walls and
replacing columns. Guilford restored the large, carved
mahogany doors in the dining room, moved a curved window
in the drawing room to its original position overlooking steps to
the garden, and remodeled the elegant morning room with
windows that opened to allow air to sweep through the house.
Located on the ground floor rear of Greenway were the
pantries, kitchen, and scullery.

The master bedroom on the first floor had both an
oversize bed for Agatha and a twin bed for Max. Nearby, there
was a separate set of dressing rooms for them both, a study
used by Max, plus a guest bedroom and bathrooms. The
sweeping arrangement of the rooms allowed for easy
movement between them with minimal disturbance to others.
The top floor held Rosalind's room, which was left in its original
condition, and several additional bedrooms for guests, as well
as baths and staff quarters.

The garden was a tangled mess of overgrown flowering
bushes and trees, some specimen items, including the largest
Liriodendron tree in the country, at 165 feet, with lovely yellow
tulip-like flowers. There were rare rhododendrons, vast plots
of daffodils, and lush flowering magnolias, all in need of
pruning. Agatha personally took charge of restoring the formal
elements of the garden and designing gravel pathways
and trails.

This beautiful house with a heritage that stretched
back to the 1700s was, to Agatha, a temporary gift. Like its

previous owners, she and Max would be given time to absorb its magic, learn its history, and live amidst its glory. And then they, like the others, would pass the gift along to the next owners to ensure its legacy would be protected.

Its purchase in 1938 came at the end of an era of gentleness and refinement for Europe. Agatha knew this sophistication and grace very well, for she grew up surrounded by it and lived it as her own. While she might not have ever imagined living without servants and assorted help, she felt the dramatic shift in temperament that would soon permit the horrors of concentration camps and torture to exist—as if man's incivility to man was acceptable.

Much later, Agatha would reflect that the years between 1930 and 1938 were the most special of her life, never to be repeated moments in time. She said "they were particularly satisfying because they were free of outside shadows. As the pressure of work, and particularly the success of work, piles up, one tends to have less and less leisure; but these were carefree years still," she remembered.

Within months, however, the storm clouds of disaster would find her life and her home and impact them forever. That the world she knew was fast disappearing was scary enough; but the world about to take its place was nothing she recognized or liked, a threatening, hostile, and dangerous place, and Agatha Christie was about to discover just how precious life itself would become.

EIGHT

The Tax Man Cometh

*A good deal of red ink in my bank a/c and they don't
seem to be as fond of overdrafts as they used to be.*

Agatha Christie
written to her agent Edmund Cork

AUGUST 1938. WRITER RAFAEL SABATINI VISITED AMERICA
only once in his lifetime. It was in 1932, at a time when the long
arm of the Great Depression had swept aside profits, jobs,
homes, and hope. With twelve million people out of work, it
was a struggling yet proud country that welcomed Sabatini,
and it was that resilient spirit of America that he loved.

A charismatic man with graying hair and a large,
distinctive nose, Sabatini was half-Italian and half-British, but
called the border between Wales and England home. There,
in a house on the River Wye, he quietly produced historical
novels of imagined derring-do.

Sabatini's parents sang opera for a living—first traveling
the continent giving performances in European capitals before
settling in Portugal, and later in Italy, to teach voice. For a small
boy, it was a fantastic world of costumes, grease paint,
elaborate librettos, and music—a combination that enabled
Sabatini to mature into a natural storyteller with a flair for
romance and passion. His were swashbuckling tales of
adventure and larceny aboard pirate ships sailing the Spanish
Main, and appealed to an enormous audience of men and
women on both sides of the Atlantic.

In 1932, at the age of fifty-seven, he came to New York
to promote his newest book, *The Black Swan,* and negotiate
the sale of an earlier best-seller, *Captain Blood,* as a feature
film. Three years later, in 1935, the film's success accomplished

two things: It turned actor Errol Flynn into a superstar and writer Rafael Sabatini into a very rich man.

The Bureau of Internal Revenue, a plunderer of its own sort in the United States, took an avid interest in Sabatini, since, as a British citizen and a "non-resident alien author," he paid no taxes in America. A lawsuit was brought, and the subsequent trial in August 1938 in the Court of Appeals, Second Circuit, resulted in a ruling against Sabatini, requiring him to pay not only current taxes, but taxes on his prior earnings in America as well.

This was not good news for another non-resident alien author—Agatha Christie. Though she knew neither Rafael Sabatini nor the BIR, she was about to learn a great deal about them both. The American tax collector, having tasted the blood of one foreign writer, decided to seek out others and went right to top with the "Queen of Mystery."

Harold Ober, Agatha's literary agent in New York, was the first to raise the possibility of a problem in 1938, writing to his British counterpart, Edmund Cork, that he had hired a tax attorney on Agatha's behalf. Ober, who represented F. Scott Fitzgerald and William Faulkner, had done a brilliant job in selling the Christie legacy in America, and royalties from the United States accounted for the vast majority of Agatha's wealth. When Ober wrote to Cork that he had recruited Harold E. Reinheimer, a tax attorney who "deals with the affairs of many prominent authors," he felt quite confident that there was little cause for worry.

Yet, at that moment, Agatha *was* worried. Her beloved wirehaired terrier, Peter, had passed away, leaving a void that Max not only could not fill, but failed to understand. "You've never been through a *really* bad time with nothing in the world but a dog to hold on to,"[i] she wrote to Max when they had first met. And, of course, she was right. Max, for all his concern and consideration, saved his passionate attachments for artifacts, not canines.

The ever-increasing specter of war placed additional stress in the household. Germany had invaded Czechoslovakia the previous September, and peacetime conscription had begun throughout England to increase the size of the country's military. Max, at thirty-four, was likely too old to be considered soldier material, but still Agatha worried, for that was her way. Fantasizing, imagining, projecting.

She was working on a new book, *Murder is Easy*, although, as she knew, it never really was. There were clues to be dropped like crumbs in the forest, and with her preoccupation with world news and the continuing construction project at Greenway, it was hard to concentrate without her beloved companion. She kept Peter's picture on her writing table, but as deep as she looked into his eyes, it was not the same.

Edmund Cork had offered to buy her a puppy, and had made inquiries at Arliss Kennels, which specialized in the increasingly rare breed, but Agatha would have none of it, preferring to mourn, moping around Winterbrook House because of it.

By August 1939, the remodeling at Greenway was complete, and the family moved into their grand home, full of anticipation and a sense of privilege. Lawn parties were given, with lemonade that Max spiked with liquor, while Rosalind served champagne and Agatha drank Devonshire cream mixed with milk. If not exactly the same as the old days, it was close enough, for Agatha knew that times had changed, even along the River Dart.

Agatha's friend Dorothy North came to visit the house for the first time in September, in what was to be the end of innocence. While washing greens for a salad at the kitchen sink, Agatha was amusing Dorothy with a story about the boathouse, with its rotting bulbs and spiderwebs. It was just then that the wireless crackled alive with the news from Ten Downing Street that England had declared war on Germany. The old friends stopped talking and unconsciously held their breath as Prime Minister Neville Chamberlain spoke. His unshakable voice did not make the news any easier to hear as he said he would defeat the enemy. "Now that we have resolved to finish it, I know you will all play your parts with calmness and courage."

A maid cried, and Agatha shuddered despite commanding her mind to remain as calm as Chamberlain advised. Her body simply did not listen. She had been through war, and she hated what it did to people. The maiming was horrible enough, but it was the loss of innocence she dreaded so. *Here we are again,* she thought, and instinctively held her hand out to Dorothy, who clasped it with the tight, cold fingers of fear.

Max's response was to join the Home Guard, which Agatha described as rather like a "comic opera." Comprised of non-military locals who were judged too old for military service, they had enthusiasm, if little else. Without many weapons to speak of, the men in the community organized nightly search parties, looking to the skies and the beaches for any sign of invasion. "Some of the wives were deeply suspicious as to what their husbands were doing under this pretence of guarding the country,"[ii] Agatha remembered.

When *Murder Is Easy*[18] was published the previous June, it was positively received. The *Manchester Guardian* felt that "the story must be counted as yet another example of Mrs. Christie's inexhaustible ingenuity."[iii] Agatha followed that book with a volume of short stories, *The Regatta Mysteries and Other Stories*—the first assembled specifically for publication in the United States. The *New Yorker* labeled the collection "rather frothy but pleasant enough for summer weekend readings."[iv]

The Christie masterpiece of 1939 was saved for the end of the year when *Ten Little Niggers* debuted on bookshelves in November to astounding raves. The title, as racist as it suggests, derives from ten guests on Nigger Island just off the coast of England—an island that received "its name from its resemblance to a man's head—a man with negroid lips."[v]

So potentially offensive was the title in America that it was changed to *And Then There Were None* for its debut in 1940. In England, however, there was no mention of bias or racism in any reviews, which thought the title a mere reflection of the nursery rhyme on which it was based.

Rupert Hart-Davis, writing for the *Spectator,* labeled it "Agatha Christie's masterpiece."[vi] Isaac Anderson's review in the *New York Times* said that "the whole thing is utterly impossible and utterly fascinating. It is the most baffling mystery Agatha Christie has ever written."[vii]

Perhaps the most astonishing part of the book was Agatha's pride in it. For a woman whose ego was so small as to

---

[18] Published as *Easy to Kill* in America.

be microscopic and whose interest in reviews was so sporadic, she wrote in her autobiography about *Ten Little Niggers* with uncamouflaged pride. "Ten people had to die without it becoming ridiculous or the murderer becoming obvious. I wrote the book after a tremendous amount of planning, and I was pleased with what I had made of it. It was clear, straightforward, baffling, and yet had a perfectly reasonable explanation.... It was well received and reviewed, but the person who was really pleased with it was myself, for I knew better than any critic how difficult it had been."[viii]

Ten Little Niggers/And Then There Were None went on to sell one hundred million copies over the years and ranks as the top-selling mystery novel in the world.

The last book Agatha wrote before the start of the war, *Sad Cypress,* was published in March 1940, but not without a spirited fight over the cover jacket. Although Agatha had no legal right to dictate artwork, she had written to her agent, Edmund Cork, declaring that the teal blue cover was "AWFUL...so common!!"[ix] while adding that her idea was that "a black and white jacket would be very arresting and striking."[x]

The always tactful Cork replied that Collins had already printed the jackets and "seem a little loath to destroy them, but of course, they will do so if you feel strongly about it."[xi]

Worse still, the book received only passing marks from the critics. The *New York Times* said that it was "not the best of the Christie achievements,"[xii] while *The Scotsman* said, "*Sad Cypress* is slighter and rather less ingenious than Mrs. Christie's stories usually are."[xiii]

The Germans were relentless in their pursuit of war and eventually the planes did come, of course. The Home Guard saw them, some flying directly over Devon and Greenway, dropping bombs in the neighborhood but causing little damage. Messerschmitts buzzing, then darting back into the night. Nothing glamorous about these planes or pilots. To Agatha, they harbored hatred and carried death.

Determined to make some positive contribution to the war effort, Max moved to London and, at the request of the founder of the British Institute of Archaeology at Ankara, volunteered to help raise funds and supplies for Erzincan, Turkey, which had been struck by a deadly earthquake that took thirty-nine thousand lives. Agatha, now nearly fifty, remained at Greenway with Rosalind and returned to the dispensary at Torquay, where she updated her skills in the pharmacy, noting that, "On the whole it was much simpler than it had been in my young days; there were so many pills, tablets, powders and things already prepared in bottles."[xiv]

Soon after the bombings in Devon, Agatha joined her husband in London, where they stayed in Sheffield Terrace— albeit briefly, since a land mine struck directly across the street, destroying the neighboring homes and damaging the top floor and basement of number 58. Among the casualties: Agatha's beloved Steinway, which was "never quite the same." The war was moving closer, faster now, and any pretense of normality was forgotten behind black-out drapes and the wail of sirens.

Their home badly damaged, and with Rosalind at Greenway, the Mallowans moved into a little flat on Lawn Road near the Hampstead Heath parkland. Five years earlier, Lawn Road had been transformed by ultra-modern concrete structures designed by Canadian architect Wells Coates, and it was here that Agatha would spend most of the war years alone. Her beloved aide-de-camp, Carlo, went off to work in a munitions factory, leaving her dog, James, a Sealyham terrier, in Agatha's care at Lawn Road for the duration of the war.

Thanks to the effort of Lord George Ambrose Lloyd, who admired Max's work with the Turkish Relief, Max had been accepted in the intelligence wing of the RAF. With his language skills in Arabic, it was natural that he would be assigned to the Middle East. Nearly a decade after they married, Agatha and Max parted. It is said that the tugging of taffy makes it sweeter. It was like that for this pair—the separation pulling at their hearts on a daily basis until they were reunited again.

Agatha went to work at the University College Hospital in the dispensary, returning home at night to Lawn Road Flats to write. The first wave of loneliness was absorbed in work and in the company of Carlo's Sealyham, and in scattered breaks back to Greenway to visit Rosalind.

Agatha's daughter, now nearly twenty-one, considered herself to be a woman. She was no longer the teenager who giggled with friends at private jokes and imagined flirtations. And while never one to share intimacies with her mother,

Rosalind now became distant in the way children sometimes do when struggling to find their independence.

But Rosalind *wasn't* independent, for she depended on her mother for housing and funds. Her brief effort to join the Woman's Auxiliary Air Force, and later the Auxiliary Territorial Service, was more illusion than reality, acting as she thought she should; doing her part without feeling the need. Yet Rosalind's mind was really on love—a rather clandestine love, at that.

Agatha's first clue that something was afoot came with the discovery of her daughter's blunted cigarette butts crushed in an ashtray next to the upstairs telephone—the mystery writer discerning that long private conversations were taking place with someone. Just *who* became known with Rosalind's casual comment that she had decided to marry Hubert Prichard—tall, handsome, intelligent Hubert, a soldier with the Royal Welch Fusiliers, one of the oldest regiments in the army.

Hubert had frequented Abney Hall in the company of Jack, who was in the same regiment. And while it was Aunt Punkie who brought him to Greenway, it was Rosalind who kept inviting him back.

Twelve years Rosalind's senior, Hubert had inherited Pwllywrach, a large manor home that had been in the family for years, near the rolling green countryside of Colwinston, at the Vale of Glamorgan in Wales.

"I suppose you want to come to the wedding, Mother?" was the way Agatha received her invitation from her only daughter.[xv] Agatha did want to come. She *insisted* on it, in fact, despite Rosalind's seeming reluctance to include her in the ceremony—which was part independence, part reluctance to be overshadowed by her famous mother. All of which is how, the following Monday, the wife-to-be and the mother-of-the-bride traveled by train to the North Wales village of Denbigh—famous for glove manufacturing, an unfinished church, and the marriage of Agatha Christie's daughter, age twenty, to Hubert Prichard in the registrar's office on High Street, on June 11, 1940.

The tax situation in America remained unresolved, and this worried Agatha so much that her letters to Edmund Cork mostly concerned her dwindling financial resources. "Have you managed my finances in case of my sudden demise," she wrote in June, aware that a bomb might strike her house, with her in it, at any time.[xvi]

"Am I going to get some money from America soon?" she asked the following month. "A good deal of red ink in my bank a/c and they don't seem as fond of overdrafts as they used to be."[xvii]

Her agents and attorneys on both sides of the Atlantic argued and fretted over the fact that the American tax revenue service had essentially frozen Agatha's assets in the United States, pending payment of taxes. Her British taxes also needed to be paid, but her accountants were waiting to receive money from America, the source of most of her income. In the meantime, Agatha continued to write.

One, Two, Buckle My Shoe[19] was released in England in November 1940. When Agatha's American agent, Harold Ober, received the manuscript of the book, he wrote Edmund Cork that "I'm afraid I don't like this book quite as much some of the others..."[xviii] It was scarred by the pervasive darkness of war, not the quaintness of St. Mary Mead. Yet to Maurice Richardson, reviewing for *The Observer*, Agatha Christie could do no wrong. "If [she] were to write about the murder of a telephone directory by a time-table, the story would still be compellingly readable."[xix]

Possibly the *more* important point to make was that Agatha Christie was writing *at all*. As the bombs dropped around London in late 1940, she refused to venture to a bomb shelter, preferring to stay in her apartment on the second floor of the Lawn Road Flats. She would grab her hot water bottle, her fur coat, and cover her face with a down pillow as glass shattered and walls shook. When the noise stopped, she bravely went back to typing, as if nothing had happened.

"Broken windows, bombs, land mines, and rockets— all these things would go on, not as something extraordinary, but as perfectly natural.... They were an everyday happening,"[xx] she wrote, and the hit parade of books continued still.

The constant threat of death in London during the Blitz had another effect on Agatha. In the time available to her outside of the dispensary, she had decided to stockpile some books as annuities for her loved ones. Max was gifted the rights to *Sleeping Murder*, featuring the spinster sleuth Miss

---

[19] Published in America as *The Patriotic Murders*. The paperback version was titled *An Overdose of Death* (1953).

Marple, while Rosalind was given *Curtain*, the final case for Hercule Poirot.

The air raids continued through much of 1940 and well into 1941. Thus, Agatha's thirty-eighth book, *Evil Under the Sun*, was pressed into existence in the worst of times. The result was classic Christie—mystery, humor, and glamour swirled in an exotic setting. Set off the coast of Devon, in the heat of the summer, immaculate Hercule Poirot stood in the sand in his crisp white suit, worrying that his hair color was running down his neck. He sensed murder, and of course it arrived—all without a hint that the world around Agatha Christie was in turmoil.

The reviews for *Evil Under the Sun* were excellent in early 1941, with E. R. Punshon asking in the *Manchester Guardian*: "Is it going too far to call Mrs. Agatha Christie one of the most remarkable writers of the day?"[xxi]

Punshon was unaware that no sooner had Agatha finished that book, than she was working on two others, concurrently. *N or M?* was published in 1941, *The Body in the Library* in 1942. "One of the difficulties of writing a book is that it suddenly goes stale on you," Agatha said. "Then you have to put it by, and do other things—but I had no other things to do. I had no wish to sit and brood."[xxii] Brood she did not.

Yet, the more she wrote, the less she earned, based on the freezing of her earnings from the U.S. At one point in the early forties, she even contemplated selling Greenway, and no doubt *would* have if a ready buyer with cash had been found. There were loans advanced by the bank against future earnings and pleadings made between agents, with Edmund Cork finally suggesting that more books were the only answer.

"Do I gather from your letter that you are urging this sausage machine to churn out a couple more of the same old hand?" Agatha asked—this reference to herself as a sausage machine was the first but not the last time Agatha would use the parallel. "Feel too depressed by my financial plight at the moment. What's the *good* of writing for money if I don't get *anything* out of it?" she asked.[xxiii]

Agatha made a very good point. As Cork wrote to Ober, "It is just a nightmare having to produce for the tax gatherer no less than three-quarters of those very monies you have to retain for American taxation…. I can quite understand your finding it hard to believe that Agatha will have to find money for Income Tax on monies she has not received..."[xxiv]

Edmund was on the offensive with his American counterpart, since it was basically an American problem that affected his British client. Agatha was worried as well, but not overly so, for at this point she still believed that logical minds would prevail right along with justice. What she would *not* tolerate was invasion of privacy of any sort, and now that she was living in London full-time and working in a public dispensary, her availability to be observed and written about was markedly increased.

Since Agatha's mysterious disappearance in 1926, requests for interviews and photographs had been frequent— and denied. The excuse was always the same—"Mrs. Christie is out of the country and in a location off-limits to journalists and photographers." Often it was even true. Currently, however, no such excuse could be given. And with Agatha's contribution to the war effort, the interest was peaking.

"Hospital still standing, though flattened buildings all around," she wrote to Cork. "If they must have some kind of pictures, let them have that."[xxv]

The press was not to be so easily assuaged. In May 1941, the *Saturday Evening Post* ran an article titled "Mystery Writer, Mystery Woman" that made Agatha furious. "I will NOT be a 'Mystery Woman,'" she wrote to Cork, enclosing a copy of the piece that he had not yet read. In it, the unnamed writer said, "Mrs. Christie is something of a mystery woman. Even her agent and publisher can supply little information about her. Her manuscripts arrive without any of the explanations and interpretations in which most authors indulge. They're published, they're successful—some more than others. That's about the net of it.... Today, Mrs. Christie is doing war work for England, as is her husband. Information about the details of what they are doing is not available."[xxvi]

If the public were looking for intrigue, they would certainly have been disappointed. Without the company of her beloved Max, who had now been deployed to Cairo, Agatha was beginning to tire of the writing pace she had set, the loss of friends by death or evacuation, and the endless destruction around her. The beauty of London's buildings had been all but destroyed. In fact, when Buckingham Palace was bombed, Queen Elizabeth, wife of then King George, said she was glad it happened. "It makes me feel I can look the East End in the face," she declared, referring to the most heavily bombed section.

It would have been quite simple for someone of Agatha's celebrity to leave the country, to travel to Canada or another neutral zone, and it was suggested several times by Edmund Cork that she do just that. But Agatha did not want to leave her home simply to feel safe. Agatha wanted to be with her husband. To accomplish that goal, she began a campaign to gain a magazine assignment to write about the war and thereby receive the necessary government clearances to travel to Cairo.

"Mrs. Mallowan tells me that her husband, who is now in the Air Force, is to be drafted in the Middle East Headquarters some time this summer, and, of course, it is very difficult for her to accompany him—or join him in Cairo," Cork wrote to his American counterpart, Harold Ober. "She has asked me whether I can do anything to facilitate it. There is very little we can do at this end, but it occurred to me that if America is going to be interested in a woman writer's view of Middle East conditions, it might be possible to get some articles commissioned."

Ober attempted to involve *Colliers Magazine* or the *Saturday Evening Post,* both of which had printed serializations of Agatha's books in the past. In the end, however, there was little interest, and the idea was eventually dropped.

By the end of May, Agatha wrote that if she could not get to Cairo, the next best thing was "the exact job I should like in England...dispenser to a doctor in Wendover."[xxvii]

Cork was appalled at the thought of his star writer working for a local doctor and responded, "My own feeling is that you should be doing a much more important job than the Wendover one."[xxviii]

Frustrated and angry over her seeming inability to be seen as anything other than a writer, Agatha wasted little time in rebuking her agent. "Dear Mr. Cork, It is all very well to say I ought to be doing a 'more important job.' What job? Just make a constructive suggestion! ... Now you tell me what your idea of an interesting important job is for me, because if I'm not going to get overseas, I need one!" She signed the note "Agatha Mallowan."[xxix]

Cork's suggestion, if it qualifies as one, was that Agatha should continue to do what she did best—write. He suggested she adapt her books to plays, a relatively easy process for her to accomplish and the potential for a lucrative payday spread over years of royalties.

Cork had been quietly looking for backers for plays based on several of Agatha's books and finally found a willing financier in B. A. (Bertie) Meyer, who had helped commission the St. Martin's Theatre in London's West End. Meyer offered to produce *Ten Little Niggers* as a play and to pay Agatha £100 plus five percent royalties from the box office receipts. All it required was a script and a signature—both of which an increasingly excited Agatha was prepared to provide—and did. To her surprise, Meyer also expressed interest in having her adapt *Death on the Nile* as a play to star Agatha's friend, Francis L. Sullivan.

The change in Agatha seemed to take place overnight. Inspired by Meyer's confidence, Agatha suddenly was a playwright, mixing with actors and writing to Max, "I am very theatrical now, and call all the most frightful people 'Darling.'"[xxx]

She launched herself aggressively into writing a new ending for *Niggers,* which, as it now stood, had every member of the cast murdered before the final curtain, leaving no one left to tell the story. "At that moment, writing plays seemed to me to be entrancing, simply because it wasn't my job," Agatha wrote, "because I hadn't got the feeling that I *had* to think of a play."[xxxi] It was during this effort that Agatha received a surprise note from the British Admiralty requisitioning Greenway House for use by the American military.

She was actually thrilled to loan her home to the cause of freedom—yet another way to contribute to victory. In the course of two weeks, Agatha had all the furniture removed from the rooms (storing it in the drawing room) and packed all of the family's personal belongings for safekeeping. And then she wrote to Max.

"I stayed for a little while after the men had gone and then I walked up (outside) and sat on the seat overlooking the house and the river and made believe you were sitting beside me." She was aware that the house might be bombed by the Germans or damaged by the Americans—that she might never see it again. "All my happy memories are of the garden and you planting your magnolias and I making my path down by the river," she added. "I thought tonight sitting there—it is the loveliest place in the world."[xxxii]

Leaving Greenway behind and returning to London was like entering an artificial world, where fires and bombs and smoke replaced sky, blotting out her recent memory of happiness. Her only refuge was in writing, so Agatha returned to her typewriter, producing *The Moving Finger,* a book she would later regard as one of her favorites. In an unusual move, *Finger* was published first in America at the end of 1942. Maurice Willson Disher, writing in the *Times Literary Supplement,* thought that "beyond all doubt, the puzzle in *The Moving Finger* is fit for experts."[xxxiii]

She quickly followed *The Moving Finger* with *Five Little Pigs,*[20] called "brilliant" by the *Times Literary Supplement*[xxxiv] when it was published in 1943. The pigs of the title refer to the five suspects in the Hercule Poirot mystery dedicated to Max's friend, Stephen Glanville.

Max had known Stephen Glanville since the mid-twenties, when he met the Egyptologist at the British Museum. Glanville was a full decade younger than Agatha, with a disarmingly childlike personality that made him instantly attractive to women with whom he was constantly flirting. With his wife evacuated with his two children to Canada, Glanville began escorting Agatha to her social functions when the invitations appeared. Flattered by the attention at a time when she was desperate for companionship, Agatha allowed herself to be entertained privately in his home. "He would call for me at the hospital and take me back to his house at Highgate to dine," she remembered.[xxxv]

She went to hear him give a lecture and wrote to Max about Glanville's "pleasant voice." She had him to dinner at Lawn Road Flats, where they toasted the publication of *Five Little Pigs* and raised a glass to Max in front of his picture. As *Ten Little Niggers* went into rehearsals, helmed by female director Irene Hentschel, it was Glanville who accompanied Agatha to the run-throughs. He joined her again on opening

[20] Published in America as *Murder in Retrospect.*

night, escorting Agatha to the St. James's Theatre on
November 17, 1943.

"Party at Prunier's afterwards," Agatha wrote Max.
"Smoked salmon and oysters, hot lobster Thermidor and
chocolate mousse. We were nine Little Niggers—the tenth was
in Tripolitania (or perhaps Cairo?)."[xxxvi] All very platonic and
very aboveboard, yet there was something a little too familiar
about his thank-you note, a little too suggestive perhaps.

"Agatha darling—Last night was really something to
remember. The whole thing was really FUN.... Best of all was
the   diverse   experience   of   Agatha: Agatha   really
nervous...Agatha   in   the   moment   of   triumph,   quite
radiant...last, and perhaps most precious, Agatha still quietly
excited, but beautifully poised and content...."[xxxvii]

In reality, Agatha was neither poised nor content. She
was restless, longing to be with Max, struggling with finances,
and writing as she could on her next book, *Towards Zero*,[21]
which she directed her agent to "vault" for publication the
following year. She was also a brand-new grandmother.

When Rosalind first discovered that she was pregnant,
she chose not to share the information with Agatha for months,
typical of a relationship that was polite but not intimate. Yet,
once   informed,   Agatha   responded   like   any   excited
grandmother-to-be, taking her daughter shopping for baby
clothes, diapers, and other maternity essentials. Rosalind
planned to have the baby in a nursing home near Abney Hall,
and was a little more than eight months pregnant when Agatha
left her in the care of her sister, Madge, and continued on to
dress rehearsals for *Ten Little Niggers,* set to open in London's
Wimbledon Theatre in Merton on September 20, 1943.

Agatha was at the opening when she received a
telegram from Madge alerting her to the imminent birth.
Racing back to Rosalind's side, Agatha arrived in Cheshire to
find that Rosalind and Hubert Prichard had a son named
Mathew, born September 21, 1943.

As the house in Glamorgan was being prepared for
mother and son, Agatha brought the pair to London and
installed them in her flat on Campden Street for a month in the
care of a nurse, with Agatha dropping by to clean and cook.
And while she was fine in the kitchen, the reality of having to

---

[21] Titled *Come and Be Hanged* in the American paperback edition.

live without staff to scrub the floors was abominable to Agatha. "My hands are like nutmeg graters from soda and soap—and my knees are sore—and my back aches," she wrote to Max.[xxxviii]

On January 17, 1944, Agatha was "well hidden away up in the balcony" for the opening night of *Hidden Hollow,* the renamed *Death on the Nile.* It was being tried out at the Dundee Repertory Theatre in Dundee, Scotland, and while Agatha thought it was well received, the play failed to find an available London theater and closed shortly thereafter.

Continuing to overload herself with work, Agatha began writing a new Mary Westmacott novel, *Absent in the Spring.* In what can only be described as an inspired weekend, Agatha began writing the first chapter, followed it with the last, and then continued for the next three days to fill in the pages in between.

"I was so frightened of interruptions, of anything breaking the flow of continuity, that after I had written the first chapter in a white heat, I proceeded to write the last chapter, because I knew so clearly where I was going that I felt that I must get it down on paper," Agatha remembered.[xxxix] With the passion of one on a spiritual mission, she wrote and then slept. "I fell on my bed, and as far as I can remember slept more or less for twenty-four hours straight through. Then I got up and had an enormous dinner, and the following day, I was able to go to the hospital again."[xl]

In contrast to the speed with which *Absent in the Spring* was conceived and written, Agatha's next book, *Death Comes As the End,* was a slow and deliberate process. Its setting was suggested by Stephen Glanville, who convinced Agatha to locate her next mystery in the historical backdrop of ancient Egypt. And it was Stephen who argued with Agatha about the ending when she finally agreed to write it.

"I am sorry to say that I gave in to him in the end. I was always annoyed with myself for having done so," Agatha said. "Up till then, on the whole, though I have given in to people on every subject under the sun, *I have never given in to anyone over what I write.*"[xli]

Based on the letters of a farmer discovered in a tomb near Luxor, *Death Comes As the End* was Agatha's forty-fourth book. Isaac Anderson, reviewing the novel for the *New York Times,* said, "Besides giving us a mystery story quite up to her own high standard, Agatha Christie has succeeded admirably in picturing the people of ancient Egypt as living persons and not as resurrected mummies."[xlii]

With Max thousands of miles away, Agatha transferred her love to her newborn grandson, making frequent visits to Pwllywrach, beginning at Christmas and continuing for the next several years. With Hubert stationed in France (he was only able to visit the baby once), Rosalind reluctantly called upon her mother for help.

"I am so happy to think of them, and that I can be 'sent for,'" she wrote to Max, for she did enjoy her time with Mathew and had even managed to keep silent rather than comment on the way the baby was being raised. Agatha wanted to surround the child with fantasy—flowers and colors and stories of faraway places. But with her husband gone, Rosalind found little time for play as she took on all the responsibility of the large home ("unheated"), the baby ("looks exactly like Hubert"), as well as all the livestock ("recalcitrant"). Just twenty-four, and without any household staff, she insisted on doing it all, while Agatha looked on and marveled, wanting to freeze the moment in time.

It was near the end of August 1944 when Rosalind received notification that her husband was missing in action. For Agatha, the world stopped as she rushed to her daughter's side, attempting to give her comfort. But Rosalind would have none of that. She allowed no weakness to permeate her crust of invincibility, and certainly not in front of her mother.

"It is terrible for Ros," Agatha wrote to Max the first week of September from Pwllywrach. "She is wonderful— never turns a hair—carries on exactly as usual—with food, dogs, Mathew, we act as though nothing has happened."[xliii]

But something had happened, they just did not know it then. Hubert Prichard had been killed in battle, and his grave was finally found and identified in October. "This is a great tragedy," she wrote to Cork. "I think they were so happy and well suited." If Rosalind cried, it was never in front of Agatha. But Agatha cried...and continued to cry, sinking into a deep depression and unwilling to struggle against it. She was crushed by the loss of her son-in-law, crushed by life, and for the first time in her life admitted that attempting to write was futile.

The war had finally won its battle against Agatha Christie. For all her courage and indefatigable strength, it had broken her spirit and her hope.

"Oh darling," she wrote to Max. "How sick I am of war and misery."[xliv]

In another few months, the war would be over, Greenway House would be returned to the Mallowans, and the slow process of rebuilding Europe would begin. Yet for Agatha, the years of bombings and destruction had taken its toll. Physically, she appeared far older than her fifty-five years. Her weight had ballooned, her legs were swollen from poor circulation, and her mind was finally worn to a blunt edge where creative thought was impossible to ignite.

"I could sleep and sleep and sleep," she wrote her husband. Yet sleep, in fact, was the one thing she did *not* do as she pushed through her days, waiting to hear when Max might be returning home. Agatha had always heard that *waiting* was the worst part, but it wasn't so. It was *not knowing* that was horrible, that void between letters when what *might* be happening takes over the imagination.

It took until early spring 1945 for Max to get his transfer back to England, and he notified his wife on April 9, "I am coming home, hooray."

Still, he did not come home. Not that week or the next, and there were no letters, either. She was restless, dissatisfied with life, and for the first time that she could remember, she had lost the memory of joy.

She traveled to visit Rosalind and Mathew in Glamorgan on the weekends and was met with an indifference that somehow fit with the mood of the country. There was a shortage of air to breathe, as if everyone in England had inhaled at the same moment. Agatha felt lost, moving in pre-programmed motion until her husband's return.

On the second Sunday in May, she caught a late train into Paddington Station, then transferred to another for Hampstead. Agatha heard the sound of her feet on the gravel, but never shifted her gaze as she walked the short distance to the Lawn Road Flats, carrying her suitcase and a bag full of kippers.

Once inside her apartment, she casually tossed her jacket aside and placed the kippers in a pan to fry, adjusting the gas on the stove top to its lowest setting. Hearing a clatter on the street below, Agatha went outside to the catwalk that stretched the length of the building and looked down over the railing from the second floor. There, below her on the sidewalk, was the bent-over figure of Max Mallowan. Except for his weight, he had not changed. Still the same Max. "He might have left yesterday. He was back again. We were back again," Agatha remembered.[xlv]

They looked at each other and laughed at their individual weight gains. Four stone between them.[22]

"What a wonderful evening it was!" she wrote. "We ate burned kippers and were happy."[xlvi]

Yet happiness has a way of being elusive, even for those with the best intentions. And as the world began to regain its footing, the Mallowans found that *some* things had not changed at all.

---

[22] Four stone equals fifty-six pounds.

NINE

The Sausage Factory

I regard my work as of no importance,
I've simply been out to entertain.

Agatha Christie

FEBRUARY 1945. THERE WAS A BEAUTIFUL WOMAN LYING naked in the library at Greenway House when Agatha Christie walked into the room for the first time in over two years. And when the British Admiralty politely asked if the woman should be removed, Agatha refused, as she was rather attracted to this female—nubile, young, and something akin to what she knew of from her years spent with Max in the Arab world as a houri.[23] This lovely lady was not a murder victim; in fact, she had never been alive. This was part of a fresco, the final image painted on the ceiling edge of Greenway by Lieutenant Marshall Lee of the 10th U.S. Patrol Boat Flotilla, based during the war in the Dart Estuary.

Lee was a talented artist in addition to being a lieutenant in the Coast Guard assigned to Flotilla 10, which used the Greenway library as their officers' mess hall during the war. Lee had painted scenes from the unit's travels "starting at Key West, Bermuda, Nassau, Morocco and so on," Agatha remembered, "finally ending with a slightly glorified exaggeration of the woods of Greenway and the white house showing through the trees."[i] The final drawing was of the woman, "an exquisite nymph, not quite finished...which [Agatha had] always supposed to represent the hopes of houris at journey's end when the war was over."[ii]

Greenway House survived the Americans in surprisingly fine shape, with the exception of some moth holes in the carpets, the kitchen "indescribable with the blackness

[23] One of the beautiful virgins promised in Paradise to all faithful Muslim men.

and oily soot of the walls,"[iii] and fourteen lavatories that had been installed in the passageway leading to it. Outside, the once splendid gardens had been allowed to overgrow, obliterating paths in a wild snarl of nature unrestrained. "How beautiful Greenway looked in its tangled splendor," Agatha thought. It took months before the place began to resemble home again, but eventually order was restored and life returned to a routine, "though not as it had been before," she said. "There was the relief that peace had at last come, but no certainty in the future of peace, or indeed of anything."[iv]

After her husband's return from the war, Agatha remained with him in London, where Max continued his work at the Air Ministry. Anxious to return as quickly as possible to archaeology, Max canvassed the various universities and museums for an employment opportunity, while Agatha continued to supply the majority of the couple's funds.

To that end, the self-proclaimed "sausage machine" continued to grind away. Her adaptation of *Appointment with Death,* written the previous year, opened in London's West End in March 1945, and closed after forty-two performances; her forty-fifth book, *Sparkling Cyanide,* was originally published in America as *Remembered Death* (an unpopular title) in February 1945. The British version followed in December. Yet it was *The Hollow,* featuring Hercule Poirot in his first appearance in four years, that gained the most notice. The book was dedicated to the Francis L. Sullivans: "For Larry and Danae, with apologies for using their swimming pool as the scene of a murder."

Agatha had become great friends with the actor (who played Poirot in *Black Coffee*) and his wife. Although she seldom went out in London during the war years, she made several trips to visit the Sullivans at their home in Haslemere, forty-four miles south of the city. "I always found it restful staying with actors in wartime, because to them, acting and the theatrical world were the *real* world. Any other world was not.... It was wonderfully refreshing."[v]

Larry Sullivan told writer Gwen Robyns that his wife "in a moment of insane optimism of the English weather, had caused a swimming pool to be made, with half-a-dozen paths leading down to it through the chestnut wood. One fine

Sunday morning, I discovered Agatha wandering up and down these paths with an expression of intense concentration."[vi] That was the beginning of *The Hollow*,[24] which the *San Francisco Chronicle* labeled "the best Christie in years."[vii]

While these projects fell under the category of "business as usual," Agatha's next book was a complete labor of love. *Come, Tell Me How You Live*, credited to Agatha Christie Mallowan, recounts the couple's adventures in Iraq and Syria and is written with a charm and humor that, more than any other book, reveals the marvelous spunk and resiliency of both the author and her marriage.

Picturing herself as large, rather matronly, and socially inept, Agatha was not at ease at social functions and admired those women who were. She wanted to be elegant, a clever conversationalist who laughed and flitted through parties in a silken ensemble that draped across her body *just so*.

This is why she often could be found in a corner *studying* a party rather than participating in it. In *Come, Tell Me How You Live*, she confessed that "I look with envy at self-possessed women flipping cigarette ash here, and there, and everywhere, and creep miserably round the room at cocktail parties finding a place to hide my untasted glass.

"For six months, I religiously smoked a cigarette after lunch, and after dinner, choking a little, biting fragments of tobacco, and blinking as the ascending smoke pricked my eyelids. Soon, I told myself, I should learn to like smoking. I did not learn to like it, and my performance was criticized severely as being inartistic and painful to watch."[viii]

Switching to wine, Agatha tried clarets, burgundies, Sauternes, Tokay, and merlot before switching to hard liquor—scotch, rum, vodka, and absinthe. Max, who had a palate for fine alcohol of all types, encouraged this effort. "My only reaction was that some tasted worse than others! With a weary sigh, Max contemplated a life in which he should be forever condemned to the battle of obtaining water for me in a restaurant!"[ix]

Failing miserably at being a sophisticate, Agatha resolved to prove her worth yet again as a housewife. While she did not scrub and clean, for those were the jobs of a maid, she loved to linger in the kitchen, preparing rich meals thick

---

[24] Published in America as *Murder After Hours*.

with cream and butter, totally unhealthy and absolutely delicious. She loved to arrange flowers from her garden, filling the house with blossoms of varying colors, and mixing them with more regard to instinct than to style.

While Agatha in an apron was popular at home, Agatha the writer was arriving in theaters in the form of *And Then There Were None,* a major feature film from 20th Century Fox. Helmed by French director René Clair and with a screenplay by Dudley Nichols (*Bringing Up Baby*), the film debuted in New York on October 31, 1945, to positive press and opened in England as *Ten Little Niggers.* Invited to both premieres, Agatha declined each, preferring at that point to remain at Greenway House in happy domesticity.

"Trying to restrain my pullets which fly into the kitchen garden," she wrote to Edmund Cork, who had begun to take on more responsibilities in handling small chores for her in London. "But they *are* laying eggs."[x]

Through all of 1946, her only released books were *The Hollow* and *Come, Tell Me How You Live*—both written in 1944. As with many in England, for Agatha and Max the year after the end of the war was a time for tidying up—lives, houses, and the country at large. The Mallowans returned to Winterbrook, which had been rented during the war. While Agatha once again had an overgrown garden to attack, Max collected his notes and wrote about his digs in Syria, documenting his successes and preparing for the potential of returning to complete his work.

There were visits with Rosalind and Mathew. ("He is so wonderful to watch," Agatha wrote to Cork, "that each minute becomes a century.") Her nephew Jack, now living in London on Chester Street, not far from Buckingham Palace, developed the habit of taking Agatha to tea at the Goring Hotel, where she found the finest clotted cream outside of Devon.

Carlo, who was suffering with pain from arthritis, left Agatha in the care of Max and retired to the south coast of England, in Eastbourne, with her sister Mary. *Hidden Horizon,* reworked and retitled *Murder on the Nile,* opened at the Ambassadors Theatre in March 1946, now without Francis L. Sullivan in the play. Writing in the *Daily Mirror,* Bernard Buckham said, "It's an Agatha Christie play, but a poor one"[xi]—a sentiment echoed by many.

In early 1947, Agatha was contacted by the BBC with the news that Her Majesty Queen Mary, wife of the late King George V, had requested a radio play by Mrs. Christie to be broadcast in honor of her upcoming eightieth birthday. "Would Mrs. Christie be so kind?" the BBC inquired. Royal request or not, Agatha had to give it some thought before agreeing to return to her typewriter. The outcome of that effort was a half-hour play titled *Three Blind Mice,* which the Queen Mother, a Christie fan, was said to have enjoyed.

It was also in 1947 that members of the Anti-Defamation League of B'nai B'rith raised serious objections to what they called "flagrant" anti-Semitic references in *The Hollow.* Harold Schiff, director of the book and literature department of the organization, took exception to the line on page 134 that read: "The raucous voice of the vitriolic little Jewess came angrily over the wires." Schiff was of the opinion that Agatha had painted the character, Madame Alfrege, as a "typical Jew and the implication to the reader will be that all Jews are grasping, unpleasant, etc."[xii]

Agatha's American publisher, Dodd, Mead & Co., made the decision to change the word "Jewess" to the word "woman" in future editions. B'nai B'rith was pleased.

In 1947, Agatha decided that after over two decades of being represented by Cork, she could and would begin to call him by his first name. No more "Dear Mr. Cork." Now, it was "Dear Edmund. Will you deal with enclosed." It was the beginning of a trend that would continue for the remainder of her life. "Dear Edmund" was to be the problem-solver: from taxes (unpaid) to travel (unbooked) to letters (unanswered) and invitations (unavailable).

Apparently forgetting the help that she received as a young girl from writer Eden Phillpotts, her note to Edmund continued, "I have let you in for someone called Wallace who wanted me to read her daughter's manuscript. Rather a nice pathetic letter," she cruelly remarked. At that point, however, Agatha wasn't feeling well. The flu, she suspected. "Sunk in listless depression." She signed the note, "Misery, yours, Agatha."[xiii]

The depression she felt was apparently short-lived, for it did not extend to the publication, in 1947, of twelve Hercule

Poirot short stories, released under the title *The Labors of Hercules*. Poirot, lamenting that the Greek hero was nothing more than "a large muscular creature of low intelligence and criminal tendencies,"[xiv] proceeded to reveal cases that loosely related to the Twelve Labors of Hercules, as depicted in ancient literature.

It was a clever theme with witty dialogue that illustrated Agatha's humor and intelligence. The *San Francisco Chronicle*'s Anthony Boucher wrote: "A finely shaped book, richly devious and quite brilliant—by far the best volume of Poirot shorts."[xv]

Though released in 1947, this was not new work. *The Labors of Hercules* was comprised of previously released short stories, mostly from the twenties. So too was her next book, *Witness for the Prosecution and Other Stories,* published only in America, in 1948. Another retread, the compilation was recognized by *The New Yorker* [xvi] as "a pretty routine sampling of Mrs. Christie's short stories, from the past twenty years."

As her publishers were aware, Agatha Christie the writer was unavailable, because Agatha Mallowan was otherwise occupied with the sand and mystery of the Middle East, having returned with her husband to Baghdad and the adventure that was Iraq. After having completed his journals on his previous work in Tell Brak and Chagar Bazar, Max had been offered a post as the recipient of the first Chair of Western Asiatic Archaeology, this at the Institute of Archaeology, a school at the University of London.

In addition to teaching seminars, the position provided for three or more months overseas at an archaeological site of his choosing. For Max, the choice was obvious, returning to Nimrud, south of Nineveh on the Tigris River, with his wife and partner.

"To many travelers, there is no more romantic spot than Nimrud," Max wrote in his memoir, "where forty years ago the bearded heads of protective stone *lamassu,* half man, half beast, stuck out of the ground outside the gates of the ancient palaces, the last of the faithful servants that guarded the warrior priest kings of Assyria."[xvii]

Agatha was thrilled to return to this special spot on earth after a ten-year lapse, and she welcomed it back into her life like the old friend it was. This time, however, there was no Orient Express; it no longer went as far as Iraq. Now, it was the age of air travel—"it was the beginning of excessive boredom and expense without pleasure"[xviii]—where speed became the real luxury, and comfort a disposable commodity.

Once in Baghdad, however, the curiosity and imagination that kept Agatha Christie young and enthused beyond her years returned, along with the heat and the cactus flowers. In a letter to Edmund Cork, in which she exalts about the sun and the food, Agatha reveals a slice of Baghdad that harbors the future.

"Even the rioting students conduce to great laziness," she wrote, "because if you go far along the main street, you get cut off from your hotel by an immense crowd that fills every inch, and whilst they are quite amiable as far as you yourself are concerned, the thoughtful way in which building bricks lay about the pavements handy for students to pick up, makes it possible to get a brick on the side of the head readily intended for the police."[xix]

Back in London, Edmund Cork had leased the 22 Cresswell Place residence to Miss V. M. Glasspool, for a term of twenty-one years at £175 per annum. It would have been quite the bargain had she not requested to be released from the lease, which was then transferred to James Richardson, who would ultimately transfer it was well.

Cork was in need of an American edition of *The Sittaford Mystery*, titled *Murder in Hazelmoor* in the United States. Alan Lane, nephew of John Lane of The Bodley Head, had left that company to form Penguin Books—the first line of all paperback editions in England, with Christie novels as one of his first releases. By 1948, he had published many of her earlier novels, and was eager to release *Murder in Hazelmoor*. Unfortunately, Collins Publishing had suffered severe bomb damage during the war and lost its records and book inventory.

After exhausting all other options, Cork wrote to Rosalind, asking to borrow Agatha's copy from Greenway, which elicited a sharp response with the requested book enclosed. "I must say," Rosalind wrote, "I should have thought you could have found a copy somewhere else. I will really be most upset if it doesn't come back in good condition."[xx]

By mid-March, Agatha was beginning to long for London—but only just barely. Imagining the queen of the ancient Persian Empire, Agatha wrote to Cork: "Esther a shadow on the horizon. One does feel so very carefree out here. Still Spring in England has been sung by many poets."[xxi]

There had been talk about a new Christie novel, which finally surfaced in the form of *Taken at the Flood,*[25] released in March, the same month that Esther's shadow was looming. As intricately plotted as the gardens at Versailles, the Hercule Poirot novel was extremely well received, even though its author was totally unavailable to the press. "A covey of nice, upper class murder suspects...comes to the attention of Hercule Poirot, who incidentally, seems to be a little less self-consciously Gallic of late," or so thought the *New Yorker.*[xxii]

Mary Westmacott surfaced with *The Rose and the Yew Tree*—a novel written in 1944 but finally completed and published four years later, in November 1948. "Miss Westmacott writes crisp and is always lucid," said the *Times Literary Supplement,* adding, however, that the "book is too vague at one point."[xxiii]

In America, *Witness for the Prosecution and Other Stories* found its way onto bookstore shelves in September 1948, in what was to become an increasingly common marketing ploy. It usually involved retitling stories published in England and pushing them on the eager U.S. book buyer as new Christie material.

She also published a new book titled *Crooked House*— a work she later repeatedly mentioned as her favorite. Though it features neither Poirot nor Marple, it does manage to weave an involved plot with an unexpected denouement, no doubt accounting for Agatha's love of the novel.

The *New Statesman and Nation* critic Ralph Partridge said that, "Mrs. Christie is a marvel. *Crooked House* is her forty-ninth contribution to detection, and her sleight of hand is still impeccable."

In the meantime, Agatha sunned, rested, photographed bits of pottery, and wallowed in what had become a structured, gracious, and altogether fulfilling life. Her absence from public view had done little to reduce her appeal, particularly from producers eager to launch stage, film, and now television

---

[25] Published as *There Is a Tide* in America.

versions of her work. While she deferred the entire process to Edmund Cork and his American counterpart, Harold Ober, her right to veto their decisions was never challenged by her agents. They had become extremely adept at tiptoeing around the mood swings of a woman who, in reality, was more about small tempests than outright hostility.

Producer Bertie Meyer was still lugging his production of *Ten Little Niggers* around England in local theaters—one of his more successful runs being at a theater in Farndale managed by Moie Charles and Barbara Toy. It was not surprising that the Charles/Toy combo would have been eager to produce another Christie at some point. What *was* surprising was that the pair wrote directly to the author and asked if she would adapt another of her books for their use onstage.

Agatha's acceptance stunned both her agents and the producers—it was so unexpected. When she asked which of the novels they would prefer, Barbara Toy immediately responded with *Murder at the Vicarage,* her feeling being that "sex and religion always goes down well."[xxiv] The play was written by Agatha, rewritten by Toy and Charles, and opened in the New Theatre in Northampton in October, before moving to the West End's Playhouse Theatre in December 1949.

A critical failure—an unnamed reviewer in the *Times* said, "Everyone has a motive for killing. Nobody, unhappily, has any good stage reason for living"[xxv]—the play managed to last through March 1950, when an eager young impresario named Peter Saunders asked for, and received, the rights to tour the production. It was Saunders who changed the title on the marquee from *Murder at the Vicarage* to *Agatha Christie's Murder at the Vicarage* and instantly got the writer's attention as well as that of the theatergoing public.

At this point, Agatha had escaped yet again to Baghdad and the sandy tells of Nimrud, where the Mallowans had moved into a new house built entirely from mud bricks, with the exception of the roof. It was a step up from their previous living accommodations that had once been part of a sheik's home, but was still "living in squalor," according to Max.

The new home had a living room, sitting room, kitchen, and an "antica" chamber for sorting through recent discoveries.

There were no bedroom accommodations of any kind inside. Sleeping was on the ground in tents, a rather muddled arrangement—especially during monsoons, which, for the first several years, were unseasonably frequent.

Nimrud is the modern name given to Kalhu,[26] the ancient capital of Assyria. Perched like a hidden jewel on the banks of the River Tigris, it is just south of Nineveh. Although it had been previously excavated briefly in the mid-1800s, it would be Max's efforts over the next ten years that uncovered its history and reflected its glory. And at his side, Agatha Christie was totally content to become Mrs. Max Mallowan, photographer-assistant and sometimes cook. It was here that she could truly disappear from prying eyes—and did. In her mind, she had every reason for hiding herself away from view by all, save a few Bedouins.

Back in London, the *Sunday Times* had printed a column in which Agatha was identified as Mary Westmacott, thus ending the anonymity she enjoyed with her alter ego. "How did this information get out?" an irritated Rosalind wrote Cork on February 22, 1949. "I am sure my mother will be most distressed...."[xxvi] She was.

Edmund Cork had no idea how the information was revealed, but suspected it came from the American copyright records for the book. He was, however, able to apply some salve to Agatha's wound with the announcement that Harold Ober had arrived in England with a gift—the very latest model Remington Noiseless typewriter. "What a fascinating toy!" he reported after trying out the machine.[xxvii] At the moment in Nimrud, Agatha was attempting to use a rather strange-looking typewriter equivalent from Switzerland. "Nothing much has come out of it yet, but a few ideas are floating around in my brain!"[xxviii]

Those few ideas eventually would turn into *A Murder Is Announced,* publicly acclaimed by Collins Publishing as Agatha's fiftieth book when it was put on the market in June 1950.[27] (It had followed the release of *Three Blind Mice and Other Stories,*[28] a compilation of short stories including the novella of the BBC radio broadcast of *Three Blind Mice,* which was counted in the total.) *A Murder is Announced* was to be another critical success, a mystery of which the *Toronto Star*

---

[26] Calah is the Old Testament.
[27] It was actually Agatha's fiftieth novel, but her fifty-second book, including her two books of short stories published only in America.
[28] Published in paperback as *The Mousetrap* and *Other Stories.*

said, "displays all the adroit and well-bred legerdemain one has come to expect from Agatha Christie.... This jubilee whodunit is as deft and ingenious a fabrication as Agatha Christie has contrived in many a year."[xxix]

The publisher, eager to celebrate the moment, gave a party in Agatha's honor at the Ritz Hotel in London, the red silk walls of the banquet room a royal backdrop for the "Queen of Crime." It was a fitting tribute to the nearly sixty-year-old woman, whose sales had totaled seventy-five million in the United States and one hundred million around the world.

At the event, Collins had a small printed booklet set on each dinner plate, with best wishes supplied by celebrity guests and fans. Among the entries: a note from Prime Minister Clement Attlee that read, "I admire and delight in the ingenuity of Agatha Christie's mind and in her capacity to keep a secret until she is ready to divulge it."[xxx]

As she was at all parties, Agatha was uncomfortable at this one, but held court, glass of water in hand, wondering silently at all the fuss.

Rosalind watched her mother with unveiled pride. It had not always been easy walking in the shadow of someone this revered and cherished, especially given Agatha's ability to presume her daughter to be the dependable one, in complete control, "the adult in the family."

The previous October, after five years on her own, Rosalind had remarried, inviting Agatha and Max to the wedding in the office of the registrar in London. It was a last-minute decision, the invite extended via letter.

"I don't suppose anyone will enjoy it much but you have got to be there and Max and then we shall have to come back to look after the dogs. You mustn't look too smart,"[xxxi] Rosalind added by way of warning—just in case her mother should pull out the mink.

Her new husband, Anthony Hicks, was a non-practicing attorney and Tibetan scholar who wooed Rosalind at Greenway, where she accepted his proposal. Both Agatha and Max admired Hicks, enamored of his gentle ways, his easy manner, and affection for seven-year-old Mathew. "Anthony was at the time reading Tibetan as well as Sanskrit at the School of Oriental and African Studies," Max wrote in his memoirs. "His natural brilliance was unaccompanied by a particle of personal ambition." Max thought of Hicks as the "kindest man I have ever known."[xxxii]

In August, following the large soiree, Agatha received news that her sister, Madge, had died. As with the passing of her brother, Monty, Agatha seemed to take the news of Punkie's death stoically, without overt emotion, and moved on with her life. Rosalind was more outwardly moved, remaining for days in Abney Hall, in mourning. When she left, she remanded herself to Greenway, with Anthony and Mathew along, to catch the remaining moments of summer. Despite the July sun and a moon the size of Kansas, the air was particularly damp that year, especially in the evenings. It was then that Agatha began to work seriously on preparing to adapt *The Hollow* into a play.

Rosalind, who liked the book, thought it would make a horrible play and attempted to dissuade her mother. As Agatha later wrote, Rosalind "had the valuable role in life of eternally trying to discourage me without success." Edmund Cork had gotten Bertie Meyer to agree to produce the finished play, hopefully for the following year. All of which would have been fine, if Bertie Meyer had kept his word. Fortunately, when, by the middle of 1951, he had done nothing to schedule a production, the entire play was offered to Peter Saunders, who expressed interest and suggested lunch at the Carlton Grill to discuss the particulars.

In those days, the Carlton Grill had a reputation for its sausages and meat pies—hearty stuff that set the tone for a comfortable meeting. Saunders had brought light comic actor Hubert Gregg, whom he believed to be the perfect choice to direct, despite his lack of experience. On her side, Agatha was joined by Rosalind, the naysayer, and Anthony Hicks, the voice of reason. In the end, Saunders's passion and confidence won the group over, all of whom were pulled into the vortex of his enthusiasm.

Gregg recalled Agatha at the play's rehearsals "spreading herself over a seat in the stalls and scribbling notes that would eventually be incorporated into rewrites on the play. I remember that there was this word, peremptory, that was in some speech of the character Inspector Colquhoun, investigating the crime. The actor playing the part was mispronouncing the word, which should be spoken *per*emptory.

"Agatha spoke up and bet me a pound that the actor was saying the word correctly. 'He's right you know,' she insisted, but never stopped me from changing it in any case. The next day, however, she slipped me a pound note with a wink. She wasn't above admitting a mistake, or keeping someone from feeling foolish because of theirs."[xxxiii]

Through casting maneuvers and money shortfalls, Saunders managed to keep his word, opening the play as promised in the Cambridge Arts Theatre on February 10, 1951, with Jeanne De Casalis in the lead.

At this point, Agatha had conveniently returned to Baghdad, allowing her to legitimately miss opening night, but she saw to it that her presence was felt with gifts of flowers for all the stars. "Something rather exotic for Jeanne De Casalis and probably tulips of different colors for the others,"[xxxiv] she instructed Cork from Iraq, making mention that the play was opening on St. Agatha's Day—a major omen.

The very same week, tragedy struck Max, whose mother was diagnosed with incurable abdominal cancer and died within two weeks. Agatha, who had written Cork to take care of all the expenses for her mother-in-law's care, labeled her quick passing a "great blessing." Max was devastated, grieving long distance, unable to return for the funeral.

The day Max got the news of her death, he cried the slow tears of sadness as Agatha held his head like a mother, stroking his thinning hair and listening to the broken cadence of sobbing. The afternoon heat was dry and intense, a nice change from the sudden rains that had greeted them when they first arrived. In the air was the smell of lamb cooking in the distance, and the braying of a camel. But Max missed it all; he had fallen asleep in her arms.

If she minded the rustic, near-slumlike living conditions, she never mentioned it; she willingly slept in her tent, inside her sleeping bag, positioned on a carpet placed directly on dirt. It was, quite simply, home.

The Hollow, the American rights for which had been sold to Lee Schubert of Schubert Theaters, began what was a successful two-month tour, with a London opening scheduled

for June 7 at the Fortune Theatre. While pleased at the play's
success, the thought of another opening night was "awful to
face," Agatha told Cork in a letter that also announced she was
headed back to England in May. "Why couldn't you get it on
before I return?" she asked.[xxxv]

In March of 1951, *They Came to Baghdad* was
released, Agatha's absence noted by some reviewers—the
majority of whom found the spy thriller well done. Anthony
Boucher of the *New York Times* called it "the most satisfactory
novel in some years from one of the most satisfying of
novelists."[xxxvi]

In addition to becoming quite a best-seller, the book
held the distinction of being the first written in Agatha's new
writing room, added on to the mud-brick house in Nimrud for
a cost of £50. It was a little square addition on one end of the
house, labeled with a sign that read: "Beit Agatha" (Agatha's
House). Just like the third-floor space on Sheffield Terrace, this
was her sanctuary, off-limits to all except her typewriter, table,
two chairs, and two paintings by Iraqi artists: "One of a sad
looking cow by a tree; the other a kaleidoscope,"[xxxvii] which,
when examined closely, turned into "two donkeys with men
leading them through the suq."[xxxviii]

The setting and seclusion in Agatha's House worked
their magic on her imagination as she completed two new
books—*Mrs. McGinty's Dead,* a Hercule Poirot mystery, and
They Do It With Mirrors, a Miss Marple entry. It was also in
this room that Agatha started to work on her autobiography,
less out of ego than a sincere desire to have her story told
correctly; and it is for that reason that multiple quotes have
been taken from that book and used here.

Eventually returning to England after a four-night stay
in Baghdad, Agatha was plunged back into the role of
celebrity, attending a performance of *The Hollow* at the
Fortune Theatre and another at the Ambassadors in Covent
Garden when the play moved there on October 8, 1951. With
Saunders ensuring Agatha's name was marqueed above the
title, she was extremely happy with the production, if not the
prying eyes attendant on her appearance at the event.

Throughout the previous summer, there had been
moments of total isolation at Greenway followed by flutters of

public activity, including a rare visit by a group of total strangers, tourists from Sweden, who had written to Agatha while in Baghdad. Mr. Lionel Hewitt was bringing a "little group," mainly schoolteachers, to tour England and asked quite casually if he might simply drop by Greenway with them for a visit while touring the River Dart.

"Miss Christie will be very pleased to see you and your Swedish party on July 13,"[xxxix] Hewitt was told in a response from Cork's office. Additionally, the note suggested that the mystery writer was prepared to offer "hospitality" in the form of a buffet lunch—this, despite the discovery that there were twenty-five in the group.

Others were not so fortunate. A group of travelers who wanted to "camp" on the grounds of Greenway was turned down, as was the features editor of *Pictorial Press,* who wrote asking for a photographic tour of Agatha in her home. "Dear Edmund, Please get me out of this unless you strongly advise it,"[xl] she wrote.

It would be a common response, growing in regularity as the years progressed. With the onset of the fifties, Agatha had already written her best work, yet her popularity was about to explode, and requests for her time expanded exponentially.

It was not that she was writing less well now; it was more that she spent less time at it, while devoting more time to assisting Max with his archaeology, lathering her grandson with her unique brand of affection, tending to the gardens, playing the piano, cooking, and, of course, eating. Quite simply, her work became less of a priority, and the plots less complicated as a result.

There was still the matter of overdue taxes in the United States, only a partial resolve having been reached with the payment of just over $160,000 for the years 1931 to 1941. Negotiations continued for amounts still due for more recent years, with lawyers fees escalating as they entered the twelfth year of fighting the tax structure within the U.S. legal system.

While still determined to write a book a year, between her tax worries and her devotion to her family, Agatha's incentive for writing two or more was gone. "If I wrote two books a year, I should make hardly more than by writing one, and give myself a great deal of extra work."[xli]

Another compilation of stories titled *The Underdog and Other Short Stories* was published only in America, all featuring vintage Hercule Poirot. With two unpublished manuscripts ready for 1952, as well as a new Mary Westmacott novel, *A Daughter's a Daughter*, based on unpublished material from the thirties, Agatha was free to turn her creative energy to stage plays and began adapting *Three Blind Mice* for the theater. This she found an easy task, having structured the original radio production to be heard rather than read.

It was just after Christmas when she called Peter Saunders to invite him to lunch. After a pleasant meal laced with reminiscences and talk of the future, and just after drinking her last sip of coffee, Agatha slid a brown paper bag across the table with a smile. "For you," she said. "Don't unwrap it until you get to the office." Pushing back from the table, she hurried out the door, smiling all the while.

As instructed, Saunders did wait until he returned to his office and upon opening the package found the completed script for a play called *The Mousetrap*, the retitled *Three Blind Mice*. Anthony Hicks had come up with the new title when it was discovered that a moderately successful existing play called *Three Blind Mice* was already in production in the West End.

By the second week of January, Agatha and Max were bound for Baghdad, yet again leaving Edmund Cork to handle settling the terms of production on the new play with Peter Saunders. His first job was to have copies made of the only script, minus the stains from the rings of Agatha's coffee cup on the cover.

Agatha was in Baghdad, yet to set out for Nimrud, when word reached her of the death of George VI, King of England and the British Dominions, on February 6, 1952. Only months earlier, the king had had his left lung removed for a malignant tumor, the result of his heavy smoking. Even so, his death came as an enormous shock. Agatha attended a memorial service in Baghdad, which was, she wrote to Cork, "very impressive with all the Iraqi cabinet attending"[xlii] as well as a procession of sheiks. Describing her clothing as "unfortunately rather lurid," she called into play her one black dress, which was used at times of somber reflection.

Mrs. McGinty's Dead, Agatha's fifty-fifth book, arrived on bookshelves in America that same month and was published in March in Great Britain to moderate acclaim. "The plot may not scintillate like other Christies, but it's perfect and the characters are wonderful," according to L. G. Offord, writing in the *San Francisco Chronicle*. The book was dedicated to Peter Saunders, "in gratitude for his kindness to authors."

By March 1952, Agatha was writing again, though feeling somewhat left out of news from Great Britain, having yet to receive her normal parcel of letters and memos from home. "There seems to be a rather sinister peace on the home front," she wrote to Cork at the beginning of March. Two days later, she learned why.

Before leaving Greenway for the season, Agatha had hired a new housekeeper named Mrs. McPherson, who had come with excellent references and a pledge to help turn the market gardens of the Devon house into a commercial enterprise. Mr. Brisley, the Greenway House gardener for the previous three years, did not take easily to the newcomer and went from being a poor gardener to being a horrible one—the distinction visible in every part of the grounds.

Upon seeing the condition of the property, Rosalind was forced to dismiss Brisley, which meant dismissing Brisley's wife, Agatha's excellent cook, as well. It was not until Cork went on vacation to the south of France that the Greenway "issue," as it came to be known, turned histrionic. Cork made his one and only visit to the property when he was summoned back to England with the news that Mrs. McPherson had attempted to end her life inside the boathouse where she was living. "So far as I can see," Cork wrote, "she hasn't done a stroke of work, and has incurred heavy bills for repairs and improvements—especially to Ferry cottage [the boathouse], which I regard as most improper."[xliii]

After auditing her records, Cork discovered that the woman had been gambling heavily on the horses, as well as charging £850 with a number of local craftsmen. He located bills that had remained unpaid for four months, and it took him until June to eventually straighten out the debacle by sending out eighteen letters of apology. "Mrs. Mallowan much regrets the circumstances in which this credit was obtained in her name," Cork said as he enclosed a check as payment in full to each business.

To their credit, Rosalind and Anthony moved down to Greenway to take direct control of the situation, allowing Agatha to report back to Cork at the end of the year that the Greenway garden "looks *wonderful*. All bursting with plants and lettuces, etc."[xliv]

In September 1952, *They Do It With Mirrors* (released in the United States as *Murder with Mirrors*) was labeled by Drexel Drake in the *Chicago Sunday Tribune* as "strikingly inferior to Agatha Christie's long established level."[xlv] It was quickly followed by *A Daughter's a Daughter,* a Mary Westmacott book that traced the lives of a mother and daughter—the daughter tall and tempestuous, always judging, perhaps inspired by Rosalind.

Despite their differences, or maybe because of them, Agatha and her daughter were now closer than ever—physically, when Agatha and Max were in residence at Greenway House, and mentally, joined in an alliance to capitalize on, and protect, the Christie legacy.

It is true in love, as it is in life, that sometimes the greatest successes are launched with a whisper, their potential impact missed. So it was with *The Mousetrap.*

Peter Saunders opened the production on October 6, 1952, at the Theatre Royal in Nottingham. It was a successful premiere as these things go, moving on to tour around England under the direction of Peter Cotes—to the New Theatre in Oxford, the Manchester Opera House, Liverpool's Royal Court Theatre, the Theatre Royal in Newcastle, the Grand Theatre in Leeds, and the Alexandra Theatre in Birmingham—before opening in London's West End at the Ambassadors Theatre on November 25, 1952.

Agatha missed opening night, having caught the production in Nottingham, where she lamented that she had laced it with too much humor, detracting from the mystery. "Don't worry!" Peter Saunders told her. "My pronouncement is that it will run over a year. Fourteen months I am going to give it."

"It won't run that long," Agatha cautioned. "Eight months perhaps. Yes, I think eight months."[xlvi] And with that began what was to become a phenomenon unequaled in the history of the theater.

TEN

One for the Books

OCTOBER 3, 1952. TWENTY-NINE-YEAR OLD RICHARD Attenborough was pacing backstage at the Theatre Royal in Nottingham, England. The grand, gilded palace of performance, built in 1865, was a magnificent backdrop for productions, having been the home to hundreds of plays, operas, and musicals over the years. For Attenborough, the opulence of the theater only added to his problem. Everything about it was larger than life. Yet, here he was, an up-and-coming film actor, about to open as the star in a play that he was certain would fail.

"We didn't think it was very good," Attenborough later admitted, which was probably due to nervous uncertainty about his future at that moment in his career. Attenborough's wife, Sylvia Sims, who had also signed on for the initial tour of the play, watched as her husband paced and fretted, certain he was right about its chance for success. At the moment, it did not matter that the playwright was in the room. Actors know what they know, and these actors sensed disaster.

Agatha Christie, while not above worry, was certain that their fears were unfounded and told both of her stars to go to bed and sleep easy. "The play will have a fine little run," she said, which, unfortunately, did not inspire the greatest confidence.

When the "little run" managed to get the play and the stars to London's West End six weeks later, the audience and critical reaction were surprisingly positive. "Even more thrilling than the plot is the atmosphere of shuddering suspense," John Barber wrote in the *Daily Express*. "No one brews it better than Agatha Christie."[i]

While Agatha was pleased at its reception for Peter Saunders and his performers, she was even more excited for Mathew—for she had gifted her nine-year-old grandson with the copyright to the play, and therefore all of her royalties from the production. At the time, he was unaware of the inheritance or the trust set up in his name to accept any monies from it.

The version of the play that was performed that night was substantially different from the one she had handed Saunders nearly a year before. The original had two set changes and ten characters, reduced by opening night to eight characters and a single set. Agatha had pruned the play herself, within the course of a single evening.

At sixty-two, she had lost none of her mental vigor and only occasionally found her ankles to be so swollen that walking was painful. The previous September she had fallen at Greenway and broken her wrist, necessitating a compromise with tradition. With her arm in a cast, there was to be no more typing on her portable machine for a while. Suddenly, she was a thoroughly modern woman courtesy of a Cork-inspired present—a Dictaphone machine.

The concept of being able to dictate her books into a machine intrigued Agatha. A wonderful conversationalist once she overcame her initial shyness with people, Agatha embraced the challenge of learning the Dictaphone Time-Master machine with enthusiasm. For its part, the Dictaphone company, thrilled at the prospect of adding the "Queen of Mystery" to their list of celebrity clientele, sent a representative to her apartment in Swan Court, Chelsea,[29] to personally demonstrate the machine.

Never one to be mechanically gifted, the nevertheless eager student absorbed the instructions and began using the machine, sending off the recorded "belts" to Cork's office for transcription. Cork, in turn, sent the belts to the Mrs. Jolly Bureau, where E. S. Harwood Jolly, the owner-operator, thanked Cork for employing her firm, before reporting back some distressing news.

"It is unfortunate that the Dictaphone Company did not explain more fully how to treat these belts when in transit,"

---

[29] After the war, Agatha had given up her flat on Lawn Street and purchased Flat #48 at 28 Swan Court in Chelsea. This served as her London writing space while in the city.

Mrs. Jolly wrote after receiving the damaged belts in the mail.[ii] Only able to transcribe portions of the book notes, she refused to charge for her service.

Having already finished writing two new books during the wet summer months in Devon, *After the Funeral*[30] and *A Pocketful of Rye*, Agatha was dictating the first elements of *Destination Unknown*, a new action-thriller. After a few more lessons in shipping and receiving, the Dictaphone company was able to renew Agatha's confidence in their equipment, which she would be comfortable using for the remainder of her life.

This was to be a British device, of little use in Nimrud or on the excavation sites. There, the trusted portable typewriter still reigned supreme, even if the hunt and peck was becoming slighter slower and less impulsive.

Along with the Dictaphone, Agatha ordered a new car, one that would hold the entire family when a gathering was in order. The automobile Cork suggested was a Humber Super Snipe Saloon—a fine car—but not large enough for the Mallowans, who eventually purchased a Humber Imperial seven-seater Saloon from the Rootes Ltd. car dealership in Piccadilly.

Gathering the family together for picnics, treasure hunts, and teas on the lawn, Agatha was never happier than when surrounded by Max, Rosalind, Mathew, and Anthony. In the evenings, Agatha would sit herself in her big worn reading chair, the floor lamp behind her positioned just so to cast its light over her shoulder and illuminate the invariable manuscript she held.

Pulling her spectacles a short distance down her nose, she would clear her throat—more as an announcement that the evening was beginning than for auditory purposes—and begin to read a chapter from an upcoming book. This was the ultimate private performance, the world's greatest mystery writer reciting her lines, unraveling her plot, and seeing who among the group could correctly identify the culprit.

There were always certain givens on these family reading nights: Max would finish his cigar and fall fast asleep, only to be jarred awake at chapter's end as everyone guessed a name; Rosalind would declare the mystery so transparent as

---

[30] Published in America as *Funerals Are Fatal.*

to be insulting to the public; Anthony would deduce the criminal using logic, though without success; and Mathew, the most enthusiastic of all, would hang on his "Nima's" every word. The coming of fall meant less time together, as the Mallowans prepared to leave yet again for the Middle East.

The 1953 season in Baghdad was one that began with rest. Agatha had traveled there via Rome, where she caught the flu and spent the first three days in bed. "The hotel was absolutely thick with cardinals and magenta sashes and pectoral crosses," she wrote to Cork. "Max and I probably breathed over a cardinal in the lift and hence the cause of the Pope's flu."[iii]

After recovering, the Mallowans traveled to Syria, where they visited friends, and then on to Baghdad, where an overworked Agatha sat on the balcony of her room at the Hotel Zia, overlooking the Tigris, and absorbed much needed sun. Before leaving London, she had begun work on a theatrical version of *Witness for the Prosecution*, a short story that she originally felt lacked the depth to be adapted as a play. Her impression changed shortly after the opening of *The Mousetrap*, when Peter Saunders suggested that *Witness* would make an excellent production.

Agatha immediately and vehemently disagreed, advising Saunders to "write the play himself," if he thought it had such potential. While not the most skilled of playwrights, Saunders was nevertheless not above taking a challenge. He tried his hand at the most rudimentary of plays and gave the finished product to Agatha before she left for the Middle East. While there was little in Saunders's script that Agatha found salvageable, there was a structure that inspired her enough to take over the project herself.

Though she wrote most of the stage play before leaving London, she changed the ending in Baghdad and sent it off via some "Embassy lads" to Saunders in London. "I devoutly hope this won't turn out to be Saunders' folly—anyway he seems to be rushing upon his doom!" she wrote to Cork.[iv] Agatha needn't have worried.

When *Witness for the Prosecution* premiered in the 1,640 seat Winter Garden Theatre in Covent Garden, it had a cast of thirty actors and two mammoth sets, including one that recreated the inside of the Old Bailey courtroom. Opening night, October 28, 1953, was a sellout, and an evening that Agatha Christie would never forget.

The play was very well received, and as the final curtain dropped, the cast bowed in unison toward the upper box where Agatha was seated. The audience, taking their cue, turned to face the box as well, and gave the play's author a standing ovation. Richard Attenborough, who had rushed to the Winter Garden from performing in *The Mousetrap*, was there. So too actor John Mills. As the applause grew to pandemonium, an embarrassed Agatha stood and left the box. Passing by Peter Saunders, she whispered with a smile, "It's rather fun, isn't it?"

Looking back at the moment, Agatha wrote in her autobiography, "I was happy, radiantly happy, made even more so by the applause of the audience." In a career full of successes, this particularly evening was special. "Yes, it was a memorable evening. I am proud of it still," Agatha later added. "And every now and then, I dig into the memory chest, bring [the program] out, take a look at it, and say, 'That was the night, that was!'"[v]

Philip Hope-Wallace, writing in *The Guardian,* said that the night "was a great success," adding, "Justice has been done and has been seen to be done. We nod approvingly, at which moment Mrs. Christie says in effect, 'Oh you thought *that* did you?' and with an unforeseen twist of the cards, lets us see how wrong we were."[vi]

In the *Observer,* Ivor Brown said that "the jury's verdict is only the beginning of a story that has as many twists as a pigtail."[vii]

The play opened on Broadway one year later, in 1954, at the Henry Miller's Theatre in New York, with Agatha's friend, Francis L. Sullivan, in the lead. The *New York Herald Tribune* labeled it a "walloping success."[viii] *Witness* won the New York Drama Critics' Circle award as the Best Foreign Play of the Year, with Sullivan and actor Patricia Jessel (who had crossed over from the British production) both garnering Tony Awards for their performances.

When Cork invited Agatha to lunch in London, it was always a festive time. The opportunity to share a meal with her old friend, while keeping business discussions to a minimum, was a joy anticipated through the years. On one occasion, during the final preparations for the British production of *Witness for the Prosecution,* Cork asked legendary film star Margaret Lockwood to join their table at the Mirabelle. Margaret announced that she was interested in playing comedy, quite against type, since she had made her reputation lately portraying sinister villainesses. She wanted to commission a play by Agatha Christie written especially for her. Six weeks later, Agatha had completed that play, now titled *Spider's Web,*[31] which Peter Saunders promised to produce the following season.

Greenway House, now successfully operating as a commercial garden, was a full-time residence for Agatha in the summers, with the views of the river and the ever-changing landscape continually providing breathtaking splendor. Mathew Prichard had been admitted to Estree, a preparatory school in Woolhampton House, Berkshire, where he was turning into an accomplished cricket player, and he continued to visit in summer at Greenway, accompanied by his mother and stepfather.

As the years progressed, Greenway became more and more of a place of rest, while Agatha's actual writing took place in her London flat, or on the dig in Nimrud. As the demands on her time increased with the enormity of her popularity, however, the woman behind the writer attempted to retreat even further into the privacy of her own mind.

It was a cocoon that allowed few things to penetrate. Yet no matter how she attempted to insulate herself from reality and a world changing around her, Agatha Christie was not able to completely escape the harsh glare of publicity—most visible in the form of photographs. There was no kindness there, as pictures from the period show an aging, matronly woman with a be-pearled neck and manicured nails.

It was a photographic shoot for the German weekly news magazine *Der Spiegel* that finally caused Agatha to revolt. She was at Greenway when she received a photograph to approve that she found so disgusting, she wrote to the photographer, "I think this is a dreadful photograph, and I would not even say it was an interesting study."[ix]

---

[31] Margaret Lockwood's character was named Clarissa after Agatha's mother.

Having second thoughts, she sent the letter and photo to Edmund Cork. "Look here, Edmund, have I got to stand for this?" she asked. "Just about fit for the psychiatric ward is what I would say.... From now on, photography is out. I don't see why I should be continually humiliated and made to suffer," she impressed.[x] Agatha then slowly sucked on a peppermint to take the bad taste out of her mouth.

It was in late 1953 when the BBC again tried in vain to entice Agatha to sit down for a face-to-face interview on television. The network had a new program titled *Panorama* that was attracting four million viewers. The producer, Dennis Barden, assured Cork that all Agatha needed to do was "sit in an armchair, forget about the cameras, and answer some questions."[xi]

Agatha, who had little enough use for television and even less for publicity, was decidedly uninterested in the prospect. As Cork wrote to Barden, "I am afraid Mrs. Christie feels that she would definitely not like to appear on television, under any circumstances, whatever."[xii]

Agatha was demonstrating her ability to stand her ground on many fronts. She continued to deny all requests from photographers ("Choke 'em"), donated the copyrights for her new book *Hickory Dickory Dock* to Max's nephews (John Michael and Patrick Andrew Mallowan), and gifted the Church of St. Mary at Churston all monies received from her first short story in years, "Greenshore Folly," for the purchase of a stained glass window on the east wall. The current window was plain glass, and when Agatha worshiped in the church, the pane always stood out like a missing tooth, an ugly gap she was personally determined to correct.

Spider's Web opened to critical acclaim and audience applause at the Savoy Theatre on December 13, 1954. While Lockwood had the starring vehicle she wanted, much of the spotlight fell on Agatha, who by this time had three hits running concurrently in the West End. There was celebration through all of Christmas, which Agatha again spent "a bit bemused by heavy eating...and...children all around."[xiii] It was, indeed, the best of times.

Escaping to Iraq provided months of relief, through weeks of intense writing combined with the enjoyable intricacies of an archaeological dig. In 1955, at the age of sixty-four, Agatha wrote *Hickory Dickory Dock* from her little office in Nimrud while the rest of the world got to read *Destination Unknown*.[32] But it seemed that her new thriller was out of step with the times, a waltz when the world was discovering the jitterbug.

While Agatha enjoyed writing spy dramas such as *Destination Unknown*, she was now delivering them to an audience that was just learning to love James Bond—Ian Fleming's *Live and Let Die* was released only months earlier, and Fleming's hit, *Casino Royale*, had come out the previous year. Agatha was of a different age, of drawing rooms and servants and cooks that still killed live turkeys before Thanksgiving.

"The thriller is not Agatha Christie's forte; it makes her go all breathless and naïve," wrote Maurice Richardson in *The Observer* of *Destination Unknown*, a book dedicated to Rosalind's husband, Anthony—"who likes foreign travel as much as I do."[xiv]

Back in England, *The Mousetrap* was approaching its thousandth performance, an occasion that Saunders first marked by printing up silk-covered programs for the audience. It was quite a nice touch, it seemed: for business, which had begun to lag with the end of Richard Attenborough's run, was revived, the play receiving a second life. The publicity stunt did not escape Agatha, who, when returning to England, received an empty envelope from Saunders in the mail, stamped by the post office "No Contents." She responded to Cork: "Tell him less silk programs and more licking of envelope flaps!"[xv]

Peter Saunders, always one to leap at an opportunity for publicity, staged a party at London's Savoy Hotel on April 24, 1955, in celebration of *The Mousetrap*'s milestone. It was labeled by the press "A Night of a Thousand Stars." Agatha stood for an hour personally greeting guests, and when called onstage to speak to the crowd said, "I would rather write ten plays than give one speech," which was a speech unto itself. She returned home that night with a gold program commemorating the event, along with memories to last a lifetime.

---

[32] Published in America as *So Many Steps to Death*.

After a decade and a half of negotiating, Agatha's tax situation had been resolved, though not without a painful hit in the pocketbook, which left her more determined than ever to give away as many copyrights as she could afford. Between tax attorneys and agents in both England and America, it was decided that Mrs. Agatha Christie needed to become a corporation—the name decided upon being the uninspired Agatha Christie Ltd. Agatha would be an employee, and paid a small annual salary, while the company would control the copyrights that were not gifted to others.

The only slight catch in the legal maneuvering was that Agatha needed to remain alive for five years beyond the corporation's formation for all the rights to be officially in the company's name. "I wish some clever guy could do something about the five years," Cork wrote to her. "No one has been able to so far, so the Doll has just *got* to live for five years!"[xvi]

Sixty-five-year-old Agatha Christie received the letter in Baghdad, at the same moment she received notification that her "garden" account at Lloyds Bank was overdrawn by £4. "Dear Edmund," she responded. "The Doll will do her best to live another five years. In order to do so, she must not worry. I shall not. I shall enjoy them. Rosalind can be counted upon as a brake lever, oiled with persistent pessimism."[xvii]

The response was pure Agatha, at ease in the trenches of Nimrud, where the weather was failing to cooperate. "Dust storms and thunderstorms alternatively. But we are digging a very promising spot, boxes and boxes of winged genii and devils to avert evil are coming up, and yesterday a large something of broken ivory and charred wood has appeared and is being lovingly cleared," she wrote. [xviii]

By April 1955, Agatha and Max had returned to London, where she learned that she had been awarded the Edgar Award from the Mystery Writers Association for *Witness for the Prosecution*. Agatha, of course, refused to receive the honor in person in New York, sending Edward Dodd of Dodd, Mead and Co., her American publisher, in her place.

Agatha was legitimately thrilled when Edmund Cork informed her that Queen Elizabeth II and her husband, the Duke of Edinburgh, were attending a performance at the Theatre Royal in Windsor to see the touring company of

Witness for the Prosecution in repertoire. Eschewing the royal box to sit in orchestra seats in the stalls, the Queen and her entourage were enthralled by the play, and told Agatha as much backstage, where the author was presented, along with Peter Saunders and members of the cast. For the child who had dreamed of knights in armor on white horses whisking her away on an adventure, *this* was the next best thing.

In September 1955, Max and Agatha celebrated their silver wedding anniversary at Greenway House with a black-tie party that gathered old friends and associates, including Sir William Collins, grandson of the founder of Collins publishing. Edmund Cork, unable to attend, sent a silver candlestick as a gift. Agatha thanked him with a note ("the kindness of our friends has put the seal on our happiness")[xix] and had provided him with her own gift of sorts—the manuscript for her next book, *Dead Man's Folly*, as well as assurances that she was working on the next Mary Westmacott, *Burden*, and the stage play of her 1944 novel, *Towards Zero*.

Queen Elizabeth showed her appreciation for Agatha's work on New Year's Day 1956 by bestowing upon the mystery writer the Commander of the Order of the British Empire (CBE). It was an honor that Agatha accepted with a certain degree of dignity and a heavy dose of humility. "The worst of a C.B.E. seems to be the amount of congratulations one has to answer— many people one hardly knows. Anyway, I feel it is one up to the Low Brows,"[xx] she wrote, while noting that the Iraqi press was now incorrectly referring to her as "Dame." Agatha was not in England to accept the honor, having traveled with Rosalind, Anthony, Mathew, and Max to Tripoli, in Africa, for a relaxing sightseeing vacation.

As the Hickses headed back to England, the Mallowans continued on to Iraq for yet another season of digging. The now familiar routine was pleasing to all, including Agatha's publishers, who understood that Nimrud time was writing time.

The reviews for Agatha's sixtieth book, *Hickory Dickory Dock*, were kind, if not abundantly so. Not that it mattered. What little importance Agatha had attached to reviews in the past was now completely overcome, the author finally becoming more confident of her own talent and strengths.

Peter Saunders staged *Towards Zero* at the St. James's Theatre for a short run in September 1956, though critics found the plotting a bit too complicated for the length of the play. "Compactly full of all the ripest ingredients," said the *Times*.[xxi]

Towards Zero aside, there was one critical opinion that *was* creating a real problem and that concerned "Greenway Folly," the short story donated to Church of St. Mary at Churston and assigned to the Exeter Diocesan Board of Finance. Agatha had approved a design for the new stained glass window—the Good Shepherd surrounded by daffodils, primroses, plus the harvests of the sea, forest, and farms. The window had been created by a local craftsman named Paterson, who lived in Bideford, north of Devon. He had his design approved by both Agatha and the church, assembled his piece of art, and was now anxious to install it on the east wall of St. Mary's. The problem was neither with the church nor the window. The difficulty was with "Greenway Folly," an Agatha Christie short story no one wanted to buy.

"I hate to be pest," Edmund Cork wrote to Dorothy Olding, an agent in Harold Ober's office, "but the Bishop of Exeter's lawyers are being horrid about 'Greenway's Folly.' They say they find it difficult to believe that Mrs. Mallowan would have presented the church with a story that would not sell!"[xxii] It was the ecclesiastical version of "No Good Deed Goes Unpunished."

After unsuccessfully trying for months to sell the short story to any American magazine, Cork authorized Agatha Christie Ltd. to buy the rights back from the church for a cash payment of £1,000. "Obviously the window must go up,"[xxiii] Cork wrote to Agatha in explaining his decision, which Agatha found "very humiliating" but "correct."[xxiv]

Almost as humiliating was the assertion from a French millionaire that Agatha's character, Mrs. Christina Nicoletis, owner of a student hostel in *Hickory Dickory Dock*, was based on his mother, whom he claimed once owned a hostel where Agatha and her mother had stayed. Cork wrote to Agatha, asking for any information she could supply to him to stem threatened legal proceedings.

"I invented the name Nicoletis!!" Agatha responded from Iraq. "M. Nicoletis must be obsessed by having a disagreeable mother. It's terrible that if you invent a character, it should come out to be so true to life!"[xxv] She didn't like this kind of accusation. No, she did not like it at all. Her thoughts were far too original to be accused of pulling plots from others. Had she been at home, she would have spread some clotted cream on a scone and gotten over her mood with the first bite. As it was, she bit into a fig, and suddenly missed England enormously.

There was to be no such confusion in Agatha's next book, *Dead Man's Folly*, in which the setting known as Nasse House is a thinly disguised version of her own Greenway, a first for any of the writer's novels. "A minor Christie," was how Frances Iles, writing for the *Manchester Guardian*, summed up the book[xxvi]. Sales were high, as usual, despite mediocre reviews, when the book was released in December 1956. At the same time, Agatha was packing for another trip to Iraq and carefully avoiding the inherent publicity surrounding the publication of *Burden*—the first Mary Westmacott novel to reveal Agatha Christie as its author.

Agatha Christie Ltd., now benefiting directly from the sales of her books, was immediately a major microcosm of detail—the tracking of copyrights of books with varying titles in Great Britain and America, rights issues with plays and productions, short stories and their adaptations, plus dealing with the ever-eager film producers, who were only too anxious to be awarded the privilege of the Christie label. It was not, however, a happy place for the corporation's appointed secretary, a man named Patrick Lavery, who had a nervous breakdown of sorts and resigned soon after accepting his postion. Edmund Cork nominated his daughter, Pat, for the post, since she "knows something about the Agatha Christie market."

The visit to the dig site in 1957 would prove to be a short one, for Max had been awarded a gold medal in archaeology by the University of Pennsylvania. Not as adverse to publicity as his wife, Max planned on receiving the award in person, with Agatha by his side, before spending a few days touring the country. The prospect of an American vacation, with the spotlight totally on her husband, had Agatha giddy with schoolgirl excitement as she planned their free time, including a trip to the Grand Canyon.

Agatha wrote that she was dashing from their return flight from Baghdad to a salon to have her hair and nails done "so as not to alight in New York looking like a savage."[xxvi] That accomplished, the Mallowans then took a BOAC flight, first class, from London to New York (for the cost of £342.90 for two). Arriving in Queens at Idlewild Airport,[33] the Mallowans were met by Dorothy Olding from the Harold Ober Agency, who wrote her colleagues in England, "I must say that Agatha is certainly full of bounce considering how little time she had between the Baghdad flight and the New York one. I'm quite enchanted with her and everybody in the office is too."[xxvii]

The official presentation was a flawless and brief one, followed by a tour of Philadelphia before taking a train trip to Los Angeles, with a stopover in Colorado at the El Tovar Hotel. Resplendent in tones of canyon brown, the El Tovar had hosted many celebrities, including Teddy Roosevelt and the Westerns writer Zane Grey, so the staff was prepared for the "Queen of Mystery." The absence of press was fundamental to the level of enjoyment Agatha experienced, having told Cork she preferred to stay at the Auto Lodge if it meant no publicity.

Sending a postcard from Lipan Point on the South Rim of the Canyon, Agatha enthused, "Enjoying myself terrifically. In fact, couldn't be enjoying myself more! Must do this all again!! Yours, A-M."[xxviii]

Traveling next to Los Angeles, Agatha was invited to the Goldwyn Studios, where the sets were being constructed for the film version of *Witness for the Prosecution*, starring Charles Laughton, Tyrone Power, and Marlene Dietrich. Agatha reported back that all was going well on the film, which— under the direction of Billy Wilder (*Sunset Boulevard*)— was true.

She had no way of knowing that what she considered "dream casting" almost did not happen. Tyrone Power, in a grand funk over his personal life, did not want the part. Wilder wanted to hire Kirk Douglas, who also turned it down. Marlene Dietrich was interested, but mainly because of Tyrone Power, on whom she had a crush. And Charles Laughton was not interested in his role unless the part was substantially expanded.

In the final analysis, it was money that converted the holdouts. Power received $300,000 plus a percentage of the

[33] The current JFK Airport in New York.

gross; Dietrich received $100,000 and dinners with Power; Laughton received $70,000 and the largest part; with the ultimate winners being the fans, and Agatha Christie, who was treated to her favorite film adaptation to date.

Agatha and Max returned to London in May 1957, continuing almost immediately down to Greenway House. This was a period in Agatha's life where she placed her own writing second to Max's career, as he was intent on publishing a major book detailing his findings at Nimrud. He began to campaign Cork to represent the project.

Rosalind had taken a life insurance policy out on her mother for £100,000, in case of her death in advance of the five-year probation period before the benefits of Agatha Christie Ltd. became effective. There was a slight delay in issuing the policy, for as Cork wrote to Rosalind, "Between you and me, the Medical Superintendant [sic] is concerned about your mother's weight..."[xxix] Agatha seemed to be the only one not worrying, for as she wrote to Cork when seeing an unflattering picture in *Paris Match* magazine, "One doesn't really (thank the Lord!) know just how awful one looks, owing to seeing oneself at the best advantage, full face. It's the profiles that are so frightful."[xxx]

4:50 from Paddington[34] was published in November 1957, though Agatha barely noticed, for she was far more nervous about the upcoming premiere of the feature version of *Witness for the Prosecution*, the rights for which had been sold at a record-setting £116,000, and these rights gifted by Agatha to Rosalind.

The reviews of the film were universally positive, and the box office returned millions of dollars. The trade newspaper *Variety* said, "[Charles] Laughton, sage of the courtroom and cardiac patient who's constantly disobeying his nurse's orders, plays out the part flamboyantly and colorfully. His reputation for scenery chewing is unmarred via this outing."[xxxi] Bosley Crowther of the *New York Times* wrote, "there's never a dull or worthless moment...the air in the courtroom fairly crackles with emotional electricity..."[xxxii]

Peter Saunders was eager for yet another play, much to the consternation of Edmund Cork, who attempted to rein in Agatha's enthusiasm for the theater and keep his "sausage

[34] Published in America as *What Mrs. McGillicuddy Saw!*

machine" focused on the much more lucrative books. In the end, she accomplished both, producing *Ordeal by Innocence*, to be published as part of Collins now-traditional "Christie for Christmas" marketing campaign, while Saunders received *Verdict*, which Agatha thought her best play, other than *Witness for the Prosecution*.

At the time, *The Mousetrap* was about to become the longest-running play in London, hitting its 2,239th performance. There was to be yet another party at the Savoy, again with the stars, the press, the photographers, and this time television cameras as well—pure agony for Agatha, but an evening she was determined to endure.

Sequestered in Winterbrook working on yet another play, *The Unexpected Guest*, Agatha constantly found her mind wandering, unable to concentrate. *What if they make me give a speech?* she thought. They were, of course, certain to expect her to say *something*. It never seemed to be enough just to write, to provide the words that entertained while she stayed safely hidden away.

When she went into London to buy a new dress for the evening, the fear really never left her—that gnawing in her stomach, a sort of nervous energy that was strong enough to boil water were it put into a pot on the stove. Still, she had done these events before, and once more she was determined to overcome whatever anxiety surfaced. She owed Peter Saunders that much—and more.

The evening of the party, he had asked her to arrive at the private banquet rooms early—to avoid the incoming press and photographers, as well as to preserve her own entrance for her grand introduction. She arrived alone—the family would come along later—and walked as directed up to the porter guarding the doors.

She was elegant in a dark draped dress with gauzy sleeves that covered thick arms, the right dress strap accented at the bodice by a diamond broach. Her nails had been polished and her hair especially coiffed, in that special style she never thought to change since the thirties. She wore a triple strand of pearls (the expensive ones she saved for these occasions), diamond earrings, elbow-length white gloves, and carried a small evening purse painted with flowers.

Approaching the porter, she smiled and announced that she was there for the party. "No admission yet, madam," the guard said. "Another twenty minutes before anyone is allowed to go in." She hesitated, wanting to speak, but only for a second. But that second was a second too long, for with that, Agatha Christie, guest of honor and writer of the longest-running stage show in London, apologized to the man and left.

Fortunately, she did not make it far, for after walking the corridors of the hotel alone, weighing her options and settling on none, Agatha was spotted, looking lost in the hotel's lounge, by Peter Saunders's general manager Verity Hudson, who guided her back to the event. When asked why she hadn't said who she was, she offered only, "I just couldn't. I was paralyzed." [xxxiii]

In the *Daily Mail*, the reporter covering the party mentioned the moment, having heard about it later during the event. "A silver-haired middle-aged woman with a motherly smile walked into the Savoy Hotel last night and was stopped by a porter as she approached the banquet hall where a big theatrical party was about to begin. 'Your ticket please, ma'am,' said the porter. But she didn't have a ticket. She was the guest of honor." [xxxiv]

In her autobiography, Agatha remembered her own frustration, feeling like a fraud at her own event. "Whatever I feel is not really shyness," she wrote. "I suppose, actually, the feeling is...that I am pretending to be something that I am not, because, even nowadays, I do not quite feel as though I am an author. I still have that overlag of feeling that I am *pretending* to be an author." [xxxv] At that moment, Mrs. Agatha Christie Mallowan had completed sixty-nine books, fifteen plays, and over a hundred short stories, and was translated into one hundred five languages around the world.

ELEVEN

The Movie Years

*Lord Mountbatten...escorting [Agatha] out of the dining
room at midnight and raising her arm in farewell...
shy as always, she enjoyed this occasion to the full.*

Max Mallowan
Mallowan's Memoirs

MAY 23, 1958. "AN IMPROBABLE VERDICT—PLAY BY
Agatha Christie Booed."[i] So read the headline of the London
Times in its critique of *Verdict*, which had opened at the
Strand Theatre in Aldwych the night before. And that was a
favorable review.

Perhaps Peter Saunders would have been wise to heed
an early omen that Agatha's play *Verdict* was going to fail—
and fail miserably. Sailing high from the success of *The
Mousetrap* party at the Savoy, Saunders pushed along through
rehearsals for the play and decided to place his name on the
vast curved marquee on the outside of the theater—a corner
location—making it visible for blocks.

He had visions of "Peter Saunders Presents VERDICT"
lighting up the West End like a beacon, much as Agatha
Christie had done nine years before with *Murder at the
Vicarage*. Unfortunately, due to a lighting malfunction, the sign
announced "Peter Saunders Resents VERDICT," which he no
doubt did after reading the reviews the following morning.
Other than the *Times*, the London papers ravaged the play
with such intensity that Saunders was obliged to send Agatha
reprints of the laudatory praise papering her after the debut of
Witness for the Prosecution. "Read these again. They will take
your mind off *Verdict*," he said.[ii]

Agatha, as usual, was unaffected by the criticism and
instead concentrated on delivering yet another play, *The
Unexpected Guest,* which opened the following August amid
Saunders's usual fanfare, this time to a slightly better reception
and with Agatha's name over the title. The success of a play in
London, however, was not Agatha's priority at the moment.
She was extremely worried about events in Iraq, where a
revolution had toppled the old regime, and the country was
declared a republic under military control. The ramifications
for Max's archaeological digs were uncertain, but from what
information could be determined, entry back into the country
might be denied, and future exploration rendered impossible.

Agatha captured the tension of that revolution in her
next book, *Cat Among the Pigeons,* a Hercule Poirot mystery
that took notice of a revolt in the small Middle East Arab state
of Ramat. *The Observer's* Maurice Richardson mentioned
"some nice school scenes with bogus sheiks sweeping up in
lilac Cadillacs to deposit highly scented and busted houris for
education"[iii] in his review.

As anticipated, Max's travels to Iraq and Nimrud were
restricted after 1959, a year fraught by the sudden and
unexpected death of Harold Ober from a heart attack.
Although his team in New York was thoroughly prepared to
continue representing Agatha through the efforts of Dorothy
Olding, the absence of Edmund Cork's strong ally in the U.S.
could not easily be dismissed.

Cork had been involved in intense negotiations to sell
the film and television rights for Agatha's books to MGM
England, and the constant pressure from the roller coaster of
offers and counteroffers were taking their toll on Cork's health
as well. "The MGM deal has almost destroyed me," Cork
wrote to Rosalind. "Its fluctuations have been too numerous
and violent to be believed."[iv]

Agatha seemed blissfully unaware of trouble at home
as she traveled with Max to India, Pakistan, and Persia before
joining Rosalind and her family in Ceylon. It was part vacation
and part celebration, for Max had been named to the Queen's
New Year's Honors List in 1960, and awarded a CBE, just as
his wife before him.

Agatha wrote in her distinctive scrawl from the Mount Lavinia Hotel in Ceylon, gossiping with the latest news. "Two rude photographers that attempted to photograph me bathing were (I think) foiled by Rosalind and Mathew rushing between me on either side," Agatha wrote to Cork. "I hope successfully, as it was a particularly ungainly attitude I was in at the moment. (Practically a close-up of a big behind.)"[v]

Agatha and Max returned to London in time to attend the opening night performance of *Go Back for Murder,* a play she had written the previous year, based on her book *Five Little Pigs.* Peter Saunders had placed the production at the Duchess Theatre in Covent Garden, one of the smallest proscenium theaters in London. Its arrival in the West End unfortunately coincided with the hiring of a new theater critic at the *Daily Mail.* In an effort to create a large impact with his first review, he declared *Go Back for Murder* "Inconceivable tedium" and added, "I don't care how rich Miss Christie is, this stinks!"[vi]

Edmund Cork wrote to Rosalind that the production generated "the most malicious press we have ever had—not even excepting *Verdict.*"[vii]

There was to be no new Christie novel in 1960, the year in which Agatha turned seventy, though a collection of short stories was released under the title *The Adventure of the Christmas Pudding and a Selection of Entrees.* Of particular interest was Agatha's foreword, in which she told of Christmases past and her wonderful memories of the holiday at Abney Hall. Jack Watts had sold the manor house for £17,000 pounds in 1958 to the city of Cheadle, who used it initially as its town hall. Agatha dedicated the book to the Abney's "kindness and hospitality."

Greenway House continued to provide its own generous hospitality to guests and family, with awards being generated for the produce and flowers in its garden. The summer of 1960 was a leisurely one, not overly warm, but sunny enough for Agatha to wade at the beach and enjoy her afternoon bathing. Although she was writing a bit on her next novel, *Pale Horse,* she did not consider it a particular priority, focusing on watching her grandson play cricket, now his favorite sport. She also assembled a collection of short stories,

Double Sin and other Stories, a compilation rated by the *New York Times* as "Grade B Christie."[viii]

The editor of the French magazine *Femmes d'Aujourd'hui* wrote to ask for an interview, to which Agatha replied to Cork: "Nothing I'd hate more than writing articles on 'les grands subjets finimins.' Tell them so!"[ix]

She entertained Larry Bachmann and his wife, Jean— Larry being the MGM producer assigned to jockey her films through the studio pipeline. "Fortunately, they liked dogs," Agatha wrote to Cork, "as the house is entirely given over to Rosalind's dogs, children and their problems. One dog wishes to kill two of the others & the cook's dog is in heat—so a busy time is had by all."[x]

MGM had decided that the first Christie novel to be dramatized under their multi-picture deal would be *The 4:50 from Paddington,* to be adapted by David Osborn and written by David Pursall and Jack Seddon. Their choice to play the frail, spinster sleuth Miss Jane Marple: the oversize character actress Margaret Rutherford.

Rutherford accepted the role with some hesitation, but not because of her physical appearance—large, frumpy, with a face like a startled bloodhound, unlike the book's description of petite Miss Marple. Instead, the stumbling block was that the plot involved murder. Unknown at the time, Rutherford's father had beaten her grandfather to death and was sentenced to an asylum for the mentally ill. While she never knew her father (having been told he was dead), she nevertheless carried the stigma and dislike of violence for her entire life.

It was to Agatha's credit that, in the end, Rutherford accepted the role due to the intelligence of the elderly sleuth from St. Mary Mead. Though Rutherford notified MGM on Christmas Day, 1960, that she would play the part, it would take several weeks before Agatha was informed. During that time, the film was in production, rushing along to meet its premiere date in 1961 as the retitled *Murder, She Said.*

Agatha saw the film with her family in the Royal Theatre in Torquay on September 17, 1961, quietly entering the theater unnoticed. "Frankly, it's pretty poor!" she wrote that evening to Edmund Cork. She further thought that the photography was horrendous—"very poor by modern standards of films."[xi] She did, however, respect Margaret Rutherford as a performer. When asked her opinion by writer Gwen Robyns, Agatha responded through a secretary, "While she thinks Miss Rutherford is a fine actress, she bears no resemblance to her own idea of Miss Marple."[xii]

The reviewer for the *Christian Science Monitor* remarked that Rutherford, outfitted in a "regular tarpaulin of a sweater," created the effect of a "warmly bundled English bulldog."[xiii] The reviewer was no doubt unaware that Rutherford wore her own clothing for the part.

"It is mainly Miss Rutherford's show," A. H. Weiler wrote in the *New York Times*. "[She] dominates most of the scenes with a forceful characterization that enhances the humor of her lines and the suspense in the 'Murder.'"[xiv]

While *Murder, She Said* was running in the theaters across Europe and in America, Agatha was writing her sixty-eighth book at age seventy-one. Titled *The Mirror Crack'd from Side to Side*, the Miss Marple novel was dedicated with class to "Margaret Rutherford, in admiration." When it was published in 1962, the novel met with modest praise. Maurice Richardson, writing in *The Observer*, said, "A moderate Christie; bit diffuse and not so taut as some."[xv]

With her eyesight becoming weaker and her hearing dimmed, Agatha continued to keep a full schedule unimpeded by her age. Ironically, it was her far younger husband who appeared to be faltering. In the spring of 1962, Max suffered a stroke, and while he was not seriously impaired physically, it scared him and made him hesitant. The unfortunate outcome was that Max became cautious and abridged his activities when exercise might have benefited his health.

"Between you, me and the gatepost, [Max] has suddenly come to look twice his age, and pretty feeble," Edmund Cork advised Dorothy Olding in a confidential note.[xvi]

Before his stroke, Max had resigned his position at the University of London and accepted a fellowship at Oxford's All Souls College. There would no longer be a need to teach or lecture. Now he was being paid to prepare his Nimrud manuscript and to mentor others in archaeology. He was being assisted with his "life's work," as he called it, by Barbara Parker, Nimrud's secretary and photographer for many years.

Packing canes, orthopedic shoes, and rheumatism medicine, the Mallowans continued to travel in the fall of 1962, attending the Bayreuth Festival, the monthlong tribute to Richard Wagner and his operas held annually in his German hometown. Mathew, just out of Eton College and a huge fan of opera, joined his grandparents for the trip. He studied the scores before each performance with Agatha, who was openly lauded by the tourists visiting Bayreuth Festspielhaus. "I must say I got a standing ovation at Bayreuth," she wrote Cork upon her return, speaking of signing hundreds of autographs and the perks it generated at her hotel, the Reichsadler.

Now requiring a cane to assist her walking, due to painful and swollen ankles, Agatha refused to alter the Mallowans' plans to visit Persia and Kashmir, areas that are now Iran and Pakistan. Here, in the Middle East, Agatha felt quite at home, despite the constant turmoil that boiled just under the political surface. It was the beauty of the countryside and the varied marketplaces that intrigued her, while Max sought out and found ancient dig sites that continued to yield historical riches.

Prior to the trip, Agatha had accepted an offer from Larry Bachmann at MGM to try adapting Charles Dickens's *Bleak House* as a film script and had jumped enthusiastically into the assignment. She was not entirely out of her element here, having written a film version of *The Spider's Web* in 1956, based on her play. While her *Web* script was never used, her adaptation was ultimately rewritten by Eldon Howard and Albert G. Miller for a Danzinger Productions Ltd. feature, starring Glynnis Johns, and was released in 1960 in England and Germany.

Agatha's *Bleak House* script, completed in April 1962, was two hundred seventy pages—far too long for a two-hour feature film that would normally run just over one hundred pages. This, of course, Agatha realized, and she had expected to edit the document upon her return to England. At over eight hundred pages, the original book presented an extraordinary editing challenge, and eventually, after several tries and £10,000 paid for her services, Agatha was taken off the project, and the film ultimately abandoned.

One film that did get made, however, was *Murder at the Gallop*, with Margaret Rutherford again playing Jane Marple. It was an adaptation of Agatha's *After the Funeral,* which originally was a Hercule Poirot mystery. Larry Bachmann, when deciding on the book, also decided to switch detectives. It was not a change that reviewers noticed, but one that disgusted the ever vigilant Mrs. Christie. Bachmann had moved the film's location to a riding school, where Miss Marple was placed undercover. The original Poirot novel was set in Enderby Hall, bearing no small similarity to Abney Hall, the manor house that had been close to Agatha since her childhood, with its fourteen bedrooms and as many servants.

"These travesties" is the way Agatha referred to the senseless changes, a complaint that Bachmann put down to "an old lady without the first instinct for making film."[xvii] The plot now concerned the last will of the just murdered Old Enderby, who has been apparently frightened to death. His relatives, staying in the family home—Gallop House and Riding Academy—are all suspected of the crime. To see Margaret Rutherford mount a steed and ride off into the sunset after the hounds was more than Agatha could bear. "I get an unregenerate pleasure when I think they're not being a success," Agatha wrote Cork, who attempted to defend the plot vulgarities by stating that they were well within the rights of their contract to freely adapt her themes.

Enjoying Margaret Rutherford in person was a totally different experience. Agatha went to the *Murder at the Gallop* set and introduced herself to the famous star. "This delightful woman came down to see me on the set," Margaret Rutherford remembered just before her death, "and when we met face to face, we instantly clicked. I completely overcame my first tentative prejudices about Christie crime and became most fond of Jane Marple."[xviii]

But the image of Margaret Rutherford galloping to the hounds was unshakable and made Agatha even more indignant. In the course of refusing to attend the film's premiere, she sent a letter to Larry Bachmann sarcastically asking him not to "kill Margaret Rutherford by making her embrace too many outdoor sports."[xix]

At the time that *Murder at the Gallop* was in preproduction in the summer of 1962, Agatha's nephew, Jack Watts, unexpectedly died. Several months later, in December, it was Archie Christie's turn to suffer a fatal attack. Ironically, Mathew Prichard had only recently attempted to connect with his grandfather, writing him from Eton about the possibility of meeting. Archie was excited about finally getting to see his grandson after nearly twenty years. Plans were made and dates set, but Archie died several days before the arranged meeting.

In 1958, Archie's wife, Nancy Neele Christie, had succumbed to cancer, at which point Agatha wrote to her former husband for the first time since their divorce, expressing condolences and acknowledging the decades of happiness that Archie and Nancy had shared. If there were any remaining issues between them, the letter of condolence indicated none, and Archie responded, thanking Agatha for her kindness in writing. Now, he too was dead.

Agatha took these deaths and the death of her childhood friend, Nan Kon, in 1959, with such calm and acceptance that those in her family worried she would break down from grief months after the events. This was, however, not the case, for Agatha had long adapted the serene Middle Eastern approach to her own mortality and that of those she loved. She accepted death as she accepted birth, with a sense of flow in a grander scheme.

Archie had lived long enough to see his ex-wife headlined across the pages of every newspaper in England with the celebration of the tenth anniversary of *The Mousetrap* on November 25, 1962. It was another wonderfully joyous event, again at the Savoy, and again with a giant cake—this one weighing a half-ton. Dame Sybil Thorndike helped Agatha wield a giant sword to cut the first slice, as Peter Saunders looked on proudly.

Dressed in a shimmering green gown, Agatha radiated confidence, so much so that when it came time to make a speech, she stepped to the stage and did what she thought was impossible—she spoke extemporaneously to her guests. "This is awful," she began with a sigh, when she realized that no one was going to save her from a speech. "I know I haven't been any good at making speeches, and usually someone has come to the rescue, and made my speech for me. But nobody's going to do it tonight, so I've got to do it myself.

"Anyway, the great thanks and really heartfelt gratitude I feel for this great party tonight and the goodness of everybody. And the terrible excitement of having a play run for ten years, longer than any other play. Sometimes I really can't believe it's me. I mean, it's not at all the sort of thing that would happen to me. I mean, if I were writing a book, it wouldn't be a person like me who had written a play that runs for ten years.

"Don't let anybody say that nothing exciting ever happens to you when you are old. It does. It's just as nice to be seventy-two as it is to be young. And tonight, it couldn't be more exciting."[xx]

Rosalind watched her mother leave the stage to tremendous applause, Agatha beaming at her bravery as she returned to her seat. "You ought to have taken more trouble, Mother," Rosalind said critically, "and prepared something properly beforehand."[xxi]

Agatha was given a gold-bound copy of the original script of the play and accepted it gleefully, noting that "Gold is so nice to have in your room, because it only wants a handkerchief and a bit of spit to keep it clean."[xxii] It was by all accounts a triumphant night. And as for *The Mousetrap*, its curtain continued to rise and fall, and rise again, month after month.

Soon after Archie's death, what was to be Agatha's final West End production opened at the Duchess Theatre, which was by then owned by Peter Saunders. *Rule of Three* was actually a trio of one-act plays—*The Rats, Afternoon at the Seaside*, and *The Patient*. Fittingly, the final curtain for Agatha's career as a playwright was a fresh form for her, still adventuring into new frontier.[35] "It is a harmless, naïve evening," according to the *Times*, which knew better than to be overly harsh to the elderly but still creative writer, with her legions of fans.[xxiii]

The previous year UNESCO declared that Agatha Christie was the best-selling author in the English language, having been published in 105 countries. With her own output slowing down, Agatha released a single book in 1963, the Hercule Poirot novel *The Clocks*. Half thriller, half mystery, the book was convincing enough to many reviewers, with fans doing their part to keep sales figures at their highest. "*The Clocks* is delightful enough for its depiction of a retired and

---

[35] Agatha was to write another play, *Fiddler's Three* in 1972, but the production never found success while touring in the provinces and was never produced in the West End.

very elderly Hercule Poirot, impatient with inactivity and eager to act as even an armchair detective."[xxiv]

When *The Clocks* was published in previews, Agatha, Max, Mathew, and two of his friends had traveled to Salzburg, Austria, for the annual Salzburg festival, where Mozart's *Così fan tutte* and *Die Zauberflöte* (The Magic Flute) plus Strauss's *Der Rosenkavalier* (The Knight of the Rose) were the favorites of the group.

Agatha loved traveling with Mathew. His youth made her young again. His smile and those of his friends—two Oxford chums, Ellis Wisner and Roger Angus—were wind in her hair. How she envied them their freedom. While she was staying in luxury, they were camping and driving around in a beat-up Vauxhall Victor estate car. Nothing wrong with her hotel, but it was just a hotel. The boys were on an adventure, and she wanted to share every moment of it—from side trips to the Austrian countryside to visits to dusty museums.

Pulling herself back to London, she returned to work on her next novel, *A Caribbean Mystery*, while Max finished his book, *Nimrud and Its Remains* (despite having had a lingering and severe flu attack). When the Mallowans finally made it to Winter Palace Hotel in Luxor for their winter vacation, it was a time of relatively good health and satisfaction in goals accomplished. "I'm sitting in the sun feeling placid as a sacred cow," Agatha wrote to Edmund Cork, painting the image of her legs splayed in the heat and light, the Nile with its boats in the distance.[xxv]

The calmness and serenity were not about to last, however, for early in March 1964, *Murder Most Foul* proved true to its title. Loosely based on *Mrs. McGinty's Dead*, Agatha had objected to MGM adapting that book, since she thought of it as "one of my best books."[xxvi] She hated the title (labeling it "trite") and told just that to Larry Bachmann, who went right ahead with his adaptation in any case.

The resulting film managed to mangle the original story to such an extent that Agatha raged in protest. The Mrs. McGinty of the original title ran a boarding house and was whacked on the head. In the film, she was turned into a barmaid/actress and was hanged. Hercule Poirot, who investigated the original crime, had now been replaced by

Miss Marple (in the figure of Margaret Rutherford), who joined the barmaid's former acting company to track down the murderer. It was not well received by either Christie fans or the critics, with the *New York Times* commenting, "While Margaret Rutherford's talents are still obvious, it is clear she is struggling mightily in an unimportant cause."[xxvii]

Yet as horrible as Agatha thought *Murder Most Foul* to be, it was a minor offense compared to MGM's next effort in the Rutherford/Marple collection—a piece of mystery meat titled *Murder Ahoy!* The script was sent to Agatha in March by Larry Bachmann. Not based on any Christie book, it merely made use of her characters in a story of MGM's own creation. Agatha's response was both instant and vitriolic.

"I return you this farrago of nonsense," Agatha wrote to Edmund Cork's daughter Pat. "Why on earth can't MGM write their scripts, engage Margaret Rutherford to play an old lady, Miss Sampson, have plenty of cheap fun, and leave me and my creations out of it?" she asked.

> The shock to me is to find that possibly MGM have the right to write these scripts of their own featuring my characters. That, neither I or Rosalind seem to have known. When Edmund talked to me a week or two ago, he mentioned it only as a suggestion on MGM's part that we could refuse. Surely this must be so?[xxviii]

Agatha was appalled at the possibility and even more astounded when it turned out to be accurate. Her contract with MGM allowed them to utilize her characters, in any movie of their choosing, including those totally of their own creation.

"I don't suppose there could be any misery greater for an author than to see their characters completely distorted," she lamented. Her distress brought her writing to a halt, and so complete was her horror at the thought that MGM could produce more of these movies that she insisted that her contract with the studio be immediately revised.

At the center of the brouhaha was Edmund Cork, who had knowingly allowed this provision to remain in the original contract and had apparently not clarified it completely to Agatha. "I feel personally most discouraged and ashamed about the dealings with MGM.... We have really let my mother down very badly over this whole deal," Rosalind wrote to Cork.[xxix]

Letters to Larry Bachmann produced some concessions on the part of MGM over their right to misuse Christie's characters in original films, and an agreement was struck to limit Agatha's credit on the production. Her name was removed from above the title, and Margaret Rutherford's name enlarged, with the note that she was portraying "Agatha Christie's Miss Marple" in small print.

Edmund Cork defended himself in a letter to Anthony Hicks, detailing the concessions made by MGM: "If anyone belittles what we have done, I can only say that they know nothing about the film business!" He signed the letter "Cork."[xxx]

Larry Bachmann attempted to placate Agatha by writing soothing words and platitudes. *Murder Ahoy!* was to be shot, regardless of Agatha's feelings, and, moreover, it was being pushed through the production process for an early release. Additionally, word reached Agatha that MGM was planning a comedy to star Zero Mostel as Hercule Poirot. At this point, there was no explanation that would satisfy the irate author.

Agatha paced the lawn between Winterbrook and the Thames back and forth in frustration. It was all too impossible; all out of her hands, yet how? Certainly she had *some* rights, yet Edmund Cork seemed useless to explain, or change it, or rectify the situation that was now clearly out of control. Several times she started to write to Larry Bachmann, and each time she destroyed her ramblings. She was, after all, a writer. But her emotions were now in control—or more precisely, out of control.

"Soft words butter no parsnips (a saying of my nursery days!)," Agatha finally responded to Bachmann. "I deeply resent the way all this 'Murder Ahoy' business was sprung upon me.... It is, to me, a matter of an author's integrity. To have one's characters incorporated in somebody else's film seems to me monstrous and highly unethical. I do not see how you can expect me to feel anything but deep resentment at your high-handed action or to pretend otherwise, and I still feel it questionable that you really have the right to act as you have done."[xxxi]

The movie was released in July 1964, while Agatha conveniently was on a trip to Zurich. A. H. Weiler, writing in the *New York Times*, found "lots of dialogue, only a bit of which is truly funny, and a modicum of action, which is rarely exciting, intriguing, or comic..."[xxxii]

Fortunately for Christie fans, the "real" Jane Marple returned to bookstalls in November 1964, when *A Caribbean Mystery* was published to critical praise. It was as if an old friend had been awakened from a coma and returned to the living, for there was the slender spinster, obviously older, but just as wise, on vacation on the fictional island of St. Honore.

"A most encouraging return to very near her best unputdownable form," is how Maurice Richardson referred to the book in his review in *The Observer*.[xxxiii]

And it was with no small amount of happiness that the critic in the *New Yorker* wrote, "As always when we read a book by Agatha Christie, we think, 'What on earth would we do without this talented vigorous lady?'"[xxxiv]

On September 21, 1964, Mathew Prichard celebrated his twenty-first birthday, and as he did, *The Mousetrap* was closing in on its five-thousandth performance. His mother and stepfather had moved permanently down to Greenway House the previous March. They occupied Ferry Cottage on the property, in order to take a more active role in both the running of the gardens and supervising the affairs of Agatha Christie Ltd., though they still kept their home Pwllywrach and visited it regularly.

Max had taken to speeding in their new Humber Super Snipe Series IV with its 125-horsepower engine, while Agatha began work on her next book, *At Bertram's Hotel*. The book would start a guessing game when it was published the following year, as to which real hotel Agatha used as her model for the fictional Bertram's. The guessing to this day widely favors Brown's Hotel, one of the most historic in all of London, and a Mayfair favorite for its afternoon tea.

Private letters between Agatha Christie and Edmund Cork suggest otherwise, however. "I think it is important that any similarities between Flemings Hotel...should be cut out," Cork wrote upon receiving the manuscript in March 1965. "We have not altered the name of [hotel manager] Capello, but I think it should be changed, as it is too similar to Manetta, who is the real proprietor of Flemings."[xxxv]

The book was praised in the press and sold 50,000 copies between its release on November 15, 1965, and the end of the year. Frances Iles, writing in *The Guardian,* felt that the denouement was too far-fetched to be believed, but asked, "Does the plot matter so much with Mrs. Christie? What does matter is that one just can't put any book of hers down."[xxxvi]

While *At Bertram's Hotel* was one of Agatha's most popular best-sellers, two weeks earlier Collins Publishing released one of her rarest, titled *Star Over Bethlehem and Other Stories.* Authored under the name Agatha Christie Mallowan, it was a book of Christian poetry and tales, aimed not at children, as is commonly thought, but at the adult market. Max referred to the tales as "Holy Detective Stories" and thought them "perhaps her most charming and among the most original of her works."[xxxvii]

As his Christmas present, Agatha sent Edmund Cork the original manuscript for her autobiography, on which she had been working for twenty-five years. Though still missing its last chapter, which she would add the following year, Agatha had decided to end her life story at age seventy-five, for "as far as life is concerned, that is all there is to say."[xxxviii]

Earlier that year, she had received a letter from the new president of Dodd, Mead in New York, Phelps Flatt ("what a name!" remarked Agatha, adding, "I don't think I much take to [him]").[xxxix] She mentioned the letter in one she wrote to Edmund Cork and referred to the constant requests from writers to write her "authorized" biography. "I turn them down as I am not dead yet."[xl]

Yet in a rare interview she gave to journalist Frances Wyndham, published in the February 26, 1966, edition of the *Sunday Times,* she said, "I've been rather enjoying jotting down silly little things that happened when I was a child. There'll be a bit about my work, I suppose, but not much. If anybody writes about my life in the future, I'd rather they got the facts right."[xli]

A personal friend of Phelps Flatt was working on a detailed bibliography of Christie books and was allowed to visit her at Greenway for several days over this period. Gordon

Clark Ramsey taught at Worcester Academy, a boarding school in Massachusetts, and was granted his audience, for that's what it was, as a courtesy to Flatt, who published the book *Agatha Christie: Mistress of Mystery* in 1967, but without biographical material as promised.

Ramsey did, however, hear about the residual MGM brouhaha and the continuing uproar over the studio intent on dramatizing Hercule Poirot on the big screen. *The ABC Murders* had been released in August 1965, with Tony Randall as Poirot. The director, Frank Tashlin, was best known from directing a half-dozen Jerry Lewis films and took a slapstick approach to comedy.

It took until the fall before MGM decided to end its contract with Agatha Christie Ltd., but not before filming a new adaptation of *Ten Little Indians,* without any input from Agatha herself. The film had an oddball cast that mixed American idols Hugh O'Brian and Fabian with British classic actors Wilfred Hyde-White and Stanley Holloway. At ninety-two minutes, its length was as short as its box office run.

When Agatha looked back on 1966, what she remembered most was travel. First there was a trip to Paris in January, where the Mallowans stayed at the Ritz Hotel and were treated like royalty. Max thought the room rates were royal as well, despite being given a room at the discounted rate of £18, including breakfast. He preferred the elegance of Le Bristol Paris to the *"mauvais* style" of the Ritz.

After a party given by Collins Publishing for Max's *Nimrud and Its Remains,* the Mallowans traveled to Belgium in June, where they visited a museum dedicated to Hercule Poirot. In August they toured Switzerland ("the air, the air," Agatha exclaimed) and stayed on Lake Thun ("Don't forward anything on to me at Merligen unless it can't be helped!! No letters is the greatest joy in life...").[xlii] And on September 11, 1966, they arrived in America, where they would remain for the remainder of the year. Max had been booked on an extensive lecture tour that was to take him to Harvard and Princeton before speaking in Baltimore, Maryland; Washington, D.C.; Cleveland, Ohio; Austin and Dallas, Texas; Sante Fe, New Mexico; Los Angeles, Berkeley, and Palo Alto, California; Chicago, New York, and Philadelphia, with his final lecture at Yale.

Agatha and Max spent a week resting in New York prior to beginning their tour, with Agatha shopping for what she labeled "outsized knickers"—a very large bathing suit capable of accommodating her girth during her sporadic swims. Her next priority was visiting the grave of her father's parents—the Nathaniel Millers.

The visit to Greenwood Cemetery in Brooklyn took place the day after the Mallowans' arrival—a "bright, sunny and moderately warm day," according to an office assistant who accompanied Agatha and Max.[xliii]

Writing to Edmund Cork, Agatha said that the "whole of Greenwood Cemetery looks like Luxor.... Granite monoliths everywhere."[xliv] She next took a tour of Easthampton, Massachusetts, twenty miles across the Connecticut border, to see her grandparents' original home. "How beautiful all New England is this time of year!"[xlv] she wrote. And of Vermont: "The first real butter I've tasted in years!"[xlvi]

She complained about American trains ("the lunch was practically inedible"), found joy in American architecture and museums, and thought Austin was "very civilized." Unfortunately, work was never far from her mind—her British publishers had decided to repackage a group of short stories, titled *Thirteen for Luck,* that they said were aimed at younger readers. "Several people came up to me in the States and said 'I believe you are writing for teenagers now.' It is *not* true. I say so to everyone.... Haven't I got *any* control over how things I have written come into?"[xlvii] she asked Edmund Cork. Of course, the answer was no...not really. Covers and titles were at the discretion of the publisher.

What *did* please her, however, was the reception in November of her newest book, *Third Girl.* Though it was a Hercule Poirot novel, it was Agatha's attempt to update her image, writing about the modern girls of London, though almost apologetically. She did not approve of the stringy hair of the Beatles generation and the drug culture that had sprung like weeds in pavement cracks. She took notice of dirty fingernails and ill-fitting clothing, leaving the critic from *The Observer* to note: "After this, I shan't be a bit surprised to see A.C. wearing a mini-skirt."[xlviii]

With the new year about to start, Agatha paused to reassess her life. What she saw made her unhappy. The world in which she found herself was familiar yet unrecognizable. To her, the *civil* had disappeared from civilization. She was seventy-six years old and still struggling to earn a living, even with the new corporate arrangement regarding her copyrights. She hated the way she looked despite all her efforts and felt worn out for the first time in her life.

She vented her feelings to Edmund Cork in a manner that suggested her frustration. "Both you and Harold Ober Inc. have got to consider *me*," she wrote, "and what I feel. I'm not a performing dog for you all. I'm the *writer,* and it's misery to be ashamed of oneself."[xlix]

Agatha was ashamed because she had lost control. She had *not* received a breakdown of her royalties and had *not* been asked about titles for a new collection that the publishers labeled the Greenway Edition. "Now then, any other complaints, Agatha?" she asked. "Yes...," she answered to no one in particular. "I must see some information about my finances! And you are the horse's mouth. I seem to have blown off a lot of steam now, so best wishes for the new year once more. Love to all, Yours, Agatha."[l]

Fortunately, 1967 proved to be the year of change. Mathew Prichard had spent the previous summer at Greenway House, having graduated from Oxford. In the fall he began to work in the publishing business, after being offered a job by Allen Lane at Penguin Books. And by May, he was married to a beautiful girl named Angela Maples. She had been a frequent guest at Greenway House, and in a letter to Edmund Cork, Agatha wrote, "We are delighted about Mathew. She is a *very* nice girl."[li] Agatha was right. Mathew had chosen well.

This was also the year that Mathew sold his rights to *The Mousetrap*. In an interview in 2002 with the *Daily Mirror's* Tony Purnell, Mathew said he had "no regrets" over selling the rights to Peter Saunders, who continued to make a fortune from the run. "We made an arrangement that neither of us would ever say the sales amount."[lii]

Perhaps due to Agatha's strong letter of the new year, Edmund Cork strove to keep her updated on various new editions of old books, and when a presentation was made to create a board game out of her Poirot books, Cork sent Agatha the rules and the artwork, only to be told, "I really can't make head or tail of any of this.... It's all very ugly.... The things you wish on me!"[liii] As if she hadn't asked for it herself.

In June, the 1962 Humber Super Snipe was traded in for a Volvo Estate Car and gifted to Max, who continued to break the speed limit with regularity. In July, Agatha had her ears treated in an effort to improve her deteriorating hearing. And in August they flew to Ljubljana, Yugoslavia, to celebrate their anniversary on a two-week vacation. In October, while traveling alone in Iran to deliver a lecture, Max suffered a second stroke and was hospitalized, though again without severe physical consequences. Despite her own ailments, compared to her younger husband, Agatha was healthy, and wrote to Edmund Cork about Max, "Waiting and wondering is Hell!"[liv]

By the time Max returned home to Winterbrook, Agatha's seventy-third book, the supernatural *Endless Night* was published to surprise critical acclaim. "It is really bold of Agatha Christie to write in the persona of a working class boy who marries a poor little rich girl..."[lv] the review read in the *Times Literary Supplement*.

There was little time to celebrate yet another novel, despite its success, for the Mallowans had planned a farewell trip to Iran. They still called it Persia, in tribute to the land and the people they loved. This time, there would be no more digging through sand for lost cities, no lamb cooked over a kerosene stove or tea brewed with water from the Tigris. This was a farewell, for age and politics had changed their ability to move freely among the people. And when they left, they did not say good-bye or even take one final look, for this place could never be forgotten, and never was.

With the New Year's Honor's List, Max was awarded a knighthood, making him Sir Max Mallowan to his Lady Agatha Christie. In 1971, it would be Agatha's turn, being honored as a Dame of the British Empire and invited to dine at Buckingham Palace. It had been a long journey for the little girl with the imaginary Kitten family, or the hoop that became a train or a pony. But she was finally what she had always dreamed of being—royalty, a lady of court.

There would be more books, of course, each slightly less clever than the last: *By the Pricking of Thumbs* in 1968 ("Not her best though it has patches of her cozy euphoria and aura of the sinister")[lxi], *Hallowe'en Party* in 1969 ("Poirot seems weary and so does the book")[lvii], and then, in 1970, *Passenger to Frankfurt: An Extravaganza.*

When Dorothy Olding, in New York, received the manuscript for *Passenger to Frankfurt*, she immediately wrote Edmund Cork a letter of warning: "Confidentially, I was disappointed in the book. It seemed to me a bad imitation of a spy story and a damned weak one at that." It was Olding who insisted that the subtitle "An Extravaganza" be added, hoping to alert readers that this was a little left of the normal Christie fare.

In the *New York Times*, A. J. Hubin attacked the book and the author. "[This] book doesn't really come off; in fact, it doesn't come off at all. This is doubly sad because I suspect Miss Christie has thrown more of herself...into this book than any other."[lviii]

Olding, however, picked another section of the review to send to Cork. In it, A. J. Hubin said, "Everyone is entitled to write a bad novel and Miss Christie's standing will suffer less from one than others. But somebody should interpose himself and discourage its publication. It does nothing for the reader or her reputation."[lix] After underlining the last two sentences, Olding asked Cork, "Do you suppose they mean us?"[lx]

The simple fact was that it would have taken tremendous courage, and total disregard for the two agencies profit-and-loss sheet, to have spoken up and advised Agatha that it was time to stop writing. It would also have likely killed her, for writing was her life.

Her grandson, Mathew, had moved into Pwllywrach in Wales, and began to raise a family of his own; Max had finished his great work, *Nimrud and Its Remains,* and was devoted to his research; Anthony had his garden and Rosalind was the official custodian of the copyrights. And Agatha, well, she had her writing. And write she did.

Nemesis followed in 1971 ("Not a Christie classic but the old hand is astonishingly fresh and the mixture as relaxing as a hot bath")[lxi], plus *The Golden Ball and Other Stories,* a book of previously published short stories. *Elephants Can*

Remember in 1972 ("This is vintage Christie. But it is, alas, not
very good.")[lxii] and *Postern of Fate* in 1973. This was to be the
last novel Agatha would ever write. It was her eightieth book,
published in her eighty-third year. Though bent with age, hard
of hearing and with difficulty seeing, she still produced her
"Christie for Christmas" one last time.

It was a comfortable book, full of nostalgia for a time
long gone. It was Agatha remembering her life, and it was a
sad farewell. Newgate Callendar, writing in the *New York
Times Book Review,* was not happy to have to say, "It is sad to
see a veteran author working under nothing but
momentum...Sorry."[lxiii]

There were still moments of glory for Agatha, and she
never failed to rally to enjoy every one of them. There was a
letter in 1971 from Madame Tussaud's, inviting Agatha to be
measured for a waxwork for their grand hall. Agatha was
excited by the prospect and obliged, even though walking was
more difficult than ever. She had fallen at Winterbrook the
previous June and thought she had bruised her hip. After
enduring a week of pain, she had the hip x-rayed, and it was
found to be broken. Surgery followed at Nuffield Orthopedic
Hospital in Oxford, and while the hip eventually healed
completely, her walking never returned to its former stride.

The following year, while spring cleaning, Agatha
came across the typewritten script for *Akhnaton,* a stage play
that she had written in 1937 but had never been produced. Set
in ancient Egypt, the play was a serious drama centered on the
Pharaoh's effort to convert his people to worship one God. With
twenty-two characters and eleven scene changes, the play was
nearly impossible to produce—Agatha knew that—and was
only saved from extinction by her insistence that her publishers
produce a printed version of the script, which they did the
following year.

Also in 1971, United Artists surprised Agatha by
releasing a version of *Endless Night* as a feature film. It was an
insulting exercise in concocted horror starring Hayley Mills
and George Sanders, who committed suicide before its
release. The London *Times* called it a "film rotten with the
stink of red herrings."

Agatha was still irate when Lord Mountbatten approached her to request the rights for his son-in-law, John Brabourne, to produce an all-star feature for EMI Films of *Murder on the Orient Express*. At this point, Agatha wanted nothing more to do with films and initially wouldn't even discuss it. Eventually, however, the politeness of Lord Mountbatten prevailed. There were many meetings scheduled at the Savoy Grill—Agatha with her retinue and John Brabourne with his. Eventually, it was the enthusiasm of Lord Mountbatten that succeeded in convincing Agatha of his confidence in his son-in-law, and once Agatha agreed, the rest of her family members fell in line. The resulting film stands as a glorious testament to the best of Agatha Christie.

It was filmed by director Sidney Lumet in a style that evoked the glamour of the thirties—Agatha's glamour. The cast was top-loaded with stars led by Albert Finney as Hercule Poirot. Lauren Bacall, Sean Connery, Ingrid Bergman, Michael York, Vanessa Redgrave, and John Gielgud, among others, gave this film mystery and romance and elegance.

"The star casting didn't have to do with making it commercially viable," Lumet said. "It had to do with style. And bless the backers for going along with it and taking what was really a risk. It wasn't the kind of operation on which you could ask anybody to take a salary cut."[lxiv]

The *New York Times'* Vincent Canby said the film was a "terrifically entertaining super-valentine" as he glowed with praise for the capture of a bygone era.[lxv] It was as much a tribute to the Christie book as it was to the glamour of old Hollywood, who recognized the film's achievement with six Academy Award nominations.

On the evening of the film's London premiere, Agatha arrived in a wheelchair, a mink shawl over her shoulders, looking elegant and elderly but with spirit unabated. Queen Elizabeth and her entourage were in the audience, and when it came time for Agatha to be presented to the Queen, she stood up, and Agatha remained standing for the Queen's daughter, Princess Anne, to be greeted as well.

It was a glorious evening—successful for the filmmakers to be sure, but even more so for Agatha, who attended the premiere party at Claridges after the film. "She enjoyed it greatly," Max wrote in his memoirs, "and I retain the picture of Lord Mountbatten...escorting her out of the dining room at midnight and raising her arm in farewell."lxvi It was her last public appearance in London.[36]

A month and a half before the premiere, Agatha had suffered a heart attack and was largely confined to bed—albeit temporarily. "Heart much steadier and doctor lets me get up and come downstairs every other day for short time.... Boring!" she wrote to Edmund Cork.lxvii

While there would not be any new books written in 1974, at Rosalind's insistence, Agatha's publishers did produce a compilation titled *Poirot's Early Cases*.[37] The cover of the U.K. edition, illustrated by Margaret Murray, revealed a rather large foot in spats next to a dirtied travel bag. "His smartly dressed lower half seems entirely unlike him," Agatha argued via letter to Billy Collins, her publisher. She thought it made him look six feet tall—"at least."lxviii

These quibbles gave her a reason to exist, for there was little activity remaining in her life. She occasionally left the Winterbrook house, but trips to Greenway were no longer possible. Her bed was eventually moved downstairs, and while a nurse was employed, it was Max who lovingly cared for his wife, though for some of the time she was not completely aware of her behavior.

There was an episode where she chopped at her hair with a pair of scissors; another where she ranted with diminished capability about some memory of the past. Yet, for the most part, Agatha remained Agatha—though one who appeared to be progressively shriveling more each day.

Max's aide, Barbara Parker, visited on weekends and helped with organization, and cared for Max as well—his health not improving under the circumstances. Agatha liked Barbara and respected her kindness and unflappability. She took criticism without defense and compliments without denial. And then, too, she was Max's friend.

There can be little doubt that Agatha knew she was dying, slowly perhaps, but ebbing away like a character in one of her books, until she, too, would disappear into dust. She planned for her funeral without sentimentality. Her grave was to be at St. Mary's Church in Cholsey, a short distance from

---

[36] Agatha appeared at the end of November at the annual party for *The Mousetrap* but this was not a public event, and she entered and exited privately.
[37] Published in America as *Hercule Poirot's Early Cases*.

Winterbrook; the inscription on her tombstone was to be taken from Edmund Spenser's *The Faerie Queene:* "Sleep after Toyle, Port after Stormie Seas, Ease after Warre, Death after Life, Doth Greatly Please;"[38] the music to be played: Johann Sebastian Bach's "Air" from *Suite No. 3 in D.*[lxix]

More often than not, she was at peace, content to play with her dog, Bingo. The Manchester terrier, like Peter before him, was her constant companion and ally in the storm. He was the one friend that never ceased to listen, and the one never denied access. Max knew better than to even try. (The dog had bitten him more than once. That was enough.)

Now completely unable to write, Agatha was finally convinced to open the vault and release the held Poirot manuscript titled *Curtain* as the "Christie for Christmas" in 1975. Its arrival was fanfared by the critics, who marveled at this classic Christie tale. "Dame Agatha, whose recent work has shown a decline, is seen once more at the peak of her ingenuity," wrote Matthew Coady in *The Guardian.*[lxx]

The book was an instant success, selling through its initial printing of one hundred twenty thousand copies, with the American hardback rights generating $300,000 for Rosalind, who owned the copyright. Fans of Hercule Poirot were visibly moved by the book, which found him now crippled with pain, and, on the last page of the novel, he said farewell to his dear friend Captain Hastings.

"Goodbye, *cher ami.* I have moved the amyl nitrite ampoules away from the bedside. I prefer to leave myself in the hands of the *bon Dieu.*"[lxxi]

"Hercule Poirot Is Dead: Famed Belgian Detective" headlined the front page of the *New York Times* in his obituary. "At the end of his life, he was arthritic and had a bad heart," it suggested. "He was in a wheelchair often, and was carried from his bedroom to the public lounge at Styles Court, a nursing home in Essex, wearing a wig and false moustaches to mask the sign of age that offended his vanity."[lxii]

Just before the holiday, Agatha Christie was carried, like Hercule Poirot, from her bed and placed on the sofa in the living room of Winterbrook, where she received her final communion. That Christmas as the family gathered close, she observed every one of them, thankful for her blessings—and for them.

---

[38] The same verse is on the tombstone of Polish novelist Joseph Conrad.

She had caught a cold—nothing much. But then, in Agatha's fragile condition, it didn't take much to provide her an excuse to let go. She celebrated the new year with Max, and on January 12, 1976, while being wheeled in her chair from the dining room, she reached for his hand and without looking up whispered, "I'm joining my Maker," and died.

Agatha Mary Clarissa Christie Mallowan was dead at the age of eighty-five.

EPILOGUE

The Great Entertainer

In her own genre of literary work,
we must accord her the title of genius.

Sir William Collins
at Agatha's memorial service

JANUARY 13, 1976. THE DAY AFTER AGATHA CHRISTIE DIED, the lights in every West End theater in London were dimmed between ten and eleven p.m. in her honor. It was a fitting tribute to a writer who had contributed nineteen plays to their treasure chest of properties. These were her friends, these theater folk, and now they paid respect to one of their own.

Exactly as she requested, Agatha was buried in a private service at the Parish Church of St. Mary's, Cholsey, four days after her death. Rosalind saw to that. The tombstone would take longer, made by friends from her archaeological digs, who combined their efforts in carving scripted lettering and cherub sculpture. The grave was positioned in a far corner of the cemetery, away from prying eyes, for even in death Agatha remained private, a shy and modest teller of tales who had one story left to reveal to the world.

In 1976, *Sleeping Murder: Miss Marple's Last Case* was published, nine months after Agatha's death. Writing about the book in the *New York Times*, critic Gavin Lambert felt that *Sleeping Murder* was "not among [Agatha's] most skilled works, but it displays her personal sense of what she calls 'evil.'"[i] Agatha would have been pleased that Lambert noticed, for throughout her career she delighted in turning the spotlight on the fight between good and evil, with good always prevailing by the final paragraph.

Sir William Collins—delivering the eulogy at her memorial service, four months to the day after her death—suggested as much when he said that her books were the modern equivalent of medieval morality plays. This creator of intricate mystery plots was less concerned with the crime than she was with catching the criminal. Whether it was Miss Marple, Hercule Poirot, Tommy and Tuppence Beresford, Parker Pyne or Harley Quin, one Christie sleuth or another was *certain* to see that the evildoer was caught, and presumably punished.

In her will, Agatha bequeathed her Wedgwood bust of Mercury to her friend and agent, Edmund Cork, as well as a large chest that had been shipped from Damascus. A memorial fund, set up at the time of her death, split contributions received from her fans worldwide between the Little Sisters of the Poor and the Agatha Christie Trust for Children. The copyright to all her books had been allotted, of course, well before her death.

Rosalind and Anthony Hicks had long before moved into the main house at Greenway, and life continued much the same—Anthony handling the complicated business of the commercial market gardens, and Rosalind protecting her mother's rights and privacy. It wasn't long before she was doing battle, as her mother before her had, with the Christie publishers: Beginning with *Sleeping Murder*, Rosalind complained that she had not been shown the cover art for the book before its publication.

The autobiography that Agatha had written and passed along to Edmund Cork was subsequently edited and cut to produce a highly entertaining if selective look into the life of the author. *Agatha Christie: An Autobiography* was published in November 1977. Philip Ziegler from Collins Publishing did most of the editing on the book, which, in its original release, included four pages of color prints of Agatha's family portraits. These would be eliminated in later editions.

For a book that was written to document the events of her life, Agatha made many inadvertent errors of dates and facts. The majority of the book covers her youth in Torquay and family travels, revealing fascinating details, while the years 1945 to 1965 (when she ended the book, a decade before her death) received a scant twenty-three pages. There was to be no mention of the eleven-day disappearance that caused such notoriety in 1926. Agatha waved it away, like one would a pesky mosquito: "The next year of my life is one I hate recalling.... There is no need to dwell on it,"[ii] she wrote.

While Rosalind had inherited all her mother's personal possessions (Greenway House had been in her name since 1959), Max retained ownership of Winterbrook and the other homes. He was seventy-one at the time of Agatha's death and apparently not prepared to spend the remainder of his life as a grieving widower. Though he continued to see Barbara Parker, who faithfully assisted him in packing away many of Agatha's things, he began an open affair with his neighbor, the recently widowed Baroness Camoys, Jeanne Stoner.

Jeanne was an extremely attractive and colorful woman whose husband, Ralph Robert Watts Sherman Stoner, was the sixth Lord Camoys. He had inherited his title and the grand manor house Stoner Park upon the death of his father, the fifth Lord Camoys. Jeanne was friendly with both Agatha and Max, her famous neighbor across town. And with the passing of the Baron in March, the sixty-three-year-old Baroness looked to Max for comfort.

Unaware of the complicated copyright structure of Agatha's estate, Jeanne saw herself as the potential benefactress of the Christie fortune—unaware that most of it had bypassed Max Mallowan entirely. Granted, two months after Agatha's death, he certainly looked the part of the rich widower. He had taken to driving a Bentley, sported updated tweeds (without his customary vest), and began to serve cocktails instead of tea in the afternoon. This flush of youthful behavior with the provocative Baroness was doomed to failure, however, for it became common knowledge soon enough that Max, while far from poor, was not what she had hoped for financially.

Barbara Parker, on the other hand, didn't care about money. At age sixty-nine, Barbara cared about Max and had shown her devotion for over twenty years. Therefore, it did not come as a huge surprise to anyone who knew the pair when they announced their engagement and subsequently married in September 1977. Rosalind was not particularly happy with the union, preferring for Max to remain the mourning and faithful widower. She did not have to endure the humiliation for long, however, since the following July, he had an operation on his arthritic hip and, while recovering, suffered another heart attack. Max Mallowan died on August 19, 1978, and joined Agatha at rest in the Cholsey churchyard.

After his funeral, Rosalind was reported to have visited Winterbrook and marked items of her mother's for removal. The house itself was sold by the Mallowan family, and Barbara Parker Mallowan was willed £40,000 pounds by the estate, an amount equal to nearly $400,000 today. She lived until 1993 in Wallingford, where Winterbrook House was located, and was elected president of the British School of Archaeology in Iraq, remaining active until her death.

The following year, *Miss Marple's Final Cases and Two Other Stories* was released in England, based on tales originally published mostly in the forties. The *Times* reported that a "decided aroma of the confectioner's comes from some."[iii] It would be followed by the efforts of HarperCollins (Collins Publishing was merged with Harper & Row in 1987) to repackage Christie stories as if they were new product: *Problem at Pollensa Bay and Other Stories* (1991) and *While the Light Lasts and Other Stories* (1997), plus the G. P. Putnam release of *The Harlequin Tea Set* (1997).

Rosalind was extremely protective of her mother's name and copyrights, and she was particularly defensive where film adaptations were concerned. She had good reason. During Agatha's final illness in 1975, a German film of *And Then There Were None* was released, having been shot on location in Iran, featuring singer Charles Aznavor and Agatha's friend Sir Richard Attenborough. When the film, titled *Ein Unbekannter rechnet ab* in German, was released in America as *Ten Little Indians*, Vincent Canby said in the *New York Times* that it was the kind of film that "damages the reputation of everyone connected with it..."[iv]

In 1978, Rosalind sued to stop production of the film *Agatha,* based on a novel by Kathleen Tynan, depicting a fictional account of her mother's disappearance in 1926. Writing to the London *Times* newspaper, Rosalind said, "I would like to take this opportunity of saying that this film is being made entirely without consultation with any of my parents' family, is altogether against our wishes, and is likely to cause us great distress."[v] Her legal efforts to stop the movie failed, and while it received generally favorable reviews, it nevertheless permanently jaundiced Rosalind's opinion of producers' ethics.

When the EMI Group followed their enormously successful *Murder on the Orient Express* with *Death on the Nile* the same year, Rosalind visited the set and reportedly told star Peter Ustinov that Hercule Poirot looked *nothing* like he did. "He does now, Madame," he was said to have responded. "He does now." The resulting film, which was shot on location in Egypt, was another critical triumph. Although grossing nearly $15 million, it was not as financially successful as *Murder on the Orient Express* had been.

That did not, however, prevent EMI from producing its third Christie adaptation, *The Mirror Crack'd,* in 1980, with another all-star cast (Angela Lansbury played Miss Marple; Elizabeth Taylor, Rock Hudson, and Kim Novak were around for fun). With this film, EMI seemed to find its style again, with *Variety* suggesting that it was a "worthy if more leisurely successor to *Murder on the Orient Express.*" By the time EMI's fourth effort, *Evil Under the Sun,* was produced in 1982, the excitement seemed to have faded, though the formula remained the same. Peter Ustinov was back as Poirot, joined by Maggie Smith and James Mason. "The film has nothing but style," Vincent Canby wrote in the *New York Times,* "but its style goes a long way."[vi]

It took television until the beginning of the eighties to get a commitment from Agatha Christie Ltd., allowing the Christie mysteries to be adapted for the small screen. It had been something Agatha fought since the invention of the medium—her own opinion of television as only something good to hold a flower vase. Rosalind did not share her mother's view, but required considerable convincing to allow London Weekend Television to present *The Agatha Christie Hour.* It was a series of ten hour-long dramas adapted from Agatha's short stories and was extremely well received.

The series was quickly followed by two 1983 TV movies for CBS—*A Caribbean Mystery* and *Sparkling Cyanide.*

The successful broadcast of these films in turn motivated the BBC to shoot *Miss Marple* as a television series, with Joan Hickson as the spinster sleuth, beginning in 1984. By 1989, London Weekend Television joined the Christie rollout by producing the series *Agatha Christie's Poirot,* starring David Suchet in the title role. Rosalind had recommended Suchet after seeing the actor in the British miniseries of Tom Sharpe's *Blott on the Landscape.* Rosalind was extremely pleased by the productions, which remained faithful to her mother's characters and plots. Bought by Public Broadcasting in America, and later rebroadcast on the Arts and Entertainment cable network, the series was enormously lucrative for Agatha Christie Ltd., which continued to benefit from the productions.

In 1993, Rosalind Hicks founded the Agatha Christie Society to preserve the legacy of her mother's writings, assuming the role of president, with Joan Hickson and David Suchet as vice presidents in the organization. Seven years later, Rosalind and her son donated Greenway House and its gardens to Britain's National Trust, as a means of preserving and protecting the grounds and building in perpetuity.

Rosalind Hicks died in 2004, leaving an estate conservatively estimated at $600 million. Anthony Hicks died the following year. At that time, Mathew Prichard donated all the contents of Greenway House to the National Trust as well, in an effort to guarantee his grandmother's legacy would be maintained for the public, whose interest in everything Christie has never flagged.

After a $7.5 million restoration, Greenway House was opened to the public in February 2009. To visit Greenway is to step back in time, to a place the color of Agatha's favorite clotted cream. There is a hushed reverence about the place, overwhelmed by knickknacks and bric-a-brac, for Agatha was a collector of things—not expensive things perhaps, but full of memories that linger still. There in the hall is the leather chest from Baghdad, worn from daily use, as is much of the house in general. The mural remains in the dining room, shell paintings still hang in the morning room, and the drawing room still has its tatty sofas and comfortable chairs where Agatha read from her manuscripts. It takes very little imagination to hear her reading still, for this house contains more than history. There is spirit there, carefully preserved by Mathew Prichard and property manager Robyn Brown.

Look past the gardening hats on the table to the garden itself—one can see the laurels and camellias still vying for attention against the strength of ash, beech, and Monterey pine. And in the distance is the River Dart, silent in its passing.

The house and garden are a quiet tribute to a woman who doubted she could write, yet managed to sell well over two *billion* books, translated into 105 languages, making Agatha Christie the most popular modern author in the world.[vii] Thirty-three years after her death, *all* of her books remain in print— eighty-four novels and compilations of short stories, six additional novels written as Mary Westmacott, her two autobiographies, and three books of poetry. She wrote 157 short stories and had her name over the title of nineteen plays. Her production *The Mousetrap* is the longest-running stage play in history, having been performed continuously since 1952. There have been 282 performers in the various casts, during the over 23,500 performances of the show. This, for a play Agatha thought would have a "nice little run."

But then, Agatha Christie was not one to boast. There was never a need. Her work took care of that. She was content to retreat from view and methodically tell her stories, which somehow continued to form in her mind, while eating apples in her bath or washing dishes in her kitchen.

Asked about her talent, she would shrug her shoulders and smack her lips in the way she always did, and then add, "I regard my work as of no importance. I'm simply out to entertain."

APPENDIX

AGATHA CHRISTIE NOVELS & SHORT STORIES (*)
(in order of publication)
English title/American title

1. *The Mysterious Affair at Styles* (1920)
2. *The Secret Adversary* (1922)
3. *Murder on the Links* (1923)
4. *Poirot Investigates* (1924)*
5. *The Man in the Brown Suit* (1924)
6. *The Secret of Chimneys* (1925)
7. *The Murder of Roger Ackroyd* (1926)
8. *The Big Four* (1927)
9. *The Mystery of the Blue Train* (1928)
10. *The Seven Dials Mystery* (1929)
11. *Partners in Crime* (1929)*
12. *The Mysterious Mr. Quin* (1930)*
13. *The Murder at the Vicarage* (1930)
14. *The Sittaford Mystery/Murder at Hazelmoor* (1931)
15. *Peril at End House* (1932)
16. *The Thirteen Problems/The Tuesday Club Murders* (1932)*
17. *Lord Edgware Dies/Thirteen at Dinner* (1933)
18. *The Hound of Death and Other Stories* (1933)* UK only
19. *Murder on the Orient Express/Murder in the Calais Coach* (1934)
20. *The Listerdale Mystery* (1934)* UK only
21. *Why Didn't They Ask Evans?/The Boomerang Clue* (1934)
22. *Parker Pyne Investigates/Mr. Parker Pyne, Detective* (1934)*
23. *Three Act Tragedy/Murder in Three Acts* (1935)
24. *Death in the Clouds/Death in the Air* (1935)
25. *The ABC Murders* (1936)
26. *Murder in Mesopotamia* (1936)
27. *Cards on the Table* (1936)
28. *Murder in the Mews/Dead Man's Mirror* (1937)*
29. *Dumb Witness/Poirot Loses a Client* (1937)
30. *Death on the Nile* (1937)
31. *Appointment with Death* (1938)
32. *Hercule Poirot's Christmas/Murder for Christmas/A Holiday for Murder*[1] (1938)
33. *Murder Is Easy/Easy to Kill* (1939)
34. *The Regatta Mystery and Other Stories* (1939)*
35. *Ten Little Niggers/And Then There Were None/Ten Little Indians/The Nursery Rhyme Murders*[2] (1939)
36. *Sad Cypress* (1940)
37. *One, Two, Buckle My Shoe/The Patriotic Murders/An Overdose of Death*[3] (1940)
38. *Evil Under the Sun* (1941)
39. *N or M?* (1941)
40. *The Body in the Library* (1942)
41. *Five Little Pigs/Murder in Retrospect* (1943)

[1] U.S. paperback title.
[2] *Ten Little Indians* and *The Nursery Rhyme Murders* were alternate U.S. titles.
[3] Alternative U.S. title.

42. *The Moving Finger* (1943)
43. *Towards Zero* (1944)
44. *Death Comes as the End* (1945)
45. *Sparkling Cyanide/Remembered Death* (1945)
46. *The Hollow/Murder After Hours* (1946)
47. *The Labours of Hercules/The Labors of Hercules* (1947)*
48. *Taken at the Flood/There Is a Tide* (1948)
49. *Witness for the Prosecution and Other Stories* (1948)
50. *Crooked House* (1949)
51. *Three Blind Mice and Other Stories/The Mousetrap and Other Stories* (1950)*
52. *A Murder is Announced* (1950)
53. *They Came to Baghdad* (1951)
54. *The Under Dog and Other Stories* (1951)*
55. *Mrs. McGinty's Dead* (1952)
56. *They Do It with Mirrors/Murder with Mirrors* (1952)
57. *After the Funeral/Funerals Are Fatal* (1953)
58. *A Pocket Full of Rye* (1953)
59. *Destination Unknown/So Many Steps to Death* (1954)
60. *Hickory Dickory Dock/Hickory Dickory Death* (1955)
61. *Dead Man's Folly* (1956)
62. *4.50 from Paddington/What Mrs. McGillicuddy Saw!* (1957)
63. *Ordeal by Innocence* (1958)
64. *Cat Among the Pigeons* (1959)
65. *The Adventure of the Christmas Pudding and a Selection of Entrées* (1960)* UK only
66. *Double Sin and Other Stories* (1961)* US only
67. *The Pale Horse* (1961)
68. *The Mirror Crack'd from Side to Side/The Mirror Crack'd* (1962)
69. *The Clocks* (1963)
70. *A Caribbean Mystery* (1964)
71. *At Bertram's Hotel* (1965)
72. *Third Girl* (1966)
73. *Endless Night* (1967)
74. *By the Pricking of My Thumbs* (1968)
75. *Hallowe'en Party* (1969)
76. *Passenger to Frankfurt: An Extravaganza* (1970)
77. *The Golden Ball and Other Stories* (1971)*
78. *Nemesis* (1971)
79. *Elephants Can Remember* (1972)
80. *Postern of Fate* (1973)
81. *Poirot's Early Cases/Hercule Poirot's Early Cases* (1974)
82. *Curtain* (1975)
83. *Sleeping Murder* (1976)
84. *Miss Marple's Final Cases and Two Other Stories* (1979)* UK only
85. *Problem at Pollensa Bay and Other Stories* (1991) UK only*
86. *The Harlequin Tea Set* (1997) US only*
87. *While the Light Lasts and Other Stories* (1997) UK only*

AGATHA CHRISTIE SHORT STORIES
Numbers in parenthesis refer to order of publication
cross-referenced to novels list.

1. *Accident* (20)
2. *The Actress* (86, 87)
3. *The Adventure of Johnny Waverly* (51,81)
4. *The Adventure of the Cheap Flat* (4)
5. *The Adventure of the Christmas Pudding* (65)
6. *The Adventure of the Clapham Cook* (54, 81)
7. *The Adventure of the Egyptian Tomb* (4)
8. *The Adventure of the Italian Nobleman* (4)
9. *The Adventure of the Sinister Stranger* (4)
10. *The Adventure of the 'Western Star'* (4)
11. *The Affair at the Bungalow* (16)
12. *The Affair at the Victory Ball* (54, 81)
13. *The Affair of the Pink Pearl* (11)
14. *The Ambassador's Boots* (11)
15. *The Apples of the Hesperides* (47)
16. *The Arcadian Deer* (47)
17. *At the Bells and Motley* (12)
18. *The Augean Stables* (47)
19. *The Bird with the Broken Wing* (12)
20. *Blindman's Buff* (11)
21. *The Bloodstained Pavement* (16)
22. *The Blue Geranium* (16)
23. *The Call of the Wings* (18, 77)
24. *The Capture of Cerberus* (47)
25. *The Case of the Caretaker* (51,84)
26. *The Case of the City Clerk* (22)
27. *The Case of the Discontented Husband* (22)
28. *The Case of the Discontented Soldier* (22)
29. *The Case of the Distressed Lady* (22)
30. *The Case of the Middle-Aged Wife* (22)
31. *The Case of the Missing Lady* (11)
32. *The Case of the Missing Will* (4)
33. *The Case of the Perfect Maid* (51, 84)
34. *The Case of the Rich Woman* (22)
35. *The Chocolate Box* (4, 81)
36. *Christmas Adventure* (87)
37. *A Christmas Tragedy* (16)
38. *The Clergyman's Daughter* (11)
39. *The Coming of Mr. Quin* (12)
40. *The Companion* (16)
41. *The Cornish Mystery* (54, 81)
42. *The Crackler* (11)
43. *The Cretan Bull* (47)
44. *The Dead Harlequin* (12)
45. *Dead Man's Mirror* (28)
46. *Death by Drowning* (16)

47. *Death on the Nile* (22)
48. *The Disappearance of Mr. Davenheim* (4)
49. *The Double Clue* (66, 81)
50. *Double Sin* (66, 81)
51. *The Dream* (34, 65)
52. *The Dressmaker's Doll* (66, 84)
53. *The Edge* (86, 87)
54. *The Erymanthian Boar* (47)
55. *The Face of Helen* (12)
56. *A Fairy in the Flat* (11)
57. *Finessing the King* (11)
58. *The Flock of Geryon* (47)
59. *Four and Twenty Blackbirds* (51, 65)
60. *The Four Suspects* (16)
61. *The Fourth Man* (18, 49)
62. *A Fruitful Sunday* (20, 77)
63. *The Gate of Baghdad* (22)
64. *The Gentleman Dress in Newspaper* (11)
65. *The Gipsy* (18, 77)
66. *The Girdle of Hyppolita* (47)
67. *The Girl in the Train* (20, 77)
68. *The Golden Ball* (20, 77)
69. *Greenshaw's Folly* (65, 66)
70. *The Harlequin Tea Set* (85, 86)
71. *Harlequin's Lane* (12)
72. *Have You Got Everything You Want?* (22)
73. *The Herb of Death* (16)
74. *The Horses of Diomedes* (47)
75. *The Hound of Death* (18, 77)
76. *The House at Shiraz* (22)
77. *The House of Dreams* (86, 87)
78. *The House of Lurking Death* (11)
79. *How Does Your Garden Grow?* (34, 81)
80. *The Idol House of Astarte* (16)
81. *In a Glass Darkly* (34, 84)
82. *The Incredible Theft* (28)
83. *Ingots of Gold* (16)
84. *Jane in Search of a Job* (20, 77)
85. *The Jewel Robbery at the Grand Metropolitan* (4)
86. *The Kidnapped Prime Minister* (4)
87. *The King of Clubs* (54, 81)
88. *The Lamp* (18, 77)
89. *The Last Séance* (18,66)
90. *The Lemesurier Inheritance* (54. 81)
91. *The Lernean Hydra* (47)
92. *The Listerdale Mystery* (20, 77)
93. *The Lonely God* (86, 87)
94. *The Lost Mine* (4, 81)
95. *The Love Detectives* (51, 85)
96. *Magnolia Blossom* (77, 85)

97. *The Man from the Sea* (12)
98. *The Man in the Mist* (11)
99. *The Man Who Was No. 16* (11)
100. *The Manhood of Edward Robinson* (20, 77)
101. *Manx Gold* (86, 87)
102. *The Market Basing Mystery* (54, 81)
103. *The Million Dollar Bond Robbery* (4)
104. *Miss Marple Tells a Story* (34, 84)
105. *Mr. Eastwood's Adventure* (20)
106. *Motive vs. Opportunity* (16)
107. *Murder in the Mews* (28)
108. *The Mystery of Hunter's Lodge* (4)
109. *The Mystery of the Baghdad Chest* (34, 87)
110. *The Mystery of the Blue Jar* (18, 49)
111. *The Mystery of the Spanish Chest* (65, 86)
112. *The Nemean Lion* (47)
113. *Next to a Dog* (77, 85)
114. *The Oracle at Delphi* (22)
115. *The Pearl of Price* (22)
116. *Philomel Cottage* (20, 49)
117. *The Plymouth Express* (54, 81)
118. *A Pot to Tea* (11)
119. *Problem at Pollensa Bay* (34, 85)
120. *Problem At Sea* (34, 81)
121. *The Rajah's Emerald* (20, 77)
122. *The Red House* (11)
123. *The Red Signal* (18, 49)
124. *The Regatta Mystery* (34, 85)
125. *Sanctuary* (66, 84)
126. *The Second Gong* (49, 85)
127. *The Shadow on the Glass* (12)
128. *The Sign in the Sky* (12)
129. *Sing a Song of Sixpence* (20, 49)
130. *SOS* (18, 49)
131. *The Soul of the Croupier* (12)
132. *The Strange Case of Sir Arthur Carmichael* (18, 77)
133. *Strange Jest* (51, 84)
134. *The Stymphalean Birds* (47)
135. *The Submarine Plans* (54, 81)
136. *The Sunningdale Mystery* (11)
137. *Swan Song* (20, 77)
138. *The Tape-Measure Murder* (51, 84)
139. *The Theft of the Royal Ruby* (66)
140. *The Third Floor Flat* (51, 81)
141. *Three Blind Mice* (51)
142. *The Thumb Mark of Saint Peter* (16)
143. *The Tragedy of Marsdon Manor* (4)
144. *Triangle at Rhodes* (28)
145. *The Tuesday Night Club* (16)
146. *The Unbreakable Alibi* (11)

147. *The Under Dog* (54, 65)
148. *The Veiled Lady* (4, 81)
149. *A Voice in the Dark* (12)
150. *Wasps' Nest* (66, 81)
151. *Where There's a Will* (49)
152. *While the Light Lasts* (86, 87)
153. *Within a Wall* (86, 87)
154. *Wireless* (18)
155. *Witness for the Prosecution* (18, 49)
156. *The World's End* (12)
157. *Yellow Iris* (34, 85)

MARY WESTMACOTT NOVELS
(in order of publication)

1. *Giant's Bread* (1930)
2. *Unfinished Portrait* (1934)
3. *Absent in the Spring* (1944)
4. *The Rose and the Yew Tree* (1947)
5. *A Daughter's a Daughter* (1952)
6. *The Burden* (1956)

AGATHA CHRISTIE SPECIALTY BOOKS

1. *The Road to Dreams* (1924) (Poetry)
2. *Come Tell Me How You Live* (1946) (as Agatha Christie Mallowan) (Biography)
3. *Star Over Bethlehem and Other Stories* (1965) (Christian stories and poetry) (as Agatha Christie Mallowan)
4. *Poems* (1973) (Poetry)
5. *Agatha Christie: An Autobiography* (1977) (Biography)

AGATHA CHRISTIE PLAYS & ADAPTATIONS

1. *Alibi* (Dramatized by Michael Morton from the novel *The Murder of Roger Ackroyd*) (1928)
2. *Black Coffee* (1930)
3. *Love from a Stranger* (Dramatized by Frank Vosper from the short story *Philomel Cottage*) (1936)
4. *Akhnaton* (1937)
5. *Tea for Three* (Dramatized by Margery Vosper from the short story *Accident*) (1939)
6. *Peril at End House* (Dramatized by Arnold Ridley) (1940)
7. *Ten Little Niggers/Ten Little Indians* (1943)
8. *Appointment with Death* (1945)
9. *Murder on the Nile/Hidden Horizon* (1946)
10. *The Murder at the Vicarage* (Dramatized by Moie Charles and Barbara Toy) (1949)
11. *The Hollow* (1951)
12. *The Mousetrap* (1952)
13. *Witness for the Prosecution* (1953)

14. *Spider's Web* (1954)
15. *Towards Zero* (1956)
16. *Verdict* (1958)
17. *The Unexpected Guest* (1958)
18. *Go Back for Murder* (1960)
19. *Rule of Three* (1962)
20. *Fiddlers Three* (1972)
21. *A Murder is Announced* (1977)
22. *Murder at the Vicarage* (Dramatized by Leslie Darbon) (1977)
23. *Cards on the Table* (Dramatized by Leslie Darbon) (1981)
24. *Murder Is Easy* (Dramatized by Clive Exton) (1993)
25. *And Then There Were None* (Dramatized by Kevin Elyot) (2005)

AGATHA CHRISTIE FILMS

1. *The Passing of Mr. Quinn* (Based on the short story *The Coming of Mr. Quin*) (1928)
2. *Die Abenteurer GmbH* (Based on *The Secret Adversary*) (1929)
3. *Alibi* (Based on the stage play from the novel *The Murder of Roger Ackroyd*) (1931)
4. *Black Coffee*
5. *Le Coffret de laque* (*Black Coffee*) (1932)
6. *Lord Edgware Dies* (1934)
7. *Love from a Stranger* (Based on the stage play from the short story *Philomel Cottage*. Released in the US as *A Night of Terror*) (1937)
8. *And Then There Were None* (1945)
9. *Love from a Stranger* (Released in the UK as *A Stranger Walked In*) (1947)
10. *Witness for the Prosecution* (1957)
11. *Spider's Web* (1960)
12. *Murder, She Said* (Based on the novel *4.50 From Paddington*) (1962)
13. *Murder at the Gallop* (Based on the novel *After the Funeral*) (1963)
14. *Murder Most Foul* (Based on the novel *Mrs. McGinty's Dead*) (1964)
15. *Murder Ahoy!* (An original movie with some elements of *They Do It with Mirrors*) (1964)
16. *Gumnaam* (uncredited adaptation of *And Then There Were None*) (1965)
17. *Ten Little Indians* (1966)
18. *The Alphabet Murders* (Based on *The A.B.C. Murders*) (1966)
19. *Endless Night* (1972)
20. *Murder on the Orient Express* (1974)
21. *Ten Little Indians* (1975)
22. *Death on the Nile* (1978)
23. *The Mirror Crack'd* (Based on *The Mirror Crack'd From Side to Side*) (1980)
24. *Evil Under the Sun* (1982)
25. *Ordeal by Innocence* (1984)
26. *Desyat Negrityat* (*Ten Little Niggers*) (1987)
27. *Appointment with Death* (1988)
28. *Ten Little Indians* (1989)
29. *Innocent Lies* (Loosely based on the novel *Towards Zero*) (1995)
30. *Mon Petit Doigt M'a Dit...* (By the Pricking of My Thumbs) (2005)
31. *L'Heure Zéro* (*Towards Zero*) (2007)
32. *Le Crime Est Notre Affaire* (*Partners in Crime*) (2008)

ENDNOTES

Prologue

i   Christie, *Agatha Christie*, p. 353
ii   Ibid., p. 354
iii Ibid.
iv   Ibid, p. 357
v   *Daily Mail*, December 6, 1926, p. 9.
vi   *Westminster Gazette*, December 8, 1926, p. 1.
vii *Westminster Gazette*, December 7, 1926, p. 1.
viii Ibid.
ix   *Daily Mail*, December 8, 1926, p. 10.
x   *Daily Mail*, December 7, 1926, p. 9.
xi   Ibid.
xii Ibid, p. 10.
xiii *New York Times*, December 6, 1926, p. 1.
xiv *Daily Mail*, December 7, 1926, p. 10.
xv   Ibid.
xvi *Westminster Gazette*, December 7, 1926, p. 1.
xvii *Daily Mail*, December 9, 1926, p. 10.
xviii *Daily News*, December 7, 1926, p. 10.
xvix *Westminster Gazette*, December 9, 1926, p. 1.
xx   Ibid.
xxi *Westminster Gazette*, December 8, 1926, p. 1.
xxii *Westminster Gazette*, December 9, 1926, p. 1
xxiii *Daily Chronicle*, December 10, 1926, p. 4.
xxiv *Daily News*, December 11, 1926, p. 7.
xxv *Daily Chronicle*, December 10, 1926, p. 4.
xxvi Ibid.
xxvii *Daily Mail*, December 11, 1926, p. 9.
xxviii *Daily News*, December 10, 1926, p. 9.
xxix *Daily Mail*, December 13, 1926, p 9.
xxx *Westminster Gazette*, December 14, 1926, p. 1.
xxxi *Daily News*, December 14, 1926, p. 5.

Chapter I-Mrs. Miller Has a Baby

i   Kipling to Norton, letter, October 30, 1896, Houghton Library, Harvard University
ii   Morgan, Agatha Christie: A Biography, p.6.
iii Christie, Agatha Christie, p. 22.
iv   Ibid, p. 14.
v   Ibid, p.43.
vi   Ibid, p. 27.
vii Ibid, p. 31.
viii Ibid, p. 39.

ix   Ibid, p. 36.
x   Ibid, p. 48.
xi   Ibid, p. 63.
xii Ibid, p. 69.
xiii Ibid, p. 71.
xiv Placard, Fräulein Uber, 1894.
xv   Letter, Frederick to Clara, undated.
xvi Letter, Frederick to Clara, undated

Chapter 2-Coming of Age

i   Letter, Frederick to Clara, undated.
ii   *Agatha Christie: Official Century Edition*, New York: Harper Paperbacks, 1990, p. 11.
iii Thompson, *Agatha Christie*, p. 41.
iv   Christie, *Agatha Christie*. New York: Dodd, Mead & Company, 1977, p. 118.
v   Ibid, p.113.
vi   Ibid, p.115.
vii Ibid, p.156.
viii Ibid, p.170.
ix   Ibid, p. 181.
x   Ibid, p. 197.
xi   Ibid, p. 195.
xii Letter, Phillpotts to Agatha, undated.
xiii Christie, *Agatha Christie*. New York: Dodd, Mead & Company, 1977, p. 200.

Chapter 3-Mrs. Archibald Christie

i   Christie, *Agatha Christie*, p. 213.
ii   Letter, Archie to Agatha, August, 1912.
iii Recorded interview, Imperial War Museum, October 16, 1974, Catalog number 493.
iv   Christie, *Agatha Christie*, p. 230.
v   Ibid., p. 234.
vi   Ibid.
vii Ibid, p. 238.
viii Letter, Archie to Agatha, December, 1915.
ix   Christie, *Agatha Christie*, p. 257.
x   Christie, *Agatha Christie,* p. 258.
xi   Ibid.
xii Ibid, p. 265.
xiii Ibid, p. 267.
xiv Ibid.

Chapter 4-The Mystery Writer

[i]   Christie, *Agatha Christie*, p. 277.
[ii]   "Mysterious Affair at Styles," *Times Literary Supplement*,
       February 2, 1921.
[iii] Christie, *Agatha Christie*, p. 276.
[iv]   Ibid. 281.
[v]   "Secret Adversary," *Times Literary Supplement*, January 26, 1922.
[vi]   Letter, Agatha to Clara, undated.
[vii] Christie, *Agatha Christie*, p. 296.
[viii] Morgan, *Agatha Christie*, p. 94.
[ix]   Christie, *Agatha Christie*, p. 301.
[x]   Letter, Agatha to Clara, undated.
[xi]   Letter, Agatha to Clara, October 19, 1922.
[xii] Christie, *Agatha Christie*, p. 313.
[xiii] Ibid. p. 283.
[xiv] "Murder on the Links." *Literary Review*, April 14, 1923.
[xv]   "Murder on the Links." *New York Times*, March 25, 1923.
[xvi] "The Man in the Brown Suit." *New Statesman*, October 11, 1924.
[xvii] "The Man in the Brown Suit." *Saturday Review of Literature*,
       December 13, 1924.
[xviii] Christie, *Agatha Christie*, p. 346.
[xix] Ibid. p. 343.
[xx]   Ibid. p. 337.
[xxi] Ibid. p. 352.
[xxii] "The Murder of Roger Ackroyd." *New York Times*, July 18, 1926.
[xxiii] "Books." *New York Herald Tribune*, July 25, 1926.

Chapter Five-My Name Is Neele

[i]   *Daily News*, December 7, 1926, p. 9.
[ii]   *Daily Express*, December 7, 1926, p. 1.
[iii] *Westminster Gazette*, December 7, 1926, p. 1.
[iv]   *Daily News*, December 7, 1926, p. 16.
[v]   *Daily Mail*, December 7, 1926, p. 9.
[vi]   *Daily Chronicle*, December 8, 1926, p. 6.
[vii] *Westminster Gazette*, December 9, 1926, p. 1.
[viii] Ibid.
[ix]   *Daily Mail*, December 9, 1926, p. 15.
[x]   *Westminster Gazette*, December 10, 1926, p. 1.
[xi]   *Daily Mail*, December 10, 1926, p. 9.
[xii] Cade, *Agatha Christie and the Eleven Missing Days*, p. 108
[xiii] *Daily News*, December 13, 1926, p.7.
[xiv] *Westminster Gazette*, December 17, 1926, p. 1.
[xv]   *Daily News*, December 17, 1927, p. 8.
[xvi] *Westminster Gazette*, December 17, 1926, p. 2.

Chapter Six- Finding Agatha

i   *Saturday Review,* February 5, 1927.
ii   Christie, *Agatha Christie,* p. 365.
iii   Ibid., p. 366.
iv   Ibid, p. 364.
v   Cuppy, "Books," *New York Herald Tribune,* August 12, 1928.
vi   Christie, *Agatha Christie,* p. 442.
vii   Ibid, p. 362.
viii   Ibid, p. 368.
ix   Ibid, p. 374.
x   Ibid, p. 377.
xi   Ibid, p. 383.
xii   Ibid, p. 387.
xiii   Ibid, p. 389.
xiv   *Outlook,* March 29, 1929.
xv   Cuppy, "Books," *New York Herald Tribune,* March 17, 1929.
xvi   *New York Times,* September 22, 1929.
xvii   Christie, *Agatha Christie,* p. 396.
xviii Ibid, p. 401.
xix   Mallowan, *Mallowan's Memoirs,* p. 44.
xx   Ibid, p. 403.
xxi   Ibid.
xxii   Ibid, p. 402.

Chapter Seven- Mrs. Max Mallowan

i   Letter, Agatha to Max, undated; Thompson, *Agatha Christie,* p. 291.
ii   Letter, Evelyn to Nancy; Carpenter, *The Brideshead Generation,* p. 82.
iii   Mallowan, *Mallowan's Memoirs,* p. 26.
iv   Letter Max to Agatha, undated; Thompson, *Agatha Christie,* p. 290.
v   Letter, Agatha to Max, undated; Thompson, *Agatha Christie,* p. 300.
vi   "Black Coffee," *Times,* December 9, 1930.
vii   Christie, *Agatha Christie,* p. 453.
viii   Ibid, p. 454.
ix   "Mystery at Hazelmoor," *New York Times,* August 16, 1931.
x   Cuppy, "Books," *New York Herald Tribune,* August 23, 1931.
xi   Letter, Agatha to Max, undated; Morgan, p. 201.
xii   Letter, Agatha to Max, undated; Morgan, p. 202.
xiii   "Peril at End House," *Times Literary Supplement,* April 14, 1932.
xiv   Anderson, "Peril at End House," *New York Times,* March 6, 1932.
xv   Cuppy, "Books," *New York Herald Tribune,* May 5, 1933.
xvi   Mallowan, *Mallowan's Memoirs,* p. 195.
xvii   Christie, *Agatha Christie,* p. 475.
xviii Ibid.
xix   Partridge, *New Statesman and Nation,* October 14, 1933.
xx   Christie, *Agatha Christie,* p. 479.
xxi   Ibid, p. 481.
xxii   Mallowan, *Come, Tell Me How You Live,* p. 20.
xxiii Ibid, p. 21.

xxiv Anderson, "Murder in the Calais Coach," *New York Times*, March 4, 1934.
xxv "Murder on the Orient Express," *Times Literary Supplement*, January 11, 1934.
xxvi "The Listerdale Mystery," *Times Literary Supplement*, July 5, 1934.
xxvii "Murder in Three Acts," *Saturday Review of Literature*, October 6, 1934.
xxviii Anderson, "Death in the Air," *New York Times*, March 24, 1935.
xxix "Murder in Mesopotamia," *New York Times*, September 20, 1936.
xxx Anderson, "Murder on the Nile," *New York Times Book Review*, February 6, 1938.
xxxi "Appointment with Death," *Saturday Review of Literature*, September 10, 1938.
xxxii Christie, *Murder for Christmas*, p. 82
xxxiii Anderson, "Murder for Christmas," *New York Times*, February 12, 1939.
xxxiv Christie, *Agatha Christie*, p. 493.

Chapter Eight – The Tax Man Cometh

i Thompson, *Agatha Christie*, p. 308.
ii Christie, *Agatha Christie*, p. 498.
iii "Murder Is Easy," *Manchester Guardian*, July 11, 1939.
iv "Regatta Mysteries and Other Stories," *New Yorker*, June 24, 1939.
v Christie, *Ten Little Niggers*, p. 71.
vi Hart-Davis, "Ten Little Niggers," *Spectator*, December 15, 1939.
vii Anderson, "And Then There Was None," *New York Times*, February 25, 1940.
viii Christie, *Agatha Christie*, p. 484.
ix Letter, Agatha to Cork, January 6, 1940.
x Letter, Agatha to Cork, January 12, 1940.
xi Letter, Cork to Agatha, January 11, 1940.
xii Irwin, "Sad Cypress," *New York Times Book Review*, September 15, 1940, p. 19.
xiii "Sad Cypress," *The Scotsman*, March 11, 1940, p. 9.
xiv Christie, *Agatha Christie*, p. 498.
xv Christie, *Agatha Christie*, p. 502.
xvi Letter, Agatha to Cork, June 5, 1940.
xvii Letter, Agatha to Cork, July 20, 1940.
xviii Letter, Ober to Cork, January 2, 1940.
xix Richardson, "One, Two, Buckle My Shoe," *The Observer*, November 10, 1940, p. 5.
xx Christie, *Agatha Christie*, p. 304.
xxi Punshon, "Evil Under the Sun," *The Guardian*, August 26, 1941, p. 3.
xxii Christie, *Agatha Christie*, p. 504.
xxiii Letter, Agatha to Cork, undated.
xxiv Letter, Cork to Ober, January 3, 1941.
xxv Letter, Agatha to Cork, undated.
xxvi "Mystery Writer, Mystery Woman," *Saturday Evening Post*, May 10, 1941, p. 4.
xxvii Letter, Agatha to Cork, undated.
xxviii Letter, Cork to Agatha, May 28, 1942.
xxix Letter, Agatha to Cork, June 2, 1942.

xxx Morgan, *Agatha Christie*, p. 240.
xxxi Christie, *Agatha Christie*, p. 20.
xxxii Morgan, *Agatha Christie*, p. 237.
xxxiii Disher, "The Moving Finger, *Times Literary Supplement*, June 19, 1943, p. 297.
xxxiv "Five Little Pigs," *Times Literary Supplement*, January 16, 1943, p. 29.
xxxv Christie, *Agatha Christie*, p. 509.
xxxvi Letter, Agatha to Max, undated: Morgan, *Agatha Christie*, p. 245.
xxxvii Thompson, *Agatha Christie*, p 333.
xxxviii Ibid, p. 343.
xxxix Christie *Agatha Christie*, p. 514.
xl Ibid.
xli Ibid, 513.
xlii Anderson, "Death Comes as the End," *New York Times*, October 22, 1944.
xliii Letter, Agatha to Max, undated; Thompson, *Agatha Christie*, p. 349
xliv Letter, Agatha to Max, undated; Thompson, *Agatha Christie*, p. 349.
xlv Christie, *Agatha Christie*, p. 521.
xlvi Ibid.

Chapter Nine-The Sausage Factory

i Christie, *Agatha Christie*, p. 507.
ii Ibid.
iii Ibid, p. 526.
iv Ibid, p. 527.
v Christie, *Agatha Christie*, p. 504.
vi Robyns, *The Mystery of Agatha Christie*, p.124
vii Boucher, "The Hollow," *San Francisco Chronicle*, October 6, 1946.
viii Mallowan, *Come, Tell Me How You Live*, p. 46.
xix Ibid.
x Letter, Agatha to Cork, undated; Morgan, *Agatha Christie*, p.254.
xi Buckham, "Murder on the Nile," *Daily Mirror*, March 21, 1946, p. 7.
xii Letter, Bond to Ober, March 13, 1947.
xiii Letter, Agatha to Cork, January 27, 1947.
xiv Christie, *Labors of Hercules*, p. 5.
xv Boucher, "Labors of Hercules," *San Francisco Chronicle*, July 6, 1947.
xvi "Witness for the Prosecution and Other Stories," *New Yorker*, September 11, 1948.
xvii Mallowan, *Mallowan's Memoirs*, p. 242.
xviii Christie, *Agatha Christie*, p. 539.
xix Letter, Agatha to Cork, February 4, 1948.
xx Letter, Rosalind to Cork, March 1, 1948
xxi Letter, Agatha to Cork, March 19, 1948
xxii "There Is a Tide," *New Yorker*, March 27, 1948.
xxiii "The Rose and the Yew Tree," *Times Literary Supplement*, November 6, 1948.
xxiv Letter, Toy to Agatha; Morgan, *Agatha Christie*, p. 269.
xxv "Murder at the Vicarage," *Times*, December 15, 1949.
xxvi Letter, Rosalind to Cork, February 22, 1949.
xxvii Letter, Cork to Agatha, March 2, 1949.

xxviii Letter, Agatha to Cork, undated; Morgan, *Agatha Christie*, p. 270.

xxix "A Murder Is Announced," *Toronto Daily Star*, September 30, 1950, p. 19.

xxx "Tips for the Bookseller," *Publishers Weekly*, July 1, 1950, p. 39.

xxxi Thompson, *Agatha Christie*, p. 423.

xxxii Mallowan, *Mallowan's Memoirs*, p. 202.

xxxiii Author interview, 1978.

xxxiv Letter, Agatha to Cork, February 6, 1951.

xxxv Letter, Agatha to Cork, April 16, 1951.

xxxvi Boucher, "They Came to Baghdad," *New York Times*, June 3, 1951

xxxvii Christie, *Agatha Christie*, p. 542.

xxxviii Ibid, p. 543.

xxxix Letter, Hughes Massie Ltd. to Lionel Hewitt, June 11, 1951.

xl Letter, Agatha to Cork, August 10, 1951.

xli Christie, *Agatha Christie*, p. 528.

xlii Letter, Agatha to Cork, February 19, 1952.

xlii Letter, Cork to Agatha, April 25, 1952.

xliv Letter, Agatha to Cork, undated; Morgan, *Agatha Christie*, p. 293.

xlv Drake, "Murder with Mirrors," *Chicago Sunday Tribune*, September 14, 1952.

xlvi Christie, *Agatha Christie*, p. 530.

Chapter Ten - One for the Books

i Osborne, *The Life and Crimes of Agatha Christie*, p. 167.

ii Letter, Jolly to Cork, October 6, 1952.

iii Letter, Agatha to Cork, February 3, 1953.

iv Ibid.

v Christie, *Agatha Christie*, p. 534.

vi Hope-Wallace, "Witness for the Prosecution, *The Guardian*, October 30, 1953, p. 5.

vii Brown, "Witness for the Prosecution," *The Observer*, November 1, 1953, p. 11.

viii "Witness for the Prosecution," *Times, December* 23, 1954, p. 8.

ix Letter, Agatha to Alexander, February 12, 1953.

x Letter, Agatha to Cork, February 12, 1953.

xi Memo, Barden to Cork, November 24, 1953.

xii Letter, Cork to Barden, November 24, 1953.

xiii Letter, Agatha to Cork, Boxing Day, 1953.

xiv Richardson, "Destination Unknown," *The Observer*, October 31, 1954, p.7.

xv Letter, Agatha to Cork, undated; Morgan, *Agatha Christie*, p. 303.

xvi Letter, Cork to Agatha, February 10, 1955.

xvii Letter, Agatha to Cork, February 19, 1955.

xviii Letter, Agatha to Cork, March 1, 1955.

xix Letter, Agatha to Cork, September 14, 1955.

xx Letter, Agatha to Cork, January 8, 1956.

xxi "Towards Zero," *Times*, September 15, 1956.

xxii Letter, Cork to Olding, January 20, 1956.

xxiii Letter, Ober to Agatha, March 6, 1956.

xxiv Letter, Agatha to Ober, March 10, 1956.

xxv Letter, Agatha to Cork, March 21, 1956.

xxvi Iles, "Dead Man's Folly," *Manchester Guardian*, December 7, 1956.

xxvii Letter, Agatha to Cork, undated.

xxviii Letter, Olding to Cork, undated.

xxix Postcard, Agatha to Cork, postmarked 6 p.m., May 18, 1957.

xxx Letter, Cork to Rosalind, June 27, 1957.

xxxi Letter, Agatha to Cork, April 8, 1957.

xxxii "Witness for the Prosecution," *Variety*, December, 1957.

xxxiii Bosley, "Witness for the Prosecution," *New York Times*, February 7, 1958.

xxxiv Saunders, *The Mousetrap*, p. 9.

xxxv Osborne, *The Life and Crimes of Agatha Christie*, p. 185.

xxxvi Christie, *Agatha Christie*, p. 535.

Chapter Eleven – The Movie Years

i "Verdict," *Times*, May 23, 1958, p. 5.

ii Saunders, *The Mousetrap Man*, p.181.

iii Richardson, "Cat Among the Pigeons," *The Observer*, November 8, 1959, p. 8.

iv Letter, Cork to Rosalind, February 26, 1960.

v Letter, Agatha to Cork, January 11, 1960.

vi Saunders, *The Mousetrap Man*, p. 185.

vii Letter, Cork to Rosalind, March 24, 1960.

viii Boucher, "Double Sin," *New York Times*, September 24, 1961.

ix Letter, Agatha to Cork, undated.

x Letter, Agatha to Cork, August 18, 1961.

xi Letter, Agatha to Cork, September 17, 1961.

xii Robyns, *The Mystery of Agatha Christie*, p. 167.

xiii Ibid.

xiv Weiler, "Murder, She Said," *New York Times*, January 8, 1962.

xv Richardson, *The Observer*, November 11, 1962, p. 24.

xvi Letter, Cork to Olding, August 29, 1961.

xvii Interview, author with Bachmann, 1981.

xviii Robyns, *The Mystery of Agatha Christie*, p. 169.

xix Letter, Agatha to Bachmann, July 24, 1963; Thompson, *Agatha Christie*, p. 431.

xx Recording, www.all-about-agatha-christie.com, September 25, 1962.

xxi Christie, *Agatha Christie*, p. 536.

xxii Saunders, *The Mousetrap Man*, p. 134.

xxiii "Loose Ends in a Triple Bill," *Times*, December 21, 1962.

xxiv Boucher, "The Clocks," *New York Times*, October 4, 1964.

xxv Morgan, *Agatha Christie*, p. 336.

xxvi Letter, Agatha to Cork, August 23, 1963.

xxvii Weiler, "Murder Most Foul," *New York Times*, May 24, 1965.

xxviii Letter, Agatha to Pat Cork, March 18, 1964.

xxix Letter, Rosalind to Cork, March 25, 1964.

xxx Letter, Cork To Hicks, March 25, 1964.

xxxi Letter, Agatha to Buchman, April 11, 1964.

xxxii Weiler, "Murder Ahoy!" *New York Times*, September 23, 1964.

xxxiii Richardson, "A Caribbean Mystery, *The Observer*, November 15, 1964, p. 26.

xxxiv *New Yorker,* September 25, 1965.
xxxv   Letter, Cork to Agatha, April 2, 1965.
xxxvi Iles, "At Bertram's Hotel," *The Guardian,* December 17, 1965, p. 9.
xxxvii Mallowan, *Mallowan's Memoirs,* p. 204.
xxxviii Christie, *Agatha Christie,* p. 547.
xxxix Letter, Agatha to Cork, August 9, 1965.
xl   Ibid.
xli   Wyndham, "The Algebra of Agatha Christie," *Sunday Times,*
       February 27, 1966, p. 26.
xlii   Letter, Agatha to Cork, July 23, 1966.
xliii Letter, Elizabeth to Nora, October 19, 1966.
xliv   Letter, Agatha to Cork, October 28, 1966.
xlv   Ibid.
xlvi   Ibid.
xlvii Letter, Agatha to Cork, December 31, 1966.
xlviii Richardson, "Third Girl," *The Observer,* November 13, 1966, p. 26.
xlix   Letter, Agatha to Cork, December 31, 1966.
l   Ibid.
li   Letter, Agatha to Cork, February 6, 1967.
lii   Purnell, *Daily Mirror,* November 30, 2002, p. 30.
liii   Letter, Agatha to Cork, March 22, 1967.
liv   Letter, Agatha to Cork, undated; Morgan, *Agatha Christie,* p. 345.
lv   "Endless Night," *Times Literary Supplement,* November 16, 1967.
lvi   Richardson, "Pricking of Thumbs," *The Observer,* November 17. 1968,
       p. 28.
lvii   Weaver, "Hallowe'en," *Toronto Daily Star,* December 13, 1969, p. 58.
lviii Hubin, "Passenger to Frankfurt: An Extravaganza," *New York Times,*
       December 13, 1970.
lix   Ibid.
lx   Letter, Olding to Cork, November 23, 1970.
lxi   Coady, "Nemesis," *The Guardian,* November 4, 1971, p. 14.
lxii   Callendar, "Elephants Can Remember," *New York Times Book Review,*
       November 26, 1972.
lxiii Callendar, "Postern of Fate," *New York Times Book Review,*
       December 16, 1973.
lxiv   Gow, *Film and Editing,* May 1975, p. 11.
lxv   Canby, "Murder on the Orient Express," *New York Times,*
       September 25, 1974.
lxvi   Mallowan, *Mallowan's Memoirs,* p. 215.
lxvii Letter, Agatha to Cork, undated; Morgan, *Agatha Christie,* p. 372.
lxviii Letter, Agatha to Collins, undated; Morgan, *Agatha Christie,* p. 373.
lxix   Morgan, *Agatha Christie,* p. 375.
lxx   Coady, "The Last Labour of Hercules," *The Guardian,* October 9, 1975,
       p. 13.
lxxi   Christie, *Curtain,* p. 215.
lxxii *New York Times,* August 6, 1975, p.1.

Epilogue

i   Lambert, "Sleeping Murder," *New York Times,* September 19, 1976.

[ii]   Christie, *Agatha Christie*, p. 353, 360.

[iii]   "Miss Marple's Final Cases," *Times*, December 20, 1979.

[iv]   Canby, "Christie Remake in Iran Is a Global Disaster," *New York Times*, April 24, 1975.

[v]   Thompson, *Agatha Christie*, p. 502.

[vi]   Canby, "Evil Under the Sun," *New York Times*, March 5, 1982.

[vii]   Guinness World Records.

BIBLIOGRAPHY

Barbainnier, Earl F. *The Gentle Art of Murder: The Detective Fiction of Agatha Christie.* Bowling Green, Ohio: Bowling Green University Popular Press, 1980.

Barnard, Robert. *A Talent to Deceive: An Appreciation of Agatha Christie.* New York: Dodd, Mead & Company, 1980.

Bloom, Harold. *Modern Critical Views: Agatha Christie.* Philadelphia: Chelsea House Publishers, 2002.

Brabazon, James. *Dorothy L. Sayers.* New York: Charles Scribner's Sons, 1981.

Brunette, Peter. *Sidney Lumet Interviews.* Jackson, Mississippi: University Press of Mississippi, 2006.

Bunson, Matthew. *The Complete Christie: An Agatha Christie Encyclopedia.* New York: Pocket Books, 2000.

Cade, Jared. *Agatha Christie and the Eleven Missing Days.* London: Peter Owen, Publishers, 1998.

Certain Members of the Detection Club. *The Floating Admiral.* Boston: Gregg Press, 1979.

Chaney, Hanna. *The Detective Novel of Manners: Hedonism, Morality, and the Life of Reasons.* Rutherford, N.J.: Fairleigh Dickinson University Press, 1981.

Christie, Agatha. *Agatha Christie: An Autobiography.* New York: Dodd, Mead & Company, 1977.

Christie, Agatha. *Curtain.* New York: Dodd, Mead & Company, 1975.

Christie, Agatha. *The Labors of Hercules: A Hercule Poirot Novel.* New York: Berkley Books, 1984.

Christie, Agatha. *Murder for Christmas*. New York: Dodd, Mead & Company, 1938.

Christie, Agatha. *Poems*. New York: Dodd, Mead & Company, 1973.

Durkin O.P., Mary Brian. *Dorothy L. Sayers*. Boston: Twayne Publishers, 1980.

Feinman, Jeffrey. *The Mysterious World of Agatha Christie*. New York: Award Books, 1975.

Fitzgibbon, Russell H. *The Agatha Christie Companion*. Bowling Green, Ohio: Bowling Green State University Popular Press, 1980.

Gawelti, John G. *Adventure, Mystery, and Romance: Formula Stories as Art and Popular Culture*. Chicago: University of Chicago Press, 1976.

Grossvogel, David I. *Mystery and Its Fictions: From Oedipus to Agatha Christie*. Baltimore: Johns Hopkins University Press, 1979.

Haycraft, Howard. *Murder for Pleasure: The Life and Times of the Detective Story*. London: Peter Davies, 1942.

Haycraft, Howard. *The Art of the Mystery Story: A Collection of Critical Essays*. New York: Appleton-Century-Crofts, 1941.

Hurdle, Judith. *The Getaway Guide to Agatha Christie's England*. Oakland, California: RDR Books, 1999.

Keating, H.R.F. *Agatha Christie: First Lady of Crime*. New York: Holt, Rinehart & Winston, 1977.

Kenney, Catherine. *The Remarkable Case of Dorothy L. Sayers*. Kent, Ohio: The Kent State University Press, 1990.

Maida, Patricia D., and Nicholas B. Spornick. *Murder She Wrote: A Study of Agatha Christie's Detective Fiction*. Bowling Green, Ohio: Bowling Green State University Popular Press, 1982.

Mallowan, Max. *Mallowan's Memoirs*. New York: Dodd, Mead & Company, 1977.

Mandel, Ernest. *Delightful Murder: A Social History of the Crime Story*. London: Pluto Press, 1984.

Morgan, Janet. *Agatha Christie: A Biography*. New York: Alfred A. Knopf, 1984.
Osborne, Charles. *The Life and Crimes of Agatha Christie*. New York: Holt, Rinehart and Winston, 1982.

Ramsey, G.C. *Agatha Christie, Mistress of Mystery*. New York: Dodd, Mead & Co., 1967.

Riley, Dick, and Pam McAllister. *The New Bedside, Bathtub & Armchair Companion to Agatha Christie*. New York: Ungar Publishing Company, 1986.

Robyns, Gwen. *The Mystery of Agatha Christie*. New York: Doubleday & Company, Inc., 1978.

Simmons, Dawn Langley. *Margaret Rutherford: A Blithe Spirit*. New York: McGraw-Hill Book Company, 1983.

Sayers, Dorothy L. *Unnatural Death*. New York: Harper & Row, 1927.

Sanders, Dennis and Len Lovallo. *The Agatha Christie Companion*. New York: Delacorte Press, 1984.

Saunders, Peter. *The Mousetrap Man*. London: Collins, 1972.

Scott, Sutherland. *Blood in Their Ink: The March of the Modern Mystery Novel*. London: Stanley Paul & Co., 1953.

Sikov, Ed. On *Sunset Boulevard*. New York: Hyperion, 1998.

Stashower, Daniel. *Teller of Tales: The Life of Arthur Canon Doyle*. New York: Henry Holt and Company, 1999.

Symons, Julian. *Mortal Consequences: A History—From the Detective Story to the Crime Novel*. New York: Harper & Row, 1972.

Toye, Randall. *The Agatha Christie Who's Who*. New York: Holt, Rinehart & Winston, 1980.

Tynan, Kathleen. *Agatha*. New York: Ballantine Books, 1978.

Wagoner, Mary S. *Agatha Christie*. Boston: G.K. Hall & Co., 1986.

Wagstaff, Vanessa, and Stephen Poole. *Agatha Christie: A Reader's Companion*. London: Aurum Press Ltd., 2004.
Westmacott, Mary. *Unfinished Portrait*. Garden City, New York: Doubleday, 1934.

Winn, Dilys. *Murderers Ink: The Better Half of the Mystery*. New York: Workman Publishing, 1979.

Wynne, Nancy Blue. *An Agatha Christie Chronology*. New York: Ace Books, 1976.

ADDITIONAL PERIODICALS

"Escape of Agatha Christie, The." *Christianity Today*,
February 13, 1976, p. 38.
"Find Mrs. Christie Has Lost Memory." *New York Times*,
December 17, 1926, p. 4.
"Guest Challenged." *Daily News*, December 13, 1926, p. 8.
"How Investors Fared in a Single Season [1954-55]." *Saturday Review*, February 23, 1957, p. 12.
"Letter Clues in Mystery of Missing Novelist." *Westminster Gazette*, December 13, 1926, p. 1.
"Letter from the Missing Novelist." *Daily News*, December 8,
1926, p. 9.
"Letter from Mrs. Christie." *Daily Mail*, December 7, 1926, p. 9.
"Lost Memory." *Daily News*, December 18, 1926, p. 3.
"Mallowans, The." *New Yorker*, October 29, 1966, p. 51.
"May We Present Mme. Whodunit." *Good Housekeeping*,
March, 1958, p. 13.
"Message Ends Hunt for Mrs. Christie." *New York Times*,
December 8, 1926, p. 4.
"Miss Christie and Music." *Musical America*, May, 1952, p. 11.
"Miss Crowe's Body Found on Seashore." *Westminster Gazette*, December 21, 1926, p. 7.
"Missing Novelist Living at a Harrogate Hydro." *Westminster Gazette*, December 15, 1926, p. 1.
"Motors Join Hunt for Mrs. Christie." *New York Times*,
December 12, 1926, p. 12.
"Mr. Mitchell Hedges." *Daily Mail*, February 10, 1928, p. 2.
"Mrs. Agatha Christie." *Daily Mail*, February 16, 1928, p. 9.
"Mrs. Agatha Christie, Novelist, Disappears." *New York Times*,
December 6, 1926, p. 1.
"Mrs. Christie and the Real Mrs. Neele." *Daily Chronicle*,
December 11, 1926, p. 3.
"Mrs. Christie as 'The Woman Who Was.'" *Daily Chronicle*,
December 16, 1926, p. 3.
"Mrs. Christie Disguised." *Daily News*, December 11, 1926, p. 8.
"Mrs. Christie's Fate." *Westminster Gazette*, December 10,
1926, p. 1.
"Mrs. Christie Found." *Daily Mail*, December 16, 1926, p. 9.
"Mrs. Christie Found in Harrogate Hydro." *Daily News*,
December 15, 1926, p. 7.
"Mrs. Christie Found in a Yorkshire Spa." *New York Times*,
December 15, 1926, p.1.

"Mrs. Christie, Her Last Day at Home." *Daily Mail*,
December 9, 1926, p. 9.
"Mrs. Christie Hiding in Male Attire." *Daily News*,
December 13, 1926, p. 7.
"Mrs. Christie Startling New Turn." *Daily Chronicle*,
December 8, 1926, p. 3.
"Mrs. Christie's Letter to Her Husband." *Daily News*,
December 11, 1926, p. 7.
"Mrs. Christie's Journey." *Daily Mail*, December 18, 1926, p. 9.
"Mrs. Christie's Torn-Up Letters." *Daily Chronicle*,
December 11, 1926, p. 9.
"Mrs. Christie's Visit to London." *Daily Chronicle*,
December 9, 1926, p. 3.
"Murder of Roger Ackroyd." *The Nation and Athaneum*,
July 8, 1926, p. 14.
"Mysterious Milestones." *Newsweek*, June 12, 1950, p. 93.
"Mystery of Mrs. Christie." *Westminster Gazette*,
December 7, 1926, p. 1.
"Mystery Writer, Mystery Woman." *Saturday Evening Post*,
May 10, 1941, p. 4.
"New Clues in Riddle of Lost Novelist." *Daily Chronicle*,
December 7, 1926, p. 3.
"New Hit." *Newsweek*, January 3, 1955, p. 43.
"New Plans in Hunt for Two Lost Women." *Daily Chronicle*,
December 14, 1926, p. 3.
"New Plays in Manhattan." *Time*, December 27, 1954, p. 32.
"Poison Bottle Find in Novelist Mystery." *Westminster Gazette*,
December 14, 1926, p. 1.
"Police Theory in Mystery of Woman Novelist." *Westminster
Gazette*, December 9, 1926, p. 1.
"Return of Agatha Christie." *Daily Chronicle*, December 15,
1926, p. 3.
"Says Mrs. Christie Still Lacks Memory." *New York Times*,
December 16, 1926, p. 7.
"Secret of Mrs. Christie Inquiries." *Westminster Gazette*,
December 11, 1926, p. 1.
"Shoe Found on Downs." *Daily News*, December 9, 1926, p. 9.
"Specialist's Bulletin on Mrs. Christie." *Westminster Gazette*,
December 17, 1926, p. 1.
"Standard Brands." *New Yorker*, December 25, 1954, p. 42.
"Still No Trace of the Missing Novelist." *Yorkshire Evening
Post*, December 6, 1926, p. 9.
"Tips for the Bookseller." *Publishers Weekly*, April 1, 1950, p. 1593.
"Tips for the Bookseller." *Publishers Weekly*, July 1, 1950, p. 39.

"Vain Hunt for Two Women." *Daily News*, December 14, 1926, p. 7.

"What They Are Saying." *Look*, March 9, 1954, p. 23.

"What They Are Saying." *Look*, January 11, 1955, p. 7.

"Who Killed Agatha Christie?" *National Review*, February 6, 1976, p. 78.

"Woman Novelist Vanishes." *Daily Mail*, December 6, 1926, p. 9.

Burgess, Anthony. "Murder Most Fair by Agatha the Good." *Life*, December 1, 1967, p. 8.

Clurman, Harold. "Theater." *The Nation*, January 1, 1955, p. 18.

Dennis, Nigel. "Genteel Queen of Crime." *Life*, May 14, 1956, p. 87.

Duffy, Martha. "The Sweet Sleuth Gone." *Time*, September 15, 1975, p. 88.

Gibbs, Walcott. "Early Frost." *New Yorker*, September 28, 1946, p. 44.

Haverstick, John. "Author of the Week." *Saturday Review*, February 4, 1956, p. 38.

Holquist, Michael. "Murder She Says." *New Republic*, July 26, 1975, p. 26.

Hoover, Eleanor Links. "Agatha's Amnesia." *Human Behavior*, April, 1979, p. 14.

Kramer, Peter G. "Mistress of Mystery." *Newsweek*, January 26, 1976, p. 69.

Mayes, Herbert R. "Moonstones and Mousetraps." *Saturday Review*, October 17, 1970, p. 4.

McCormack, William A. "Not a Dame." *Saturday Review*, March 3, 1956, p. 21.

McKeogh, Arthur. "Our Own Four Walls." *Good Housekeeping*, February, 1931, p. 82.

Mochrie, Margaret. "They Make Crime Pay." *Delineator*, February, 1937, p. 29.

Petschek, Willa. "Agatha Christie: The World's Most Mysterious Woman." *McCall's*, February, 1969, p. 80.

Tarrant, Marguerite. "In the Money." *People Weekly*, April 10, 1978, p. 131.

Tyler, Ralph. "Curtains for Poirot." *Saturday Review*, October 4, 1975, p. 24.

Ulan, Adam. "Murder and Class." *New Republic*, July 31, 1976, p. 21.

Wallace, Edgar. "My Theory of Mrs. Christie." *Daily Mail*, December 11, 1926, p. 9.

Waugh, Auberon. "Murder at Newlands Corner." *Esquire*, July, 1976, p. 140.

Wyndham, Francis. "Algebra of Agatha Christie, The." *Sunday Times*, February 27, 1966, p. 26.

INDEX

ACKNOWLEDGMENTS

THE LIFE OF AGATHA CHRISTIE WAS ONE LIVED IN THE shadow of privacy. Ultimately, she was neither lonely nor unhappy, as many talented, rich and famous people are. She was simply Agatha—a wonderfully complicated, gracious, and shy writer of tales whose mysteries will outlive us all. Her family guards her privacy still and refused to cooperate with this unauthorized biography. Regardless, I have made every effort to separate fact from rumor and present a truthful composite of this complex woman. Where her thoughts are italicized, they are my thoughts as imagined through her mind—an inexhaustible font of creativity and wonder. Agatha, you amaze me still.

To discover her story and present it here was a collective effort of researchers, librarians, and a coterie of individuals who shared their time and stories of not only the Millers, Christies, Mallowans, and Hicks families, but of the towns of Torquay, Devon, Sunningdale, Harrogate, Wallingford, and Newlands Corner, Great Britain, as well.

I owe a special debt of gratitude to the archivists and staff at the University of Exeter Special Collections and Research Support Division in the Bill Douglas Centre, where I spent weeks inspecting over 5,000 documents and letters in their superb Agatha Christie Collection. Dr. Christine Faunch, the Curator of Archives, was always available for counseling and direction, as was Jessica Gardner, who is the Head of the Special Collections Division and cheered me on during the most moist of Exeter winters. Sue Inskit, Sue Guy, and Michael Rickard made certain I was always supplied with the sharpest pencil and most comfortable seat in the Reading Room. The smallest things mean the most. I hope to visit you again with this book in hand and express how much your kindness meant to me.

To the Surrey Constabulary, West Yorkshire Police, West Yorkshire Archive Service, Thames Valley Police: my thanks for keeping me on the path. Likewise the librarians and staff at the Colindale Newspaper Library and the Reading Room of the

British Library at St. Pancras, Great Britain. In addition, the staff in the Manuscript Division and Performing Arts Reading Room at the Library of Congress, Washington, DC.

To my friends Russell Sveda and Victor Schachter who opened their home to me in the Capitol and did yeoman's work transcribing an audio recording of Mathew Prichard, unbridled appreciation and a question: the carton of wine I consumed was for me, right? And thanks as well to Troy Stratos for his hospitality and encouragement whilst in London. I'm still waiting for the scones.

To Agatha Christie fans Andy Kress, Bob DeBenedictis, Anne Jordan, Roger Jereza, Travis Yonn, Jim McCarthy, Kevin Williams, Mike Trost, Evan Harlow, Marilyn Richards, Langston Goree, Julie McCarron, Valerie Reynolds Mueller, Maxine Potter, Anthony Joseph Melluzzo, Carole Ita White, Laurie Allen and Lu Plante, Phoebe Otis and Betty Newman, Donald Sanders, Tony Mascioli, Matt Willey, Tom Palucis, Joyce Outlaw, Nicole Murphy, Annette Warner, David Hall, plus Christine Beck who always wanted her name in a book— this one's for you.

To my faithful friend Robert Elias Deaton, appreciation for your constant encouragement and enthusiastic proofreading.

For the exceptional team at Phoenix Books, this biography is shared with you: Publisher Michael Viner, Managing Editor Dan Smetanka, Marketing Director Judith Abarbanel, Editor Darby Connor, and Henrietta Tiefenthaler, former Director of Production, who started this book on its way. And a very special thanks to Sherry Huber, who patiently edited every line of this biography. It is an honor to share it with you.

And, finally as always, to my mother, Anne, whose kindness and joy in daily life inspires us all—especially me.

Richard Hack
Fort Lauderdale, Florida